# Georg Simmel:
# Sociologist and European

the Making of Sociology series
EDITOR: RONALD FLETCHER

The Making of Sociology
vol. 1 Beginnings and Foundations
vol. 2 Developments
vol. 3 Reassessments: Consolidation and Advance?
RONALD FLETCHER

Auguste Comte
KENNETH THOMPSON

Freud and Modern Society
ROBERT BOCOCK

L. T. Hobhouse
JOHN E. OWEN

Karl Marx
Z. A. JORDAN

John Stuart Mill
RONALD FLETCHER

Georg Simmel
P. A. LAWRENCE

Herbert Spencer
STANISLAV ANDRESKI

Max Weber
J. E. T. ELDRIDGE

Sociology and Industrial Life
J. E. T. ELDRIDGE

Deviance and Society
LAURIE TAYLOR

P. A. Lawrence
University of Southampton

# Georg Simmel:

# Sociologist and European

BARNES & NOBLE

**BOOKS**

10 East 53d St., New York 10022
*(a division of Harper & Row Publishers, Inc.)*

Published in the U.S.A. 1976 by
HARPER & ROW PUBLISHERS INC.
BARNES & NOBLE IMPORT DIVISION

ISBN 0–06–494094–2

Library of Congress Catalog Number
LC 76–19974

*Produced by offset lithography by*
UNWIN BROTHERS LIMITED
The Gresham Press, Old Woking, Surrey, England
A member of the Staples Printing Group

**To the memory
of my Father**

# Acknowledgements

I should like to thank the general editor of the series, Ronald Fletcher, for all the help and encouragement which he has given me.

A substantial part of the readings in this volume consists of new translations. This work has been undertaken by D. E. Jenkinson, University of London Goldsmiths' College.

P.L.

# Contents

# Introduction

by Ronald Fletcher

Georg Simmel, the nature of his work, and the extent of his influence, form one of the most curious and intriguing subjects in the whole story of the making of sociology. He has always been numbered among those few distinguished scholars who, in their several ways, were establishing the foundations of the subject towards the end of the nineteenth century and at the beginning of our own. He is bracketed with Tönnies, Durkheim, Weber, Pareto. Yet his work has never seemed to be accepted with quite the same conviction as being as essential and fundamental as theirs. Any examination of it, however, shows that there is something strange about this.

Perhaps because of the selective translations from his writings, and their patchy availability (in various journals), Simmel has seemed to be a theorist indulging himself in speculative and philosophical explorations of human experience and behaviour in very specific social situations—such as his analysis of the socio-mental mechanisms by which men endure their lives in large and congested cities. Essays like this give the impression of a highly individual and probing mind following inclinations of interest rather than working at systematization; absorbed particularly in the very subtle socio-psychological process of human 'association'. And yet, even this alone places him—before men like Cooley and Mead and the long development of the Chicago School—as a basic contributor to the origins of what has come to be called 'interactionism'; indeed, of all those 'micro-sociological' studies (though still, with him, within a framework of 'macro'-analysis) which are among the most conspicuous theoretical preoccupations of our own day. As Everett Hughes has said: 'Like Freud, Simmel has many intellectual children, though not all of them have that wisdom which makes them know their own father.'

Similarly, as some current writers have come to abstract particular elements from sociological analysis as a whole and emphasize them selectively, Simmel has seemed the most prominent exponent of the importance of 'conflict' in society. Yet this was by no means one horn of a superficial 'two sociologies' dichotomy, but a profound exploration of the ways in which conflict actually contributes to the establishment of social and institutionalized bonds: something, of course, which Lester Ward and many others always emphasized, and which all earlier theorists understood in their continual talk about 'conflict and co-operation'. And again, this was only one aspect of his attempt to distinguish and clarify those fundamental 'forms' of human association (e.g. dominance–submission) which could be discerned in all areas of society: religion, education, politics, the family, etc. The emphasis on conflict was, in short, one aspect of a central dimension within society and sociological analysis as a whole.

This emphasis on 'social forms' has itself been taken to be a relatively limited contribution when compared with the large systems of men like Comte, Spencer, Marx, Hobhouse, and the large-scale methods of comparative sociology established by Durkheim and Weber for the satisfactory formulation and testing of theories. Simmel, it is said, is no 'system builder'. And yet, this dimension is not only at the heart of all sociological analysis, but was the basis of one important strand in the development of sociological theory: that of 'Formal Sociology'. Though Simmel's theoretical focus was sharp, it was also central, and of the widest relevance and application.

Such considerations, simple and immediate though they are, indicate at once how wide Simmel's influence has been, both in Europe and America, in stimulating analysis and contributing to the professional establishment of the subject.

Indeed, strange though it may seem, it was Simmel who, among all the European scholars of his generation, first received conspicuous attention in America. This was at the hands of Albion Small—the founding father of professional sociology in America, of the *American Journal of Sociology*, and of the Chicago School. Like other American scholars in his and subsequent generations, Small cultivated close links with German sociology, and translated and published many selections from Simmel (on 'Super-Ordination and Sub-Ordination', on 'The Persistence of the Small Group', on the influence of numbers in determining the form of groups, etc.), in the *American Journal* during the 1890s, and on the philosophy of value, the sociology of religion, the sociology of secrecy, and 'The Problem of Sociology' before 1910. Other papers were published in the *American Journal of Psychology* and the *Annals* of the American Academy of Political and Social Science. This influence continued in later generations. Charles Ellwood, for example, a (nowadays) much neglected American sociologist, actually studied under Simmel (on the advice of Small) in Berlin. Park and Burgess, too, were much influenced by him. Simmel's was the basic influence in the work of Leopold von Wiese and Vierkandt in the development of 'Formal Sociology', which became highly influential in America as 'Systematic Sociology' through the work of Howard Becker and others. And beyond these quite large and central directions, Simmel's influence was also at the root of the work of some scholars now little heard of: Hans Freyer, for example, and Stuckenberg.

Simmel, then, is a theorist whose work holds much interest and needs more searching examination than most. One thing that is certain is that his story is not yet fully told. This is why it is a particular pleasure to welcome this new book on Simmel into 'The Making of Sociology' series, and by a scholar, Peter Lawrence, who has written and compiled it with one great advantage: that of personal enthusiasm and commitment. Mr Lawrence's interest in Simmel began a long time ago, and he has gone to great lengths, including a period of work in Germany, to pursue his studies more deeply. This book—which has the merit, too, of providing new and additional translations—is an outcome of his ongoing work.

In it, some of the major and distinctive strands of Simmel's approach to theory, as well as some of his particular studies, are presented, but Mr Lawrence also emphasizes two themes which are both timely and important. Part 4 focuses on 'The Crisis of Culture', something with which we are increasingly occupied— both at the large-scale level of pitting our wits against the problem of reconstructing industrial capitalism, and at the personal level of making some satisfying sense of our own destiny. Perhaps I could quote (very selectively) a little:

> The reason for the apparent pessimism of the majority of minds regarding the present state of culture is the widening gulf between the culture of things and personal culture. . . .

The rootless, arbitrary character of modern personal life is the expression of this fact: the vast, intricate, sophisticated culture of things, of institutions, of objectified ideas, robs the individual of any consistent inner relationship to culture as a whole, and casts him back again on his own resources. . . .

The cultural malaise of modern man is the result of this discrepancy between the objective substance of culture, both concrete and abstract, on the one hand, and, on the other, the subjective culture of individuals who feel this objective culture to be something *alien*: which does violence to them and with which they cannot keep pace. There is a feeling that we are deficient in culture by comparison with the Athens of Pericles, or with, say, Italy in the 15th and 16th centuries. Yet we are not lacking in any particular elements of culture.

No increase in knowledge, literature, political achievements, works of art, means of communication, or social manners, can make good our deficiency. The possession of all these things does not, in itself, make a man cultured, any more than it makes him happy.

Well . . . Simmel addresses himself to this issue, but is it not quite plain, even in this brief extract, how close his approach is, from his own standpoint, to the malaise of modern industrial society analysed by the other sociological theorists—the alienation of Marx, the anomie of Durkheim, the great dilemma of the promise and threat of science and industrialization voiced over a hundred years and more from Comte to Weber and Hobhouse?

But there is another emphasis which is important and timely: the emphasis, within this, of the significance of Europe. Mr Lawrence's title portrays Simmel not only as sociologist but also as a European. With a newly constituted Europe being shaped about us, here is a theme which lies at the heart of our present-day concern for the making of sociology and the making of the modern world.

Suffolk
29 February 1976

# I Introduction to the Life and Work of Georg Simmel

# 1     The Scene in Brief

In 1893 the Manchester Ship Canal was opened, and in that same year
the first portion of Georg Simmel's work was made available in
English. This bizarre juxtaposition is not an invitation to compare
utilitarian and intellectual values. Rather it raises the question of
justification. Only one ship canal in Britain has been found to be
necessary, but several translations and editions of Simmel's work have
appeared. On what grounds, then, is the present volume to be
justified?

There are arguments centring on proportion and completeness.
Simmel was a prolific writer and an eclectic thinker. But considering his
stature as one of the founding fathers of sociology, he has hardly been
the subject of excessive attention. During the twenty years following his
death in 1918, the sociological centre of gravity is to be found in the
United States and the dominant interests of this period are severely
empirical: race, immigration, crime, poverty and community studies.
Robert Park, the key figure in the Department of Sociology at Chicago
in succession to the department's founder, Albion Woodbury Small,
had attended Simmel's lectures in Berlin at the turn of the century, and
recommended Simmel's works to his students, but Park is not in any
formal sense a disciple of Simmel. In the two works of theoretical
stocktaking in the United States in the second quarter of this century,
Simmel does rather badly. First, Pitirim Sorokin in his *Contemporary
Sociological Theories* (1928) delivers a formidable attack on Simmel
(of which more later), beginning with the assertion that the formal
school of sociology, with which Sorokin identifies Simmel, is far from
original and begins 'at least with Confucius . . .'.[1] To call sociologists
back to Simmel, Sorokin concludes, '. . . means to call them back to a
pure speculation, metaphysics, and a lack of scientific method'.[2]

Secondly, in Talcott Parsons's famous work,[3] Simmel suffers from his presumed irrelevance to the task in hand. That is to say, Parsons does not regard his ideas as contributing to the development of the voluntaristic theory of action with which Parsons is concerned.

Even more recently, it is noticeable that much of the secondary literature on Simmel is in the form of collections of critical essays[4] and journal articles[5] rather than of extensive monographs. Indeed, there has not been a major work entirely devoted to a discussion of Simmel's sociology for nearly half a century.[6] Similarly, while enumerations of Simmel's work available in English appear extensive, they are not impressive in relation to the extent of his original writing. Simmel's publications include four books explicitly on sociology: *Über Soziale Differenzierung* (1890; *Concerning Social Differentiation*), *Philosophie des Geldes* (1900; *The Philosophy of Money*), *Soziologie: Untersuchungen Über die Formen der Vergesellschaftung* (1908; *Sociology: Investigations into the Forms of Sociation*), and *Grundfragen der Soziologie* (1917; *Basic Questions of Sociology*). The first of these has not been translated, except in so far as parts of it are reproduced in a later work: some excerpts from this book are translated and included in the present volume. Regarding the second work, *Philosophie des Geldes*, for many years the only part of this available in English was Howard Becker's annotated translation of the table of contents.[7] More recently, some forty-three pages of the original have been translated by Donald Levine,[8] and a further ninety pages have been newly translated for the present volume. Of the two other works, the greater part of *Soziologie: Untersuchungen über die Formen der Vergesellschaftung* and the whole of *Grundfragen der Soziologie* have already been made available in English by Kurt H. Wolff and Reinhard Bendix,[9] portions of which are reproduced here. We have also sought to include further newly translated material, namely some articles on cultural topics, and two essays from Simmel's book on the implications of the First World War, *Der Krieg und die Geistigen Entscheidungen* (1918; *The War and Spiritual Decisions*). The purpose of this note on sources, however, is not simply to define the contents of the present volume, but also to indicate that substantial portions of Simmel's work have not previously been available in English—a fact which is felt to have impaired the appreciation of Simmel's thematic range and an understanding of the extent to which he is part of a European sociological tradition, sharing its concerns and problems.

Before turning to this central issue, however, some comments on the socio-political context of Simmel's life are perhaps in order. Simmel is of interest as a representative, though not always a typical representative, of both European culture before the war of 1914-18 and of Wilhelminan Germany, though there is some opposition between these two environmental forces. Europe enjoyed a certain pre-eminence in the half-century before the First World War. The European Powers were *the* Powers; Africa was at their disposal, and Asia largely so. For forty years before the First World War there were no serious wars in Europe. There was a kind of stability, and certainly one which permitted advance in scholarship. Simmel's continental contemporaries in sociology alone included Weber, Tönnies, Sombart, Michels, Pareto and Durkheim, and the Europe in which they lived was perhaps less divided by internal boundaries than it has since become. This was the Europe of the multi-national Habsburg and Ottoman empires; a Europe without passports, and the golden age of the trans-Europa expresses. The level of individual freedom for the middle classes was high. Not all states were liberal, but those which were not tended to be inefficient. Imperial Germany, however, was an exception to this generalization; it was neither liberal nor inefficient. Here was a state at the height of its powers: unified in 1871, administratively co-ordinated, successfully industrialized, and even dignified by Bismarck's social welfare legislation. But political unification had not led to parliamentary democracy, only to a façade thereof. Nor had unification been the end point of national consciousness; the twenty years before the First World War were marked by the search for colonies, by naval rivalry with Britain, by economic penetration of south-east Europe and the Middle East, and by the 'export' of military missions—to Turkey, to Japan, even to Chile. A further paradox of unification is that its architect, Bismarck, believed it necessary to protect unified Germany by alliance with other states. The German alliance system, however, eventually provoked a counter-system, and without these competing blocs of alliances, the First World War would have been impossible in the extensive form in which it took place. And German society was marked by certain inconsistencies, particularly as between economic development and dominant values. In other societies, industrialization had given rise to the preponderance of middle-class values and political forms. But, in Germany, political power was primarily in the hands of a service nobility whose values—patriotism-ethnocentrism, loyalty to emperor, honour, service, obedience, family integrity—were dominant social values. How, then, do these tensions between Germany and

Europe, and within German society, affect Simmel? Does he reflect them, react against them? Is the nature of his work determined by them?

The question may be answered in a number of ways. First, some of the contradictions of the period may be perceived in Simmel's own life and thought. His commitment is to European culture rather than to German society, yet he spent all but the last four years of his life in Berlin, the grey city facing eastern Europe. He deplored the First World War, which shattered the civilization he revered, yet he displayed a characteristically German apathy towards contemporary politics. Secondly, it might be argued that the qualified internationalism of Europe before 1914 finds its parallel in Simmel's breadth of interest. His published works include monographs on Kant, Schopenhauer, Nietzsche, Rembrandt and Goethe, he contributed to epistemology, the philosophy of history, ethics, aesthetics and the theory of culture, as well as to social theory. And thirdly, his professional career foundered in its German setting, and not only in the sense that he was the victim of antisemitism. His catholicity ran counter to professional norms of specialization. In an academic milieu which rewarded 'hard' scholar-ship, he was best known in his own lifetime as an outstanding teacher whose lectures were attended by the social élite of Berlin, whether or not they were enrolled students. In a state whose professional classes took themselves seriously, he aroused antagonism by his frequent publications in literary magazines and newspapers. And he compounded the sin of non-conformity with that of intellectual independence. His books are not replete with references to his contemporaries. As Donald Levine puts it: 'He speaks for himself, along with the immortal dead.'[10] Yet he cannot be assimilated to a stereotype of intellectual arrogance. He self-consciously declined to found a school of followers, and shortly before his death from cancer he recorded in his diary that his inheritance was, as it were, to be distributed in cash to be used in whatever way his successors thought desirable. With death imminent, he had the humility to declare that he had no substantial new contributions to make. In his life, he had an impressive circle of friends and correspondents (no less a person than Weber acted as his referee in an unsuccessful application for a chair at Heidelberg), but his own university declined to give him the status of full professor. He contributed to the development of sociology as an independent discipline, yet unlike his German contemporaries, Weber, Michels, Sombart and Tönnies, he did no empirical research. As a Jew with a cosmopolitan outlook, he was not sufficiently involved in German society to be attracted by empirical inquiry. When he finally achieved the rank of full professor, in his late fifties, it was in territorially ambiguous Strasbourg.[11] His preoccupation with the forms of social interaction may be thought of as Cartesian rather than Hegelian. His examination, and particularly his exemplification, of such forms was transcultural and a-historical. His illustrations are drawn from Ancient Rome and North American Indian tribes with equal facility. His interests are theoretical, yet his series of analyses are not systematically related. He developed a theory of sociology rather than a theory of society.

This antithetical sketch of Simmel's position emphasizes his divided loyalties and the inconsistencies in his work. And it suggests that these counterpoint certain tensions in the European situation in which Simmel's thought developed. But to concentrate on his inconsistencies, and to depict him as a European stranger in German society, is to offer an incomplete picture of his social thought. There are senses in which he was firmly rooted in the sociological enterprise of his period, and it is to this which we now turn.

## NOTES AND REFERENCES

1. P.A. Sorokin, *Contemporary Sociological Theories*, Harper & Row, New York, 1928.

2. ibid.

3. Talcott Parsons, *The Structure of Social Action*, McGraw-Hill, New York, 1937.

4. Kurt H. Wolff (ed.), *Georg Simmel, 1858-1918*, Ohio State University Press, 1959; and Lewis Coser (ed.), *Georg Simmel*, Prentice-Hall, Englewood Cliffs, N.J., 1965.

5. In 1958, the centenary of the births of Simmel and Durkheim, an edition of the *American Sociological Review* was devoted to the work of both.

6. Nicholas J. Spykman, *The Social Theory of Georg Simmel*, Atherton Press, New York, 1965 (first published 1925).

7. Howard Becker, 'On Simmel's Philosophy of Money', in Wolff (ed.), *Georg Simmel*.

8. Donald N. Levine (ed.), *Georg Simmel on Individuality and Social Forms*, University of Chicago Press, 1971.

9. Kurt H. Wolff (ed.), *The Sociology of Georg Simmel*, The Free Press of Glencoe, Ill., 1950; and Georg Simmel, *Conflict and the Web of Group-Affiliations,* translated by Kurt H. Wolff and Reinhard Bendix, The Free Press of Glencoe, Ill., 1955.

10. Levine (ed.), *Georg Simmel on Individuality and Social Forms.*

11. The provinces of Alsace and Lorraine were ceded to Germany by the Treaty of Frankfurt (1871) at the end of the Franco-Prussian War; they reverted to France by the Treaty of Versailles (1919) after the First World War.

# 2   Formal Sociology

There are two justifications for placing Simmel in the mainstream of European sociology. The main one is concerned with some of his substantive interests, and this idea will be explored in a later chapter. The other one, which we consider here, concerns the contribution Simmel made to the establishment of sociology as an independent and discrete discipline. This contribution goes under the loose and unfelicitous name of 'formal sociology'. The concept of formal sociology is adumbrated and exemplified at length in Simmel's third work on sociology, first published in 1908.[1]

The basic idea is a distinction between *form* and *content*. Simmel's starting-point is that society exists when several individuals enter into interaction (see below). This interaction will result from particular drives or purposes. As instances of such drives, Simmel mentions the erotic, the religious and the purely sociable; as examples of interacting purposes, he suggests defence and attack, entertainment and gainful employment, the provision of aid and instruction, and so on. It is clear that he regards these as examples culled from a lengthy list, comprising every drive or purpose which may draw individuals into an interactional situation in which $x$ affects $y$ and is affected by $y$; and this idea of reciprocal effect is conveyed literally by the German *Wechselwirkung*, which by convention among interpreters of Simmel is usually translated as 'interaction'. These drives, interests and purposes—phenomena residing in the individual—are what Simmel means by *content*. And content is also to be regarded, so to speak, as the raw material of form. The interaction implies that the various individual carriers of these drives and purposes constitute units. Any such unit is a 'society', or a form of sociation (*Vergesellschaftung*). So, for Simmel, *form* means forms of sociation: supra-individual interactional entities within which individuals are engaged and realize their interests.[2] Simmel regards form, of course, as an analytic construct: that is to say, forms cannot exist independently of content. And sociology is the study of such forms:

> If there is to be a science whose object is society and nothing else, then this science can only concern itself with these interactions, these kinds and forms of sociation.[3]

And furthermore, sociology will not be just an exercise in stocktaking, in matching forms with their corresponding contents, because the relationship between the two is not invariable. The same forms of sociation may exist in different contents; for example, superordination is a form of sociation, but its content may be parents *vis-à-vis* children, or officers *vis-à-vis* enlisted men. Similarly, content—individual purposes—may be realized within different forms of sociation; for instance, competition (price undercutting) and co-operation (price fixing) are different forms of economic interaction which may both serve the ends of individual gain. Thus Simmel is arguing for a sociology which studies the forms of sociation, the interactional patterns analytically separable from the individuals composing them, there being no one-to-one relationship between particular forms and contents.

Three general observations about these epistemological formulations seem in order. First, any appreciation of the importance of Simmel's contribution must be related to the historical context of sociology's development; that is, these ideas are not to be regarded as a thunderbolt for the 1970s. Secondly, it is probably fair to say that the tag 'formal sociology' is somewhat unfortunate, partly because of the rather unfavourable connotations of the word 'formal', especially in a sociological climate which is staunchly anti-determinist, and partly because the tag is not a very good indicator of what Simmel actually does as a practitioner of so-called formal sociology. That is to say, his analyses are generally regarded as stimulating and insightful, not merely as exercises in the construction of typologies. And thirdly, there is probably an associational factor serving to reduce the lustre of Simmel's ideas: although he founded no school himself, his principal self-proclaimed disciple, Leopold von Wiese, has pursued the goal of constructing an elaborate formal typology of social relations, and designates in his main work some 650 different forms of social relationships.[4] In the light of Simmel's own discussions of social forms and types, it is probably fair to say that he would not have approved of this exercise.

These preliminary comments, however, are not meant to indicate that there are no serious objections to Simmel's position; a number of critical objections are associated particularly with Theodore Abel and Pitirim Sorokin.[5] It may well be helpful to summarize these:

1. The formalistic approach is too narrow, and leaves out much which contemporary sociologists wish to study.
2. Simmel himself did not stick to his declared programme of restricting attention to the forms of sociation.
3. The distinction between form and content is not new: Simmel cannot be credited with originality.
4. The distinction between form and content is invalid since form can never be independent of content.
5. Even if the distinction were valid, and was adhered to, this would not give sociology a distinctive identity since other branches of knowledge are concerned with forms as well, e.g. constitutional law and economics.

These criticisms are not be dismissed lightly, but there are certainly a number of counter-arguments which may be called into play. First, it may be pointed out that Simmel himself was aware of the difficulties of operationalizing his form–content distinction. In *Einleitung in die Moralwissenschaft* he wrote:

> . . . the category of content and form is one of the most relative and subjective in the entire area of thought. What is form in one respect is content in another; and, upon closer scrutiny, the conceptual antithesis between the two dissolves into a merely gradual (opposition), having a determinateness which is between the general and the specific.[6]

Simmel's awareness of the problem may to some extent serve to take the sting out of the criticism.

Secondly, and to reverse the tactic, one might practise what David Matza in his study of deviance has called 'the condemnation of the condemners'.[7] Some of the above criticisms tend to be mutually contradictory, or, at least, to be unfair if applied simultaneously. It is, for instance, unreasonable to apply criticisms (1) and (2) together. For, if Simmel is to be condemned for adopting too restrictive a framework in principle, then he should be praised for breaking its confines in practice. Similarly, criticisms (3), (4) and (5), which all derive from Sorokin, are incompatible. If the form–content distinction is invalid anyway, as Sorokin argues, then it is gratuitous simultaneously to denounce Simmel for lack of originality where, in fact, lack of originality might be converted into a defence: Simmel could be depicted as having been led astray by all his precursors in folly from Confucius onwards! A similar question mark attaches to Sorokin's praise for scholars in other disciplines already engaged in the study of forms. If he were to be consistent, Sorokin would condemn, for example, constitutional historians for their pathetic naïvety in believing that the constitution (form) meant anything considered apart from the key political personalities (content).

Thirdly, there are a number of arguments which relate to sociology's stage of development in the first decade of this century, and to the available intellectual resources. The most general form of this argument would be to say that Simmel produced both a prescription *for* sociology and studies *in* sociology, and not so many people can make such a double claim at the turn of the century. Simmel's two greatest contemporaries, Weber and Durkeim, take his ideas seriously, though not uncritically; in fact, they both react more to Simmel than to each other. It is perhaps difficult for us, three quarters of a century later, to conceive of the impact which Simmel's bold if controversial legitimation of sociology made on contemporary minds. The academic dean at Heidelberg, for instance, commented as follows on Simmel's contribution:

There is no doubt that Simmel, thanks to his extensive and many-sided knowledge and the penetrating energy of this thought, is the only man capable of lifting sociology from the level of mere data collecting and general reflection to the rank of a truly philosophical undertaking.[8]

And an extension of this appraisal of Simmel as a 'founding father' of sociology is possible, though perhaps not obvious because of Simmel's independent stance. This is to say that, in terms of strict intellectual ancestry rather than the dynamics of direct influence and personal association, a number of concepts and developments may be traced back to him. He might well be regarded as the founder of the study of group dynamics; he is probably the first sociologist to engage in characterizations of social roles (though without using the term); he pioneers the concept of social distance; he is the reluctant prophet of mass society; he has produced what is probably the first analysis of the condition of the poor (analysis, not data collection); he has analysed the phenomenon of urban life; and in his essay on the metropolis and mental life,[9] he comes close to a concept of anomie. There are, of course, cases where the Simmelian legacy has been rediscovered rather than internalized.

A more particularist form of the argument which relates Simmel's thought to the context of sociology's development has been put forward by Lewis Coser.[10] Coser depicts Simmel as reacting against the two dominant forces of his time—the organicism of Comte and Spencer on the one hand, and the idealism of the *Geisteswissenschaft* school, associated with Wilhelm Dilthey, on the other—and arrives at an independent formulation. The organicists, Coser suggests, view society as an organism subject to something approaching natural laws; the idealist alternative claims a qualitative difference between *Naturwissenschaften* (natural sciences) and *Geisteswissenschaften* (humanities), so making scientific methods inapplicable to the humanities, and, indeed, in its terms society as such can scarcely be the object of systematic inquiry since only individuals have a real existence. Simmel's resolution, as outlined earlier, is to view society as an interactional phenomenon, as the totality of reciprocal effects which individuals exert and experience. In this formulation, society is pragmatically defined, yet the forms of sociation are available for discussion and analysis. It should be added that Coser's interpretation is not particularly indiosyncratic. H. Stuart Hughes,[11] for instance, maps the intellectual history of the twenty years before the First World War in terms of a reaction against positivism. In this account, Weber in particular is regarded as the towering mind of the period precisely because he was able to resolve, however precariously, the positivist-idealist dilemma in the methodology he evolved for the social sciences. There can be little doubt that the problem Simmel confronted was one critical for his intellectual epoque.

This theme of the effects of Simmel's contribution on the development of sociology has also been taken up by Ronald Fletcher.[12] At a general level, Fletcher sees Simmel aş a linkman between the social psychologists on the one hand and the structural theorists concerned, as it were, with 'large-scale social facts' on the other. Simmel, in his concern with defining the methods and area of sociology, and in his analytical resort to the concept of form, may be seen as belonging with the latter. A lot of his discussion of particular forms of sociation, however, does involve him in social-psychological analysis and in the insights of this genre. One instance of this is his analysis of the properties of dyadic and tryadic groups. Thus he may also be seen to have common ground with the social psychologists. And two particular points are suggested by Fletcher. First, that Simmel's concept of form would enable the social psychologists to link their kind of analysis with an analysis of social structure—in this sense again Simmel is the potential unifier. And secondly, the concept of form facilitates a transcending of any particular context of experience and behaviour—religious, political, familial and so on. As Fletcher puts it:

> . . . a simplified central analysis of forms had been made possible without at all losing sight of or discountenancing the density and differential qualities of experience and behaviour in each institutional field.[13]

A further way of defending Simmel against charges of arid formalism is to show that he does, in fact, rise above such limitations. This can be done by an examination of his substantive studies (a line of inquiry which will be explored in the next chapter), and also by claiming that his epistemological prescription has been misunderstood. The second alternative has been pursued most vigorously by F.H. Tenbruck.[14] Underlying Tenbruck's defence is a distinction between a psychological and a sociological conception of action systems. The psychological concept focuses on individual action systems, i.e. on individuals' actions and their reciprocal effects. Simmel, according to Tenbruck, regards this as incomplete in that it fails to account for the stable and persistent relationships exhibited by society. Interaction has unity in two senses: the empirically observable unity of the actions of a group of actors (the psychological concept), and a non-observable unity deriving from the actors' reciprocal orientations (sociological concept). These preliminaries allow Tenbruck to develop a defence of Simmel's approach along four lines. First, Simmel's concern with reciprocal orientations shows him to be involved in a sociology of meaning which precludes any charge of abstracted formalism. Secondly, it shows

Simmel as recognizing the inextricable connectedness of forms and content, since actions cannot be divorced from meanings. In other words, Simmel is not, as some detractors have claimed, setting artificial limits on sociology:

> Sociology is offered as the study of the entire realm of socio-cultural phenomena; but it must relate them to its proper object, that is, the forms of sociation.[15]

This absolves Simmel from the charge of violating his alleged prescriptions in the discussions of particular forms and social types. Thirdly (though this argument is independent of the others), Simmel is placed in line with the subsequent development of a theory of social structure, although he abjured this macro-exercise, because Simmel's forms of sociation turn out to be particular social roles, statuses and types; and also, more generally, because he recognized this level of reality. And fourthly, Tenbruck draws attention to various references to 'pure' forms in Simmel's writing and argues that here Simmel is operating with something approaching an ideal-type concept, and he quotes from Simmel's *Philosophie des Geldes* to underline this point:

> Innumerable times, we form our concepts of objects in such a manner that experience can show no equivalent of their pure and absolute character; they gain an empirical form only in being weakened and limited by opposing concepts . . . This peculiar method of exaggerating and reducing concepts yields knowledge of the world which is commensurate with our mode of cognition . . . Our intellect can grasp reality only by limitations of pure concepts which, no matter how far they deviate from reality, prove their legitimacy by the service they render for the interpretation of it.[16]

Tenbruck pursues this idea by arguing that not only did Simmel develop an ideal-type construct, but that in this he may have been Max Weber's precursor. This last suggestion is based on a comparison of the contents and publication dates of various working papers produced by the two thinkers.

Now, it may be objected that Tenbruck has read too much into Simmel. The present writer's view is that Tenbruck's interpretation is perfectly plausible (and appealing) without being compelling. It falls short of being compelling, not because of any inadequacy on

Tenbruck's part, but because Simmel himself is not sufficiently systematic or consistent. It is certainly possible to illustrate if not to prove more modest interpretations. The extrinsic general point to be made in favour of Tenbruck's position is that it serves to reduce the gap between Simmel's methodological programme and his substantive work.

Two final comments on Simmel's approach may be offered here. For readers who find Tenbruck's valorization of Simmel unconvincing, and who prefer the more modest and conventional account given at the beginning of this chapter, it must still be admitted that Simmel's prescriptions serve to focus attention on uniformities and regularities in social action. They direct us to forms and patterns which transcent 'local variations' and individual idiosyncracies.[17] And this has been the standard focus of modern sociology until the renewed interest in the last few years in social action theory, interpretations in terms of meaning, and the depiction of society as subjective rather than objective reality. However, with regard to this recent subjectivist climate it is probably still too soon to say whether it will ultimately involve a departure from the usual concern with patterns and uniformities. The 'finished products', as it were, may still refer to such uniformities in social action, although the way in which they are established will have been different.

The last point to be said is that if Simmel's formalism, as normally understood, tends to evoke an unfavourable reaction, this could be because some antipathy between formalism and individualism is assumed. In this context it is proper to emphasize that Simmel was a thinker deeply concerned with individuality who has written about changes in the concept and nature of personal freedom.[18] In his discussion of the money economy (in *Philosophie des Geldes*), he seeks to evaluate its implications for personal freedom; in some of his characterizations of social types and situations, the features which establish the parameters for individual freedom are salient; and again, in his discussion of culture, he takes cognisance of the individual's relationship to objectified culture. In short, there is no case for any stereotyping of Simmel as a personality indifferent to the claims of individuality. Indeed, as was briefly indicated in the first chapter, Simmel himself might well have enjoyed more worldly success if he had been more conformist.

NOTES AND REFERENCES

1. Georg Simmel, *Soziologie: Untersuchungen über die Formen der Vergesellschaftung*. All references are to the fourth edition, published by Duncker & Humblot, Berlin, 1958.

2. ibid., p.5.

3. ibid., p.6 (editor's translation).

4. Leopold von Wiese, *Allgemeine Soziologie*, Part I: *Beziehungslehre*, 1924; Part II: *Gebildelehre*, 1929.

5. Theodore Abel, *Systematic Sociology in Germany*, Columbia University Press, 1929; and P.A. Sorokin, *Contemporary Sociological Theories*, Harper & Row, New York, 1928.

6. Quoted by Rudolf H. Weingartner, 'Form and Content in Simmel's Philosophy of Life', in Kurt H. Wolff (ed.), *Georg Simmel, 1858-1918*, Ohio State University Press, 1959.

7. David Matza, *Becoming Deviant*, Prentice-Hall, Englewood Cliffs, N.J., 1969.

8. Quoted by Kurt Gassen and Michael Landmann, *Buch des Dankes an Georg Simmel*, Duncker & Humblot, Berlin, 1958.

9. Translated in Donald N. Levine (ed.), *Georg Simmel on Individuality and Social Forms*, University of Chicago Press, 1971.

10. Lewis Coser (ed.), *Georg Simmel*, Prentice-Hall, Englewood Cliffs, N.J., 1965.

11. H. Stuart Hughes, *Consciousness and Society*, Macgibbon & Key, London, 1959.

12. Ronald Fletcher, *The Making of Sociology*, Vol. 2: *Developments*, Nelson, London, 1972.

13. ibid., p.643.

14. F.H. Tenbruck, 'Formal Sociology', in Wolff (ed.), *Georg Simmel, 1858-1918*.

15. ibid., p.75.

16. ibid. Quotation from p.135 of the first edition of Georg Simmel's *Philosophie des Geldes*, Duncker & Humblot, Leipzig, 1900.

17. This point is also made by Lewis Coser in Coser (ed.), *Georg Simmel*.

18. Levine (ed.), *Georg Simmel on Individuality and Social Forms*, contains some of these essays.

# 3 The Analysis of Forms and Types

There is a general feeling among commentators on Simmel that his discussion of social forms and types is engaging and full of insight. With this judgement the present writer would agree without qualification. And it is probably also fair to say that this view is largely shared even by those who reject Simmel's methodological prescriptions, or who regard them as being of historical interest only. One may therefore ask: in what lies the merit and fascination of these studies? The question is particularly worth posing perhaps since there appears to be an absence of 'middle range' interpretative comment. On the one hand, there is a view which suggests that the formal sociology ideas are unimportant, but that Simmel just happened to be rather a bright fellow so that it is possible to read his essay on, say, the stranger, and be impressed by the intuitive grasp of social phenomena which it displays.

This viewpoint connects with a flattering yet patronizing image of Simmel's personality. It is what we expect from Simmel the performer: Simmel the brilliant teacher (what academic could possibly take a brilliant teacher seriously?); Simmel the urbane and frivolous, lecturing the German Sociological Association (at its inaugural session) on sociability as the 'play form' of sociation and explaining to them that a woman is more likely to wear a low-cut dress at a large party than at a small party; Simmel cracking jokes to his students and telling them that, with the advent of nicotine-free cigarettes, the appearance of feminity-free girls must be on the way. This mood is caught by Ortega y Gasset's oft-quoted quip that Simmel is a philosophic squirrel leaping from bough to bough to show his virtuosity but merely nibbling the different nuts he encounters. Or, to suggest a parallel metaphor, Simmel is seen as a butterfly sipping nectar from many flowers: butterflies are not serious creatures, but they have their charm. On the other hand, as we have indicated already, there are various discussions of what Simmel really meant, of where he went wrong and of the nature of the underlying structure of his thought. But what is there to be found in the middle ground; what is it about these analyses of Simmel's that enables them to stand alone and command interest?

As a preliminary move we might redefine the question, and point out that there are three stages, logical rather than temporal, in Simmel's treatment of the forms of sociation: (a) he decides what sociology should be all about and how it should proceed (the formal premises), (b) he chooses particular forms of sociation for discussion, and then (c) he characterizes them. The main emphasis in the critical literature has been on stage (a), and hence it is worth suggesting that it could be helpful to consider the other stages. This observation may yield one contributory answer to the question: to designate particular phenomena as forms of sociation or social types is itself a creative and selective act, and the capacity to perform it is not logically entailed by making the form–content distinction in the first place. Simmel does not anywhere claim to have discussed *all* the forms of sociation, but the ones he chooses are substantively interesting. Consider, for example, that we now regard the stranger as a distinctive social type because Simmel chose this role for analysis. And some of his choices are very strong with reference to his formal purposes: that is, he focuses on forms of wide currency, forms which, if not omnipresent, are very general; on forms with which widely varying 'contents' are associated. Superordination, subordination, dyadic and tryadic group structures would be obvious examples. The point is neatly made by Coser, who observes that conflict may be variously observed between warring nations and marriage partners.[1] An extension of this line of appraisal would be to say that, in the choice of forms, Simmel exhibits not only insight but staying power.

Donald Levine has made a quantitative check[2] showing that Simmel discusses some 123 forms of sociation, some of these themselves composite, such as the forms of change of possession (robbery, giving presents, gift exchange, tradition-sanctioned exchanges, exchange with and without fixed price) discussed in *Philosophie des Geldes*. An interesting aspect of Levine's treatment here is that he breaks down the global category 'forms of sociation' into social processes, social types and developmental patterns. In this classification, social processes include phenomena such as the formal characteristics of the small group, various forms of superordination and subordination, unification, contract, jealousy, discretion, hereditary office, and so on, though these are examples from a particularly long list. Social types are mostly what, in modern parlance, would be classed as social roles, Simmel's choices being widely distributed on a generality–specificity continuum—the woman, the bourgeois, the priest, the coquette. The developmental patterns are the rather less definable diachronic forms, such as changes in a group's nature as its size increases over time, social differentiation and its consequences, the lengthening of means ends chains to attain what is close at hand. This typology is illuminating for reasons we have pressaged in the discussion of formal sociology. The social types, although Simmel's characterization of them is not based on empirical research, are not as abstracted as the term 'formal sociology' would suggest. And the treatment by Simmel of many phenomena which Levine feels (rightly) must be categorized as developmental patterns also shows Simmel to be making numerous excursions outside the realm of what might be termed 'social statics'. So far, then, we have argued that Simmel's choice of forms is itself a creative act; that it is an act of sustained creativity—not a 'one-off' exercise in didactic illustration; and that the term 'form of sociation' (*Vergesellschaftung*) covers, in fact, not only analytic constructs, but also social roles, processes and emergent situations.

Before examining any particular example of Simmel's work, a note on the editor's strategy is perhaps relevant. We do not see the principal task of the introductory section as being to offer an anticipatory summary of the subsequent readings from Simmel, a tactic which we feel falls somewhere between the unnecessary and the vainglorious. We would see the introduction as complementary rather than reflective. This has two practical implications. First, that we should try to outline the general features of Simmel's sociological thought, thereby hopefully showing the context of the selected readings. The other is that, since the readings are necessarily selective in the sense of being only a small part of the total, one may indicate, where possible, the nature and content of writings not included. With reference to this second point, in the following discussion of Simmel's substantive treatment of forms where there is a premium on illustration, we have deliberately chosen our examples from writings of Simmel not included in this volume, with the intention of broadening the canvas a little. The only limitation we have imposed is to restrict ourselves here to writings already available in English, from sources already indicated,[3] to facilitate further reference.

Our first point about Simmel's discussion of social forms would be to argue that his treatment is not sociologistic.[4] That is, he does not account for phenomena exclusively in terms of exterior, social determinants. Or, to put the point in a positive form, he is able to offer accounts which take cognizance of actors' meanings and intentions. This capacity of Simmel's to depict in terms of subjective definitions comes out strongly, for instance, in his essay on the adventurer.[5] The starting-point in this essay, which is rather in the form of a role study of the adventurer, is a meaning premise. Events in life, Simmel asserts, may be objectively similar while at the same time having a widely varying significance for the individual's life as a whole. Thus a set of experiences have the character of an adventure, not so much because of their objective nature, but rather because they are different and, particularly, discontinuous for the individual who experiences them. The university lecturer who takes six months off to drive heavy lorries is having an adventure: the professional lorry driver is not. And for an individual to perceive an experience as 'an adventure', he must ascribe to it a beginning and an end; that is, he must view it as both temporally and qualitatively distinctive. Indeed, because these adventurous experiences are perceived by the individual as a distinctive unity, the adventure has something of the character of the work of art. It is a perceptually organized and unitary extraction from the totality of experience and sensibility. And, furthermore, the adventurer is a person engrossed in the present: the adventure is not only a subjective reality, but an immediate and vital reality. The adventurer also endows the fortuitous event which marks the departure from normality with special meaning; the adventure is not only subjectively perceived but subjectively highlighted. And Simmel also argues that, to have this capacity to endow the unusual event at the beginning of a series with heightened meaning, implies that one has a concept of purpose and being which transcends everyday conventionality, this being mirrored in the eager participation in adventure. Or, to put it differently, the adventurer treats what is incalculable as though it were calculable, and this is only possible for a person with an unconventional world view. In short, the adventure is subjectively defined, interpreted and unified, and indicates a differential conception of reality.

A more prosaic version of this theme is to say that Simmel shows a capacity to apprehend the motives and gratifications of others, a simple point which emerges clearly in, for example, his discussions of the miser and the spendthrift.[6] The miser's delight is the sheer possession of money; his delight is pure and abstracted and does not entail the acquisition of particular goods and services. It is the ultimate in deferred gratification. The miser's feeling that he controls his destiny is more intense, precisely because he never commits himself to a particular course of action (specific purchases) so that all alternatives are always open to him. His pleasure is aesthetic rather than carnal: it resides in contemplation not sensation. In contrast, the spendthrift epitomizes the foreshortened time perspective: he lives in the emphemeral present, and his pleasures are located there. Yet his pleasure lies not so much in the possession of a rapidly changing series of objects, but in the act of wastefulness itself. The key feature is not that the spendthrift is inconsistent as to the possessions he desires, but that these possessions are irrelevant to his circumstances and conventionally understood needs. The paradox is that money is important for the spendthrift, as for the miser, but its importance lies in its translation into other values. The spendthrift's purchases may be irrational in conventional terms, but for him they are acts of exquisite choice.

A second feature of Simmel's studies, and no originality is claimed for this point, is that he really does exhibit a sensitive insightfulness in appraising social phenomena. Numerous examples could be called into play here, and every Simmel enthusiast will have his own favourite. We may suggest for consideration Simmel's classic essay on the stranger.[7] Simmel considers in this essay not the man who comes today and goes tomorrow, but rather the man who comes today and stays tomorrow. The stranger is the potential wanderer; he may be going no further, but he retains a potentiality for moving on. The stranger is involved in a particular form of interaction; he is not only, by definition, outside the group—he also confronts it. The concept of the stranger refers not to those who are unknown or socially inaccessible, but to those who are present but not integrated. Strangers have been empirically conspicuous throughout history as traders, and in Europe this role has been played by the Jew. And this manifestation, trade, is significant. Trade is an innovating activity, not tied to traditional occupational placements and landownership. It is the 'soft centre' of the economic community which the outsider can penetrate. And, conversely, the stranger's connection with trade underlines his image of mobility. As a 'free floater', all members of an established group are accessible to him, yet he is bound to none of them organically—in terms of kinship, community or occupation. Hence he appraises all members of the group objectively; no member of it has a special claim on his esteem or consideration. Similarly, he has this quality of objectivity for the group. His opinion may be sought, he may become the recipient of confidences from group members who would not or could not confide in each other (equally a characteristic of the open participant observation role in field research). The objectivity which the stranger enjoys may be redefined as freedom: he is not constrained in his judgements by partisan considerations. His interactional relationship with the group is ambivalent. He is close to the group only in terms of common membership of general categories; he may share their nationality, their social status, or be bound to them by common humanity. Yet, simultaneously, he is distant from them because these shared categories are general: nationality, for instance, connects group members with other people who are not physically present or socially known. The only bonds are general, and sometimes abstract. And Simmel gives this last point a characteristic twist by saying that the phenomenon of shared general categories is pervasive, so that there is an element of 'strangeness' in all social relationships, including the most intimate. Even lovers may lose an initial sense of the uniqueness of their attachment, and become aware that they are representatives of general categories, and thus in principle substitutable. The view being offered here is that an analysis of this kind, not the result of anything we would recognize as research and not underpinned by the cumulative insights of others, is only possible for someone possessing, in C. Wright Mills's phrase, a certain 'sociological imagination'.[8]

A third and related point we would make is that Simmel has a quite literal capacity for formulation. He is able to impose order on, and put into words, things that 'we know *really*'. Consider in this connection his comments on prostitution.[9] On what humanistic grounds is prostitution open to objection? Simmel is able to formulate an answer for us. He begins by placing prostitution in the context of the money economy. It is monetary exchanges particularly which eventuate in purely transitory relationships, without emotive involvement or repercussion. The giving of money enables an impersonal withdrawal from a relationship; money is different in kind from a gift, since the latter, at least in some elementary way, is an indicator of personality and choice. And the payment of money in prostitution is congruent. An impersonal act is ratified by an impersonal means. Prostitution is not only unambiguously sensual, but it is an act in which personality factors are at zero. Both partners to the act are substitutable. Individuals who are markedly different, both in terms of personality and social statuses, may engage in it. It is, Simmel claims, the ultimate case in which two people are reduced to the status of means. Yet there are inequalities if the partners are viewed separately. What is normally for the woman most intimate and personal is given a cash value, and it is in this incongruance that the act is a degradation. This point is developed by Simmel by arguing that it is clear from observable effects and sanctions that society places different values on the sexual act for the man and the woman. It is assumed that a larger segment of the woman's personality is usually involved. This, Simmel suggests, is borne out by the differential penalties levied in primitive societies in the event of the termination of an engagement, these penalties being typically higher for the man. The woman's loss of chastity is also judged more harshly. The difference again redounds to the disadvantage of the woman in prostitution. The prostitute experiences a hopeless loss of social status, whereas the most compulsive frequenter of prostitutes may still be esteemed for other aspects of his personality or other achievements. And the felony is compounded, as it were, by the giving of money: it is this which establishes the superiority of the buyer over the seller. It should be added, however, that Simmel does not, in this essay, play the role of explicator of biologically determined verities. He is clear that his dissection is culture-bound, and points out that there are societies whose definitions of sexual honour are less disparate, and where, in consequence, less imbalance between service and remuneration exists in prostitution.

A fourth consideration may be urged in an estimation of Simmel's studies of social forms, and this has been anticipated in the earlier remarks on formal sociology. This is that some of the entities which Simmel chooses as forms of sociation meriting analysis (see Chapter 4, 'Simmel and European Sociology', below) have also been found significant by later generations; some have passed into our conceptual vocabulary. We might take as a case of this Simmel's exploration of the form of exchange.[10] It is not argued here that Simmel has produced a sophisticated theory of exchange (his particular interest, in any case, is in economical exchange), but that he has identified it as a significant form, which others, most notably Peter Blau, have developed into a general theory,[11] and which may also lend itself to particular purposes such as the integration of conflict and consensus theories of social order.[12] The ingredients are prescribed by Simmel in a preliminary way.

Most relationships, Simmel announces, can be assimilated to an exchange model. Even many which we may think of as one-sided in fact involve reciprocal effects—for instance, the journalist and his reading public, the politician and his 'followers'. Exchange is a particular form of interaction, and it thus has the potentiality of omnipresence. An exchange model of society is not static or ossified because only in the context of a mature economic system do objects have a predetermined value. Value is otherwise a reflection of variable needs and situations. Exchange relations thus have emergent properties; they are marked by relativity and reciprocity. Nor is Simmel's concept of exchange purely 'economistic'. He notes that the actor's sacrifice in an exchange transaction may itself be fulfilling, and suggests by way of illustration that people do not climb the Alps simply to enjoy the view from the top. And he recognizes the 'medial' goal phenomenon later formalized by the decision-making theorists,[13] namely, that an object may be both immediately valuable and the means to further ends. There is also a conceptual link between exchange as a basic form, and the open system approach which has been fruitful in the analysis of formal organizations. Thus we may presume that Simmel's treatment of this form contains the basis for later theoretical elaborations.

Fifthly, a feature of Simmel's studies which merits attention is the sureness with which he is able to delineate social roles or statuses with reference to society's determining view of them. We are not advancing the simple dualist argument here, as was the case with prostitution where the institution has significance in contrast to the usual context of sexual relations. The case is rather that Simmel is able to grasp the phenomenon of social situations defined for their occupants by society, though the distinction is admittedly continuous not dichotomous. Simmel's essay on the poor would be a case in point [14] where the phenomenon of unfavourable social definitions is highlighted by Simmel's quasi-ethical *point de départ*. Man, proclaims Simmel, has obligations, and in so far as he is a social being, others have corresponding obligations towards him which are his 'by right'. Thus society may be viewed as a network of rights and obligations, but with rights predominating and obligations as their corollaries. But, Simmel admits, there is some tension here between the ethical and the social. That is to say, in practice people are much more ready to claim their rights than to acknowledge their obligations. These introductory remarks are particularly salient for a consideration of the poor, since if they can feel that in asking for assistance they are simply demanding their rights, then the humiliation is considerably lessened. The problem is, however, that it is not clear to whom their claim should be addressed. Where their claim is, in fact, directed to some collectivity, such as the family, the guild or the village, with whom the supplicant has some ties, then the outcome may not be unfavourable. Less satisfactory, however, is a situation in which the poor address their claim to the needs of the rich, or where it is not the right of the receiver that counts but the obligation of the giver. Here, the motive for assisting the poor is the significance which giving has for the giver; it may earn him grace or contribute to his salvation.

This situation, however, where the poor are a means to the salvation of the rich, is a historical phase rather than a modern reality, and here arises a paradox. The welfare of modern society requires that assistance be given to the poor: this motivation removes the focus from the giver without applying it to the receiver. The institution of public assistance to the poor is exceptional: it renders a personal service to the poor and only to the poor, it relieves their misery and no one else's, whereas most public bodies directly serve the whole population (for instance public utilities). Public assistance is thus distinctive; its direct activity relates to differentiated individuals. And yet the poor are not the real end in this relief operation. The end is the protection of society in general; that is, against dissidence, disgrace and contamination. Thus the relief of the poor results from the needs of society, not the needs of the poor themselves. Indeed, it is doubtful even if the poor have the status of a means to an end, according to Simmel, since public relief neutralizes rather than utilizes them. Even the family, he suggests, may only relieve its poor to avert disgrace; the trade union may help its unemployed members to prevent them in their greater necessity from undercutting established wage rates. Simmel enlarges on this argument concerning the meaning of society's relief of the poor. In taxing the rich to relieve the poor, society does not aim at the equalization of incomes. The goal is rather to reduce the most striking anomalies, thereby facilitating the perpetuation of a differentiated society. This excercise Simmel sees, rather bleakly, as a remarkable achievement by society. That is, the needs of the poor are acute, yet society has still managed to convert their alleviation into a mechanism for maintaining the social system. In short, we have a situation in which the State has an obligation to the total society not matched by a corresponding right inherent in the poor themselves. This means that the poor cannot complain if the obligation is not fulfilled, though others can complain 'on their behalf'. Simmel comments acidly in this context that no one in Germany (of his day) is punished for torturing an animal unless he does so publicly or in a manner likely to cause a scandal.[15] Thus it is not the condition of the sufferer which determines action, but the interests of others. An indication that this is the true state of affairs is found by Simmel in the fact that, even in a democracy, those who are the object of public relief do not participate in its administration or control, in contrast to other branches of the administration. The poor may also be regarded as the victim of modernity. This is meant in the sense that increasing occupational and geographical mobility has eroded ties between (potentially) poor people and particular communities, where the community might have viewed the poor in a more personalized if still instrumental way. In the present, the poor must address their claim to the State, the most general collectivity; if poor relief is, in fact, administered on a local basis, this is not on account of any particularist ties, but simply for administrative convenience. This is disadvantageous to the poor: they loose their best weapon, the ability to excite pity through direct contact.[16] Conversely, the generous and compassionate impulses of individuals are reified in the State.

At this point in the discussion Simmel compares the role of poor to the role of the stranger. The beggar is also 'a stranger'; he is confronted by the group, yet no mechanism exists to draw him into the group in terms of specific interactions. He is the archetypal outsider. It is also of interest that Simmel refines this idea of poverty as a socially defined status, and moves into a consideration of poverty as *relative deprivation* (a concept rediscovered in the 1960s). The norms regarding poverty do not apply to the poor in general, but only to those poor who are receiving assistance. This leads us to the realization that poverty has a relative character. A person is 'poor' if he is unable to attain his ends. Now although nature determines certain general needs, for nutrition and shelter, there is no mechanism for ascertaining the level of these needs in a way which is always and everywhere valid. Different social classes have different expectations; thus there are people who are poor by the standards of their class, but who would not be considered poor in a lower class. Simmel concedes that this subjective view of poverty is not always operative: the person in the lowest category, as it were, may feel this aspirational factor less strongly. Or, conversely, the bourgeois may rise above the consumer aspirations of his class because of his personal value system. The upper-class assumption, however, is that a person may be psychologically poor in the sense that his resources are not equal to his perceived needs, but this does not necessarily mean he will apply for assistance. He is not socially poor until he has been assisted. The poor are not 'a class for themselves'; they are not united by interaction. Their only unity is the identity which society bestows on them.

This essay has been discussed at some length since it is rather a strong case of the phenomenon which we wish to illustrate. It brings out Simmel's ability to see the impersonal parameters of a social status. Not only is poverty socially defined, but the treatment of the poor derives from the needs of society rather than the poor themselves. And in advanced societies the full nature of poverty can only be grasped by resort to the concept of relative deprivation.

A sixth consideration we would urge in the estimation of Simmel's studies is that he is able not only effectively to analyse discrete social roles—the stranger, the beggar and so on—but also to come to terms with strata consisting of homogeneous role occupants. An instance of this capacity is his characterization of the nobility.[17] He shows his usual confident grasp. The nobility, like the middle class, is an intermediate structure; royalty above it, commoners below it. Unlike the middle class, however, it is usually closed at both boundaries. It has intruded itself as a bloc between the ruler and the bulk of the population, and frustrated the policies of the former (a probable reference to the nobility of the *Ancien Régime*). On the other hand, it has, on occasion, performed a mediating and therefore unifying function. Its exclusiveness, however, is likely to be challenged in a society where interests are pluralistic rather than simply hierarchical. Or, in such a society, the composition of the nobility will become less homogeneous—a point which Simmel deftly illustrates with reference to the newly created nobility of Napoleon I's period. The institution of nobility in this example may be considered democratic since it rests on the *carrière ouverte aux talents* principle; the new nobility will limit the power of the old; it may also, by virtue of its meritocratic image, revalorize the old nobility, and so on. Simmel also refers here to the case of Canton Thurgau, Switzerland, where an eighteenth-century ordinance required noble candidates for public office to renounce their nobility—a move towards élite pluralism. Simmel proceeds to the observation that many noble families in European states are of foreign extraction, a remarkable fact in view of the connection between nobility and landownership and the generally conservative attitudes of the nobility. That this is so, of course, is a tribute to the strength of assimilative processes. Two general propositions are involved here: first, the greater the initial heterogeneity of a group, the greater its need for effective, particularistic socialization; and secondly, the greater the prestige of a group, the greater its potential capacity for effective socialization. Simmel also makes a passing reference to the surprising unity of the nobility (geographically disparate) in the Habsburg Empire, surprising and instructive, Simmel claims, because of the general absence of national consciousness in the multi-national Habsburg territories and the internecine struggles of the monarchy. Again, general propositions inhere in these observations; patriotism is only one element in the value system of the nobility, and so the unity of the nobility is inversely proportional to the degree of overall national consciousness. And, again, the nobility stands between the power centre (monarchy) and the populace, so its unity is inversely proportional to the stability of the power centre. An additional point which Simmel argues in his characterization of the nobility is that, for this strata, self-definitions are the very essence. Considerations of dignity require that the noble does not work, but non-work occupations are both permitted and encouraged, namely war and hunting, even though they involve more physical exertion than many roundly proletarian jobs. And war, indeed, may even be remunerative. Ransoms on captured enemies, however, do not carry the stigma of earned income. The general case we have been urging via this and other examples is that Simmel is impressive because he is able to do a variety of things and operate at different levels. He can empathize in terms of meaning and motive, he can elucidate the significance of forms, he can grasp the parameters of a social role, apprehend social definitions, and characterize a strata with reference to the global social setting.

The remarks on Simmel's discussion of the nobility lead to a seventh point relevant to an evaluation of his studies. It was suggested earlier in this chapter that his approach is not sociologistic, that is, it does not exclude psychological or social psychological factors. It might also be regarded as multi-disciplinary, as contributing to disciplines other than sociology—in the context of his expressly sociological writings, that is. Most obviously, one can view Simmel as contributing also to political science. This has been illustrated in a small way regarding his treatment of the nobility. The classic case of this phenomenon, however, and it is probably too well known to need any further comment, is Simmel's ideas on conflict.[18] In particular, these ideas have been codified and popularized by Lewis Coser,[19] the main burden being that conflict is not necessarily disruptive and may, in a variety of ways, be a force for integration. These ideas are not only well known, but have achieved a minor notoriety, since they may be used as a set of arguments for propping up normative functionalism. What we would urge here is that Simmel's tacit contribution to political science is not limited to a few essays characterizing politically significant roles, nor even to his ideas on conflict, but is the mark of a significant portion of his work. A substantial section, for instance, of his *Soziologie: Untersuchungen über die Formen der Vergesellschaftung*, is devoted to a discussion of superordination and subordination as forms of sociation, this work having been available in English since 1950.[20] These discussions would appear to have several merits. First, Simmel is able to distinguish a variety of formal manifestations of these phenomena—subordination to a plurality, to an individual, an idea, an object, a law, and so on. Secondly, he considers the formal and situational variability of their effectiveness. Here it would not be an exaggeration to say that he anticipates at certain points the typology of compliance relations later developed by Etzioni, that is to say, obedience resulting from normative internalization, obedience deriving from a rational calculation of material benefits and sacrifices and obedience based on fear of punishment or the restriction of liberty.[21] Thirdly, he traces the qualitative implications of the various forms for individuals. Included here is the point that subordination to a rule or law may have the advantage that it is impersonal and therefore construed as less humiliating, a point rediscovered by Michel Crozier.[22] Simmel, like Crozier, regards this as varying from culture to culture. And lastly, Simmel provides his usual battery of culturally diverse illustrations, a feature which adds lustre to his writings.

We have suggested that there are various ways in which Simmel's work has a remarkably modern tone. An additional sense in which this is so is that his studies often have a character which would recommend them to the phenomenologist. To put the point shortly, he is rather good at showing how a phenomenon is built up, of what it consists. This point could be diversely illustrated, but it is perhaps most easily observable where Simmel is dealing with some topic that his detractors would hold to be trivial or frivolous. He has a certain flair for divesting himself of the assumptive encrustations of the *Lebenswelt* and laying the phenomenon bare. Consider, for instance, his essay on fashion.[23] Fashion, he boldly declares, is a paradoxical phenomenon. This is so because it stands at the point of intersection of two forces: the desire for assimilation and that for differentiation. In so far as fashion involves the imitation of an example offered by someone else, it absolves the individual from the responsibility of initiative. It is a conformist act, it renders him part of the group, it confirms a collective identity. On the other hand, fashion satisfies needs for change, contrast and differentiation. Its changing content gives the individual the stamp of today rather than that of yesterday. The two counterposed forces are both necessary conditions for fashion: because of their contrast, the one is a condition for the realization of the other.

Fashion is, in fact, inexpedient. Our clothes, for instance, may in a general way be adapted to our needs, but particular variations (wide or narrow ties) serve no practical purpose and conform to no rationale. Neither is any objective aesthetics reflected in fashion's changing content; some fashions, by aesthetic criteria, are frankly awful. This simple fact, however, is somewhat clouded since there is frequently an empirical overlap between fashion and beauty. That is to say, those most committed to following the dictates of fashion are often, in short, the handsomest men and the prettiest girls; they are also the people who in any case will take most care over their appearance, whatever the nature of any particular fashion.

Fashion is essentially a superficial manifestation, even if the desires and needs which sustain it are not. It occasionally effects 'serious' things, such as religious faith and political belief, yet they cannot really become fashionable until they have been divorced from larger human commitments. Foreignness, necessarily imperfectly apprehended, is an excellent vehicle for conveying fashionableness. This, though, Simmel notes, is restricted to 'higher civilizations'; foreignness engenders only fear among savages, whose life is not so much nasty, brutish and short as downright dangerous. The exposure to danger thus produces a fear of the unknown, rendering foreign imports unappealing. In civilized societies, however, whatever is bizarre, unusual or conspicuous exercises charm: foreignness is fanciful.

The nature of fashion requires that, at any point in time, it should be practised by only some members of a collectivity, the rest being relegated to the status of aspirants, potential adopters or downright eccentrics. This feature assumes a patterned form when fashion functions to differentiate classes. Fashion's powerhouse is the upper classes, because of their greater leisure and resources. The content of any particular fashion is likely to change for them, however, when it is socially diffused. Lower-class adoption spells upper-class renunciation. Fashion has an analogous function for personal, as opposed to stratified differentiation. Its lures are especially appealing for the individual who combines a dependent nature with a desire for prominence. And the two forces may operate together; the commonplace man achieves style and elevation through a fashionable adoption. Fashion, indeed, may be seen as something of a safety valve in society's compliance system. In other contexts, conformity is expected but does not earn honour. No prizes are given to those who keep the law and internalize the norms. Yet fashion enables the individual to conform and to individualize at the same time. As an act of conformity, it is positive; as an act of differentiation, it is legitimate and carries no sanctions. Fashion may even be viewed, Simmel suggests, as an analogue to democracy. In the same way that democracy gives individuals a spurious sense of political autonomy (it should be remembered that Simmel lived under the representative but not responsible parliamentary régimes of Bismarck's era), fashion may give him a heightened sense of his individualism.

We may pause here and note what Simmel has suggested. He has placed a phenomenon in the context of determining forces. He has ascribed motives to participants, and differentiated among them. He has indicated social and psychological functions which are served by fashion. And he has culturally relativized his account in some respects. He has further suggested what features an artefact must have to be fashionably viable. We hope this sketch may serve to illustrate our eighth point, that Simmel is able to demonstrate the way in which a phenomenon is constituted.

We would like to suggest a ninth consideration in this evaluation of Simmel's studies. Many of us were brought up on a natural science model of sociology. That is, in the belief that, notwithstanding the difficulties, sociology can and should seek to emulate the natural sciences in two ways. First, it should be nomothetic; it should seek to generate law-like propositions having considerable empirical scope. Secondly, it should seek to test its conclusions by scientific methods of a quantitive kind, having regard to the rules of evidence. This view attaches considerable importance to a statement's operationalizability. That is, on that quality or those features of a statement that allow it both in principle and in practice to be tested. This quality depends on the lucidity and precision of the statement—both with regard to the variables it contains and with regard to the relationship between them; on the correspondence between the concepts the statement contains and empirical phenomena in the observable world; and on the availability of tangible measures of the existence and variability of these empirical phenomena. In short, operationalizability demands a good deal: Simmel would say that it is a concept that may be inferred from its negation in reality. Now it will be clear that Simmel, given his period and leanings, was not himself a great man for the Chi Square test and factor analysis. Nevertheless, for devotees of this approach we would like to raise the question: does Simmel, in the arena of his over-arching German prose style, ever say anything which could, at any rate in principle, be regarded as testable? Does he himself present propositions containing two (or more) variables, where the relationship between these variables is clear, so that testing is viable? Or even if he does not explicitly formulate such propositions, can they be derived from his writings without violation of his meaning or purpose?

We would argue that he does, and there are some extant illustrations of this. Theodore M. Mills has performed this exercise regarding Simmel's contribution to group dynamics.[24] In this essay Mills assembles six hypotheses concerning dyadic and tryadic groups derived from Simmel, and nine referring to large and small interactional systems. The classic case of codifying Simmel's ideas, already referred to in another context, is Lewis Coser's systematization and refinement of Simmel's ideas on conflict.[25] We would generalize from these examples and say that Simmel's work usually does permit the derivation of formal hypotheses, and this is especially true with his writing which impinges on political science: the essays on superordination and subordination are an obviously fertile source. We have sought, however, a difficult test-case and settled for a posthumously published essay on freedom and the individual.[26] This may be regarded as a tough test-case in that the essay is value-laden, abstract and philosophic. Thus the emphasis must necessarily be on the possibility (or otherwise) of extracting clear propositions, not on the availability of empirical indicators. We suggest that the following propositions may be derived from this piece without any violation of the writer's intentions.

1. Freedom is a term to which different meanings attach.
2. These meanings vary in a patterned way from epoch to epoch.
3. Freedom in the Renaissance period denotes mainly man's desire to be conspicuous.
4. The demand for freedom in the eighteenth century is the expression of the individual's various grievances against society.
5. The demand for freedom is directly proportional to the size of the disparity between

  (a) legitimate social institutions, and
  (b) material advance and intellectual achievements.
6. The demand for freedom may be based on a belief in the natural equality of the individual.
7. The demand for freedom is likely to be based on this belief where social arrangements produce inequality.
8. The cultural emphasis on human freedom increases with the level of scientific understanding of the natural world.
9. If the grant of *liberté* is not to violate *égalité*, then *fraternité* must become an institutionalized value.
10. Individualism in the eighteenth century is quantitative: it derives from a belief in man's equality.
11. Individualism in the nineteenth century is qualitative: it derives from a belief in man's uniqueness.
12. Romanticism also derives from the 'uniqueness concept' of man.
13. Different concepts of individualism are connected with different economic principles.
14. The belief in equality connects with the principle of the free market.
15. The belief in human uniqueness connects with the division of labour.

Our treatment may be checked by referring to Levine's English translation. The general point is that it is not difficult to derive straightforward relationship-between-phenomena propositions from Simmel's writings, and where the subject matter is less grandiose than in the foregoing example, such propositions may well be candidates for operationalization in the fuller sense.

Lastly, we would like to extend an earlier argument. It was suggested a few pages back that one reason for valuing Simmel's studies was that he shows an ability to formulate, to put things into words. We may go further and say that he has not only a formal linguistic competence, but a logical capacity for constructing and developing an argument, and there exist many illustrations of this ability, notwithstanding the occasional charges of frivolity and the 'squirrel' metaphors. We might suggest, as a case in point, his essay on the metropolis and mental life.[27] Simmel declares at the outset of this essay that, for the individual, the key problem of modern life is the maintenance of his independence against society, culture and technology. In order to apprehend the quality of modern life, one needs to examine therefore both the relationship between the individual and those features of society which transcend individual existence, and the relationship between the different aspects of life promoted by the social structure.

From these generalizations, Simmel proceeds to argue that the peculiar feature of metropolitan life is the rapidity of incessant stimuli, internal and external, with which it confronts the individual. The effect of these stimuli is to intensify the individual's emotional life. The stimuli are in the form of a contrast between present impressions and past impressions; that is to say, the number and rapidity of such contrasts is greater in the metropolis than in the small town. Hence mental life in the metropolis has a primarily intellectualist character, in contrast to the more emotional character of small-town life deriving from their inhabitants' feelings about the stable features of their environment. Or, to put it in another way, the intellect is more adaptable than the emotions. Metropolitan life requires adaptability and has consequently developed ratiocinative rather than intuitive faculties. The metropolitan 'type' (with individual variations) thus reacts rationally rather than emotionally. And this form of reaction serves to protect the individual's inner life from, as it were, the violence of excessive stimuli. This general rational quality of metropolitan life has some particular manifestations: the rest of the essay really seeks to explore these and their antitheses.

One of these manifestations is the role of the metropolis as a commercial and financial centre; that is, the rational mentality of the metropolis is favourable to exchange operations. These factors, of course, are mutually reinforcing. And we may generalize from this example: metropolitan life both requires and facilitates the emergence of norms of punctuality, precision, calculativeness and impersonality. The impersonality of metropolitan life, however, has produced a psychological reaction, namely, the blasé outlook. This may be viewed as a response to over-stimulation; in the small town, both the over-stimulation and the blasé attitude are relatively absent. Although one cause of this attitude, then, is physiological overstimulation, we may also argue that, in so far as its essence is an indifference to the distinctions between things, it also reflects the predominance of the money economy. The money economy, by supplying, as it were, a lowest common denominator, tends to obscure qualitative differences.

Reserve in social relationships is a further manifestation of these tendencies in the metropolis. It is conditioned by over-stimulation and has become a protective device. These reserved norms of social conduct also make possible for the individual a high degree of personal freedom. This may be understood by considering its opposite: where the group is small, and the possibility of out-of-group relationships is limited, the group will watch over the deeds and attitudes of its members more zealously and thereby inhibit the development of a certain kind of personal freedom. The blessing of this freedom, however, is not unmixed, since loneliness is its corollary, and the feeling of loneliness may be accentuated by pure weight of numbers in the metropolis. The impersonality of the metropolis is also instanced by the fact that its life is independent of the existence of particular individuals, even its most prominent citizens, in the way that the life of the small town is not. Simmel illustrates this proposition with a case of its opposite: Weimar in the eighteenth century is not metropolitan and does depend on particular individuals for its character and lustre. The metropolis is also the site of the most extreme division of labour; Simmel offers as an example the role of the *quartorsième* in Paris—the professional dinner-party guest whose services may be engaged by hostesses needing to make the number of guests up to fourteen.

On the other hand, the impersonality and rationality of the metropolis makes the differentiation of the individual *qua* individual more difficult. This accounts for the extravagances of the metropolis in terms of fastidiousness and eccentricity; they represent attempts at 'being different'. So we see that metropolitan life both enables personal freedom and gives rise to a desire for individuation, a desire that is not easy to satisfy. These aspirations for individuation are also not advanced by modern culture, which is dominated by the external spirit; it is external to the individual, whose own intellectual development lags behind its achievements. This discrepancy is, again, a reflection of the growing division of labour. It requires from the individual an ever more one-sided achievement or specialized contribution, and in this formulation Simmel anticipates Alvin Gouldner's concept of 'the unemployed self'.[28] In the crisis of modern existence, the metropolis is central. It permits individual independence and generates a need for personal differentiation. At the same time, it is both the symbol and the quintessence of forces conducive to the atrophy of individual culture.

We would suggest that, in this essay, Simmel has done more than just put what we apprehend (and that in part because of later analysis) into words. He has consistently shown the connections between the parts of this phenomenon and its derivatives. More generally, it is hoped that some progress has been made in this chapter towards a 'middle-range' evaluation of Simmel's substantive studies. That is, towards an interpretation which lies between an analysis of the underlying structure of his ideas on the one hand, and the assertion, on the other, that he is simply an entertaining commentator. In the final chapter of the introductory section, we wish to consider other ways, apart from his methodological contribution, in which Simmel participates in the sociological enterprise of his period.

NOTES AND REFERENCES

1. Lewis Coser (ed.), *Georg Simmel*, Prentice-Hall, Englewood Cliffs, N.J., 1965.

2. Donald N. Levine, 'Some Key Problems in Simmel's Work', in ibid.

3. Namely Kurt H. Wolff, *The Sociology of Georg Simmel*, The Free Press of Glencoe, Ill., 1950; Georg Simmel, *Conflict and the Web of Group Affiliations*, translated by Kurt H. Wolff and Reinhard Bendix, The Free Press, Glencoe, Ill., 1955; Kurt H. Wolff (ed.), *Georg Simmel 1858-1918*, Ohio State University Press, 1959; Donald N. Levine (ed.), *Georg Simmel on Individuality and Social Forms*, University of Chicago Press, 1971. Levine's book may be particularly recommended: it is the most recent anthology, contains some new translations and makes available in one volume some very interesting excerpts.

4. cf. Ronald Fletcher's view of Simmel as a developmental link man already discussed in the previous chapter.

5. See in Wolff (ed.), *Georg Simmel, 1858-1918*. Originally published in German as 'Das Abenteuer' in Georg Simmel, *Philosophische Kultur: Gesammelte Essays*, W. Klinkhardt, Leipzig, 1911.

6. See in Levine (ed.), *Georg Simmel on Individuality and Forms*. Taken from Georg Simmel, *Philosophie des Geldes*, Duncker & Humblot, Leipzig, 1900.

7. See Robert E. Park and Ernest W. Burgess, 'The Sociological Significance of the Stranger', in *Introduction to the Science of Sociology*, University of Chicago Press, 1921. Also available in Levine (ed.) *Georg Simmel on Individuality and Forms*. Originally published in Georg Simmel, *Soziologie: Untersuchungen über die Formen der Vergesellschaftung*, Duncker & Humblot, Leipzig, 1908.

8. C. Wright Mills, *The Sociological Imagination*, Oxford University Press, New York, 1959.

9. Levine (ed.), *Georg Simmel on Individuality and Forms*. Originally published in Simmel, *Philosophie des Geldes*.

10. In Levine (ed.), *Georg Simmel on Individuality and Social Forms*. Originally published in Simmel, *Philosophie des Geldes*.

11. P.M. Blau, *Exchange and Power in Social Life*, John Wiley & Sons, New York, 1964.

12. R.D. Jessop, *Social Order, Reform and Revolution*, The Macmillan Press, New York, 1972.

13. H.A. Simon, *Administrative Behaviour*, Macmillan Co., New York, 1945.

14. Georg Simmel, 'The Poor', *Social Problems*, 13, No. 2, 1965. Originally published in Simmel, *Soziologie: Untersuchungen über die Formen der Vergesellschaftung*. The editor is indebted to Adrian Sinfield, University of Essex, for first drawing his attention to the special interest of this essay.

15. This suggestion finds some modern echo in Gunter Grass's novel *Local Anaesthetic*, Secker & Warburg, London, 1970.

16. For an interesting though somewhat different account of reactions to the beggar, see Olivia Manning's novel set in pre-war Roumania, *The Great Fortune*, Heinemann, London, 1960.

17. In Levine (ed.) *Georg Simmel on Individuality and Social Forms*. Originally published in Simmel *Soziologie: Untersuchungen über die Formen der Vergesellschaftung*.

18. See Chapter 4, 'Der Streit', in Simmel, *Soziologie: Untersuchungen über die Formen der Vergesellschaftung*. Available in translation in Simmel, *Conflict and the Web of Group Affiliations*, in Wolff, *The Sociology of Georg Simmel*; and, in part, in Levine (ed.), *Georg Simmel on Individuality and Social Forms*. Some extracts are included in this volume.

19. Lewis Coser, *The Functions of Social Conflict*, Routledge & Kegan Paul, London, 1956.

20. Wolff, *The Sociology of Georg Simmel*.

21. Amitai Etzioni, *The Comparative Analysis of Complex Organizations*, Free Press of Glencoe, Ill., 1961.

22. Michel Crozier, *The Bureaucratic Phenomenon*, Tavistock Publications, London, 1964.

23. Available in English in the *American Journal of Sociology*, No. 62, 1957; originally published as Georg Simmel, *Philosophie der Mode*, Pan-Verlag, Berlin, 1905.

24. Theodore M. Mills, 'Some Hypotheses on Small Groups from Simmel', in Lewis Coser (ed.), *Georg Simmel*, Prentice-Hall, Englewood Cliffs, N.J., 1965.

25. Coser, *The Functions of Social Conflict.*

26. Georg Simmel, 'Das Individuum und die Freiheit'', in Michael Landmann and Margarete Sussman (eds.), *Brücke and Tür*, Koehler, Stuttgart 1957. Available in English in Levine (ed.), *Georg Simmel on Individuality and Social Forms.*

27. Georg Simmel, 'Die Grosstadt und das Geistesleben', in *Die Grosstadt. Jahrbuch der Gehe-Stiftung 9*, (1903). Available in English in Wolff, *The Sociology of Georg Simmel.*

28. Alvin W. Gouldner, 'The Unemployed Self', in Ronald Fraser (ed.), *Work*, Vol. II, Penguin Books, Harmondsworth, 1969.

# 4 Simmel and European Sociology

In the title of this volume we have accorded Simmel the soubriquet of 'Sociologist and European'. This has not been done in the hope of increasing sales in the E.E.C. countries, but because it is believed that Simmel is an explicitly European figure in both sociological and non-sociological ways. The latter point has already been touched on in Chapter 1, where some observations on the context and style of Simmel's life were offered: he was born in Europe, travelled in Europe and never left Europe. The breadth of his interests and the quality of his work mark him out as an impressive representative of a civilization which was culturally and intellectually rich. Simmel is interested in European art, European literature and European philosophy; he thought, wrote and lectured about them, and it is clear from his pragmatic emphases and choices that, for him, culture is European culture. We will also argue later that his interest in the theory of culture is pre-eminently European. Our principal concern in this section, however, is to justify the soubriquet 'European' by showing the extent of his involvement in the European sociological enterprise, an involvement manifest in terms of intellectual orientation and problem choice rather than one of association, whether personal or institutional.

One line in this argument has already been pursued in Chapter 2. This is that Simmel provided an epistemological rationale for sociology and delimited its scope as a discrete field of inquiry. This concern, in Simmel's day, was exclusively European, and it was a task to which his two greatest continental contemporaries—Weber and Durkheim—were also committed. It is now suggested that there are two further important respects in which he participated in the sociological enterprise of his period; two respects which have, as it were, a common denominator.

This common denominator may be apprehended tangentially. It is not an accident, one may argue, that the majority of those celebrated as 'the founding fathers of sociology' were European. Nor that they are all comprehended in the period 1820 to 1920. It is not an accident, because they were, in various ways and with varying degrees of discernible directness, reacting to industrialization and the multilateral transformation of society which it implied. And industrialization occurred in this period: it occurred only in Western Europe and the United States, and it occurred in Europe first. It is the precondition for the explosion of sociological creativity; it renders 'the nature of society' a no longer unchanging and therefore taken-for-granted phenomenon; and it is a stimulus also in that the content of social change is both a challenge to characterization and an invitation to explore the precarious stability of the new order and its implications for the human condition. This awareness of having experienced epochal change may be apprehended quite simply by the terms of contrast which are basic to the thinkers of this period: the positivistic stage as opposed to the theological and metaphysical stages (Comte); industrial society as opposed to military society (Spencer); capitalism *versus* feudalism (Marx); organic solidarity *versus* mechanistic solidarity (Durkheim); society based on legal-rational authority as opposed to society based on traditional or charismatic authority (Weber); *Gesellschaft versus Gemeinschaft* (Tönnies); and so on. We will argue that Simmel, though characteristically enlarging the phenomenon under discussion, is also part of this response to the emergence of modern society, but first a more particular point may be argued. The very fact that society had changed dramatically focused attention on the problem of social order. In the face of the changes that had occurred, it could no longer be taken for granted; it became both pragmatically and theoretically problematic. The response that this evokes in the founding fathers may be clearly observed, for instance, in Weber's concern with bureaucracy and authority bases; in Tönnies's apostrophization of rational will; and, of course, most obviously in Durkheim's account of organic solidarity. What, we may ask, is Simmel's contribution to the understanding of social order?

The answer to this question is not contained, in the view of the present writer, in Simmel's rather well-known essay, 'How is Society Possible?'.[1] This piece is of interest because of the modesty of Simmel's claims, and also—a related point—because, nearly seventy years later, very little of it is open to objection. Simmel begins in this essay by claiming that Kant's axiom—namely, that the unity of the natural world inheres entirely in the observer—is inapplicable to society. In nature, the connections between the elements are imposed by the observer; in society, the connections inhere in the elements themselves, that is, in the constituent individuals. Thus society is a unity, whose simple basis is that the individuals concerned are conscious of constituting a unity. At this point, Simmel 'backs off' a little and allows that this consciousness may not be explicit; rather, the individual is aware of being involved in relationships, of determining others and being determined by them. This mediated consciousness of unity, however, is also accessible to the outsider. He may perform an act of synthesis, and if he is able to do so, the society in question becomes an objective reality for him.

The members' consciousness of society, however, is not complete. In answer to the question—How do we know that individuals have this awareness of the processes of sociation?—Simmel replies, in effect, that it simply must be so—sociation implies the individual's awareness of participating in it. The awareness is also a presupposition for the existence of 'the perfect society', but Simmel is aware that, in this sense, society may well not be perfect. In developing this idea, he points out that the individual's perceptions may be distorted or incomplete, that one individual can never 'know' another absolutely, and that social perceptions may be vitiated by a tendency to think in terms of types: the Protestant, the bureaucrat and so on. Thus the individual is only partly absorbed in society. Part of him is extra-social—his temperament, interests, worth as a personality and so on. This extra-social aspect, however, is regarded by Simmel as constituting a condition that, in other respects, man is social. (This is Simmel's use of the duality concept, viz. something only is if the possibility of its being other is experienced.) Engaging in social action puts the individual into a dual position: he is both a participant in action and is confronted by it; or, our conception of society is based on the assumption that the individual is both determined and determining. Thus society may be conceived as an objective system of contents-actions, connected by concepts and values and ordered in space and time. Some people, Simmel remarks, may see bureaucracy as a small-scale analogue of society in respect of its order and predetermined functions. Yet, in society itself, a conscious and systematic determination of functions is lacking; society may only be conceived through an analysis of man's creativity and experience. And Simmel ends this account on a note of *lebensbejahend* optimism. Every individual, Simmel believes, has a part to play, a contribution to make. He is directed towards a certain place in society by his own qualities, and the place which ideally belongs to him actually exists. This, he admits, is based upon '. . . the premise of a pre-established harmony that exists between our psychological energies, however individualized they may be, and external, objective existence'.[2] Simmel's own career does not encourage one to believe in this harmony.

What is remarkable about this essay, apart from Simmel's naïvety or idealism, depending on one's viewpoint, is the carefully balanced position that he takes up in this brief ontology of society. The individual is conscious of society, but only through his involvement in particular relationships; we may make logical inferences from a concept of the perfect society while admitting that it does not, in fact, exist; the individual is both social and asocial; and so on. Indeed, when Simmel portrays the individual as both originating action and confronted by society as objective reality, he anticipates the eloquent development of the 'duality thesis' presented by Berger and Luckmann.[3] What is unsatisfactory about the essay is that too many things are inadequately treated: the observer's capacity to comprehend a totality of interactions in which he is not involved; the precise determinants of the individual's consciousness of society; and the question of the real locus of power. And, of course, it does not in any precise way contribute to a theory of social order, since, in terms of this essay, the conditions which have to be satisfied for 'society' to be said to exist are very general.

Instead, we wish to argue that Simmel's adumbration of a theory of social order is to be found in two of his substantive works, namely, in his first book on sociology, *Über Soziale Differenzierung*, and in his later work, *Soziologie: Untersuchungen über die Formen der Vergesellschaftung* to which frequent reference has already been made. We may go further and say that the first work offers a positive theory of social order, and the second makes a negative contribution to our understanding of the phenomenon. It is the first work which we wish to emphasize, focusing in the first instance on Chapter 5 of *Über Soziale Differenzierung* (reproduced in translation in this volume as Reading 3). This chapter is entitled 'The Intersection of Social Spheres', and it contains propositions serving to explain the persistence of society.[4] It should be admitted that Simmel himself does not hammer home his points, which is why a short exegesis is felt to be helpful in this introduction. Simmel approaches the problem from the standpoint of the individual rather than from a notion of societal prerequisites. He argues that any given individual can be socially defined in terms of the number and variety of social circles to which he belongs – which, so to speak, intersect in him. Thus any (modern) society is made up of countless individuals with (sometimes overlapping) membership of numerous social circles. Society may thus be viewed as a honeycomb of multilaterally linked cells, linked through the mechanism of pluralistic membership. This is the main argument, but the chapter contains at least seven sub-arguments relating to this theme.

First, both the greater freedom of modern society (see the earlier discussion of Simmel's essay on metropolitan life, and the subsequent discussion in this section of parts of *Philosophie des Geldes*) and the maturation processes of individuals result in an increase in the overall participation rates in a variety of social circles. That is, from Simmel's standpoint in the late nineteenth century, the degree is higher than it was before (historical dimension), and, from the viewpoint of any particular individual, the degree increases as he moves into adulthood (biographical dimension). Secondly, some common interests and pursuits give rise to social circles whose membership is diverse in terms of the individuals' social origins or class affiliations. We may not find Simmel's preferred example, namely the Renaissance as a republic of scholars, wildly convincing, but the argument is at least partially valid. In our society, for instance, constituency Labour parties contain graduate professionals side by side with manual workers; voluntary and recreational associations are not heavily 'patterned' with respect to the rank-and-file membership, only with regard to the occupants of offices and leadership positions where the middle class is over-represented. And particular institutional sectors might illustrate both this point and Simmel's previous argument about historical change: our educational institutions, for instance, are more heterogeneous with regard to class background now than they were forty years ago. Thirdly, not only may the individual's relative position in any social circle vary over time, but he may also occupy different positions in different social circles at the same time. In so far as this is so, it is a further factor inhibiting the division of societal members along some unambiguous line of cleavage. Fourthly, the individual may stand at the point of intersection of hostile social circles, that is, have common membership of two or more circles generally hostile to each other: for example, Conservative trade unionists, or radical peers in Britain. Fifthly, Simmel in this discussion introduces an extrinsic self-actualization argument by suggesting that free access to recreational, interest and ideological circles may function as a counterpoise to the putative loss of security and satisfaction involved in the transition from an agrarian to an industrialized society. Sixthly, some of these social circles are 'value intensive' in that they imply commitments to group norms of, for instance, professional ethics, ideological solidarity or military honour. Social circles of this type are particularly effective as socializing agencies, since membership is voluntary and their values are thus freely embraced. Here segmental normative integration is seen as a counterpoise to possible generalized anomie. And lastly, he cites working-class solidarity, not just as a new cohesive force, but as one paralleling and conceivably compensating for the fragmentation deriving from the division of labour.

Now it is not claimed that this analysis is new for us, but both a general and a particular historical qualification seems in order. The general point is that, in this analysis, Simmel is clearly meeting a felt need, as with his delimitation of the proper area of sociological inquiry discussed in Chapter 2. The industrial transformation of society posed acutely for Simmel's generation the problem of exploring modes of social order and cohesion. The particular point is that the person generally associated with the explanation of social cohesion in industrial society is not Simmel but Durkheim.[5] Very simply, Durkheim's answer to the question is that advanced societies are characterized by an organic solidarity deriving from the reciprocal interdependence of heterogeneous societal members; or, the division of labour eventuates in different people doing different things who will need each other. Now a couple of points on the comparative Durkheim–Simmel contribution are relevant. First, it can be seen that Simmel's analysis comprehends Durkheim's, but the reverse is not true. That is, Simmel's concept of 'social circles', while admittedly somewhat imprecise, is broader than Durkheim's notion of occupational-functional specialisms. Thus Simmel, as briefly indicated, is able to draw into the discussion the whole range of associational forms and institutional affiliations. The second point, quite simply, is that Simmel's published contribution to this debate precedes Durkheim's by some three years, a fact which may not be generally recognized.[6]

We may continue this Durkheim–Simmel analysis by looking at Chapter 4 of Simmel's *Über Soziale Differenzierung*, included in this volume in translation as Reading 4. This chapter is entitled 'Differentiation and the Principle of Saving Energy', and Simmel's concern is to show what facilitates efficiency or saving of energy and what is the role of differentiation in this process.[7] Here again we have a contribution (indirect) to the understanding of social order in the sense that 'increased efficiency' will, *ceteris paribus*, facilitate, the persistence of society and vice versa. Simmel sees friction, indirectness and superfluity of means as the obstacles to efficiency: these, in fact, are all reduced by differentiation in the sense of the division of labour. Simmel's overall estimation of the effects of differentiation, however, is not unmixed. He notes as well that differentiation may, in some instances, mean division into hostile factions, as, for instance, is the case with political parties. Here the connection between differentiation and increased efficiency is somewhat doubtful, though it might be argued that there is an efficiency gain in so far as energy is released by clear-cut commitment. A firmer objection, however, is that capitalism, which achieves *par excellence* the division of labour, also implies competition and conflict which Simmel regards as antipathetic to increased efficiency. Furthermore, Simmel recognizes that, for individuals, the division of labour may imply atrophy of certain qualities, this being another emergence of the 'unemployed self' concept to which we alluded in the previous section.

An interesting feature of Simmel's discussion in this chapter is not just that it loosely parallels Durkheim's and contributes to the then contemporary discussion of social order; it also anticipates what later came to be known as the structural differentiation model—anticipates it and goes a step further. Simmel observes that the evolutionary process involves the removal of functions from individuals and the vesting of them in the community, and he also suggests that if and when their centralized administration becomes too complex, they may be returned to individuals. Simmel's examples here are typically 'broad reach'. He notes that the medieval Church attained a significant level of differentiation in the form of a specialized, celibate priesthood, bolstered by monastic institutions and an episcopal hierarchy. All this clearly serves the ends of increased efficiency in terms of Simmel's analysis, since all spiritual energy is reserved for the priestly task (hopefully). The system, however, becomes counter-productive. The rule of celibacy prevents a direct transmission of cultivated spirituality. And institutional specialization precludes a lay, intellectual contribution to the development of religious understanding. Then the Reformation, in part a response to these tensions, restores the individual's access to God for which the priest was formally necessary. The institutional working out of de-differentiation may then be observed in the more egalitarian forms of Nonconformist Protestantism, and in the abolition of the priesthood·in some sects. Simmel's second example concerns the provision of military forces. The feudal system is relatively undifferentiated in that all have the obligation to serve, even if knights have a specialist military function. In the interests of efficiency, this gives way to professional standing armies, a development which reaches its zenith in the employment of mercenaries where the specialized function is divorced even from patriotic sentiment. But this stage again is transcended when universal conscription becomes the norm, though from the standpoint of the conscripts themselves, Simmel allows that we are dealing here with a case of temporal differentiation. A good example of conscription as de-differentiation would be the system in contemporary Switzerland where only the general staff are professionals and the office of the Commander-in-Chief is elective.

A final point on the problem of social order should be made. It was suggested earlier that a positive contribution to this question is to be found in *Über Soziale Differenzierung*, and that some negative clues are also to be found in *Soziologie: Untersuchungen über die Formen der Vergesellschaftung*. In the latter case, the reference is to Simmel's fourth chapter of this work containing his discussion of conflict, already briefly discussed in Chapter 3 (see Reading 5). In this connection, one may make two simple points. First, with respect to the conflictful entities considered singly, the existence of the conflict is a force for cohesion within them. Thus, generally, conflict implies cohesive sub-collectivities. And secondly, conflict itself is a form of interaction: the existence of conflict between entities implies an ongoing relationship between them. The purpose of these observations (and Simmel's ideas may be more fully apprehended in Reading 5), is to say that we cannot assume from the existence of conflict, or from an analytical identification of its potentiality, that social order is irredeemably threatened. We cannot make this assumption, because Simmel's discussion has shown that conflict has relationship-perpetuating and cohesion-inducing tendencies.

It was suggested at the beginning of this chapter that Simmel was centrally involved in the characterization of the form of society that had emerged in western Europe by the opening of the present century: a form deriving from industrialization and its attributes. Simmel's discussion of this phenomenon is to be found principally in his book *Philosophie des Geldes*. Three excerpts from this work, to the best of my knowledge translated for the first time, are included in the present

volume (Readings 6, 7 and 8). It is hoped that they speak for themselves
and that no summarized preview is necessary. The general point to be
emphasized is simply that Simmel does indulge in an extensive
exploration of the features and antecedents of modern society, and this
fact links him with his sociological contemporaries and places him at
the centre of sociological inquiry in his period. The elements of his
interpretation are not, for the most part, new to us, but in reading
*Philosophie des Geldes* we are confronted with the phenomenon of the
unpromoted German academic whose discussion of modern society, in
1900, anticipated many of the ideas later developed by thinkers such as
Ivan Illich, Alvin Gouldner and Charles Reich. All the ideas of admass,
means–ends disjunction, anomie, personal inauthenticity, ambiguous
freedom and technological determinism are to be found here. His
treatment is also marked by some characteristic differences. His
time-scale is longer than is the case with, say, Durkheim or Tönnies; for
Simmel, the *point de départ* is the erosion of feudalism, which, in turn,
facilitates capital accumulation, industrialization and the division of
labour. Its treatment is also broad-based rather than unilateral: in
*Philosophie des Geldes*, and in some of his essays discussed in Chapter
3, the treatment of sociological, psychological, economic and cultural
phenomena converge. Hence Simmel is able to describe the dynamics
of the money economy, work out their implications for social forms,
discuss their effect on the nature of culture and show the states of mind
induced in individuals. We may also note that Simmel's appraisal is a
balanced one. He draws attention to the phenomena of impersonality,
the trivialization of human relationships, economic calousness, calculative orientations, egocentric individualism, the emergence of meaningless 'middleman' occupations, declining job satisfaction and the
impoverishment of personal culture (see Readings 7 and 8). On the
other hand, in a chapter from the same book entitled 'Individual
Freedom' (see Reading 6), he argues very plausibly that the transition
from feudalism to the money economy entails gains in personal
freedom. Very briefly, there are three strands to this argument. First,
the monetization of seigneurial obligations makes them, for the
individual who is liable, more predictable, more calculable and more
flexible in so far as he can exercise initiative as to the means whereby he
meets them. Secondly, the impersonality–anonymity implied by a
money economy is two-edged; the disadvantages have already been
touched upon, but a corresponding advantage arises for individuals.
This is, that they are able to participate in its operations without

committing themselves as whole personalities. The subjective self may be preserved inviolate behind the impersonally fulfilled function. And thirdly, the money economy provides objective universal standards in terms of which goods and services may be supplied and procured. This, again, is two-edged: it increases the total number of the individual's dependencies in the context of advanced differentiation, but it reduces his dependency on *particular* individuals. Both the universal standard and the division of labour imply substitutability and therefore choice. The number and salience of ascriptive relationships is reduced, and this is a gain in terms of autonomy and self-direction. Thus there is no straight answer to the question: is Simmel positively or negatively orientated to modern society? But his appraisal has a degree of balance. To make the obvious comparison, he does not, like Tönnies, allow his longing for an idyllic childhood in rural Schleswigland to masquerade as social theory. This is partly because he follows so many lines of inquiry (where multilateralism is the antidote to snap judgements), but probably also because the context of his life permitted a certain distance, a point which was raised in Chapter 1. This relative neutralism of Simmel's comes out in relation also the the First World War; indeed, his political non-partisanship is a *leitmotiv* highlighted by the experience of major war in his late fifties. The point can easily be made by comparisons: he was not, like Weber, an enthusiast of the German war effort; nor did he, like Durkheim, indulge in patriotic pamphleteering. And if we would turn this into a conjectural exercise, it is not likely that, had Simmel lived longer, he would have made an academic career in a Fascist state, like Michels, been decorated by Mussolini, like Pareto, or written in praise of National Socialism, like Werner Sombart. Indeed, there can be little doubt that, had his life extended into the Third Reich, he would soon have suffered the fate which in fact befell his son.[8] Simmel's condemnation of the First World War is both ethical and cultural, and it is to a brief consideration of Simmel's cultural interests that we finally turn.

Included in this volume are several excerpts from Simmel's writings on the First World War and on his contribution to the theory of culture (see Readings 9, 10, 11, 12, and 13). These have been selected partly to further an appreciation of Simmel's breadth of interest and to enable the reader to appraise the interrelations between his social thought and cultural theory. I do not wish to summarize the contents of these readings, but a few indications of the recurrent themes in Simmel's discussion may be helpful. It may be noted that Simmel's concern with culture is a further aspect of his European persona. When he discusses culture in the conventional sense, his empirical referrents are clearly the products of European art, literature and philosophy; and the tensions and problems he designates are, if not exclusively European, certainly pre-eminently European. And it should be admitted that Simmel's use of the term culture is not always consistent (and it is difficult to avoid reproducing this variability in translation). Most often, he uses it in a traditional sense to indicate the intellectual and aesthetic products of gifted people; sometimes, however, it appears in a loose anthropological sense, and sometimes as a specialized metaphor, as in 'material culture'.

Our first point would be that the form–content distinction discussed in Chapter 2 is relevant in the analysis of culture, where the form is the very essence. Thus 'the contents of culture . . . follow a logic which is independent of their cultural purpose and leads further and further away from it'.[9] Secondly, and this has been touched on in Chapter 3 in the discussion of his essay on the nature of metropolitan life, Simmel is deeply concerned by the growing disparity between personal culture and objective culture. That is, the growth of culture in all spheres—aesthetic, material and scientific—has far outstripped the capacity of the individual to keep pace with it, so that his personal subjective culture is impoverished, a development which is exacerbated by the division of labour. Simmel varies in the extent to which he sees this development as hopeless and irreversible. On some occasions, he devotes himself to explaining the nature of the act of internalization which is required for the individual meaningfully to assimilate cultural products—an enterprise which would seem to imply the possibility of the individual's 'reconquest' of culture. On other occasions, he seems to regard this as hopeless, though with the possibility of 'temporary relief' being afforded by upheavals such as war. Thirdly, he argues that, precisely because of the form–content distinction, the meaningful internalization of culture by the individual is rendered additionally problematic since it logically involves an apprehension of the cultural form. Fourthly, he believes that contemporary culture has recognized the problem, but failed to come to terms with it. The recognition is manifest in the struggle against form as such (see Reading 9), and he discusses expressionism in art and contemporary sexual morality in the light of this problem designation. And lastly, he believes that the expansion of material culture, especially of technology, has upset the individual's perceptions of means–ends relationships. That is, it has produced a plethora of means, induced confusion between means and ends, and brought about a situation in which ends, achieved by particular means, are not terminal but have further implications. All this simply adds to the ontic insecurity of the ordinary person who is already the victim of the 'culture gap' previously indicated. Throughout these discussions, strictly cultural analysis is interwoven with a consideration of social causes and effects.

Towards the end of his life, Simmel's interest in cultural questions merged with his reaction to the First World War. If we give a 'warts and all' picture, it must be admitted that Simmel's position in the war was not without blemish. In the heady days of 1914, he delivered an address in Strasbourg, to whose university he had just been 'called' as a full professor after half a lifetime of disappointments, and this address is unpleasantly war-mongering in tone. He soon retracted, however, but allowed this address to be published with three other papers, two of which are included here (see Readings 12 and 13), in a small volume entitled *The War and Spiritual Decisions*.[10] It may also be objected that traces of this war enthusiasm appear in another essay in this book, entitled 'The Crisis of Culture' (included in this volume as Reading 12). The present writer's view on this point is that this 'enthusiasm' is reasoned rather than rabid. While there is little doubt that Simmel's position here is anti-war, with his distanced subtlety he is able to review the problems he has already discussed—both cultural in a formal sense and those pertaining to the quality of modern life—in the context of the First World War. Here he notes that, in a quite simple sense, the war represents an escape from the unresolved tensions of the cultural milieu: soldiers are too busy and too frightened to be perturbed by the culture gap. There is also a less clear argument to the effect that the upheaval of war places a temporary moratorium on the growing disparity between subjective and objective culture, and possibly offers some means of breaking out of the impasse. He also suggests, and this is 'pure' Simmel, that the conditions of war upset the taken-for-granted assumptions of the money economy discussed in *Philosophie des Geldes* and in some of the essays referred to in Chapter 3. That is, the material shortages of war, heightened by the British blockade, demonstrate the inefficacy of money: in wartime, one may have abundant money but little bread. Thus war strikes a blow to the money economy in so far as it reverses the trend from intrinsic value to objective value. Similarly, capitalism's facilitation of egocentric individualism is undermined by the pragmatic demand for patriotic sacrifice. In a final essay, 'The Idea of Europe' (see Reading 13), Simmel shows his hand, but with a caution that probably reflects the exigencies of conformity in a powerful state at war, and deplores the war as having shattered the cultural unity of Europe and imperilled its creative vitality. This leads Simmel to urge not German success at arms, but a qualified Europeanism in which integrated national contributions to a European culture again become possible: for Simmel, that which is, say, characteristically French will also be *ipso facto* European. Europeanism is extolled rather than internationalism, which Simmel rejects as superficial and inadequately based on cultural internalization. Simmel may be viewed as a European chauvinist, but it was Europe's intellectual vitality and cultural achievements which he lauded, not its economic penetration of the Third World.

It is hoped that these introductory chapters may enable the reader to place the following selections from Simmel's work in context. Since such a selection necessarily omits a great deal, we have sought to redress the balance with some discussion of sections of his work not included in this volume, and have tried to present the main lines of his thought. And, in particular, we have tried to argue that there are important respects in which Simmel, perhaps better viewed as a hungry wolf than a lone wolf, is very much a part of the European sociological enterprise which was the setting for his own development and creativity.

NOTES AND REFERENCES

1. Originally published as 'Exkurs über das Problem: Wie ist Gesellschaft möglich' in *Soziologie: Untersuchungen über die Formen der Vergesellschaftung*, Duncker & Humblot, Leipzig, 1908. Available in English in Kurt H. Wolff (ed.), *Georg Simmel, 1858-1918*, Ohio State University Press, 1959.

2. In ibid.

3. P.L. Berger and T. Luckmann, *The Social Construction of Reality*, Allan Lane The Penguin Press, 1967.

4. The key word in this essay, *Kreis*, may be rendered in English either as 'circle' or as 'sphere'. We have translated it as 'sphere' in Reading 3. *Kreis*, as used by Simmel, means *any* social collectivity: the family, a work group, a professional association, any formal organization, a friendship or interest group, even a complete social class.

5. Émile Durkheim, *De la division du travail social: étude sur l'organisation des sociétés supérieures*, Paris, 1893.

6. The editor is indebted to Anthony Giddens of King's College, Cambridge, for drawing his attention to this point in a letter some years ago.

7. The translation of the key word in this title, *Kraftersparnis*, is arguable. We have opted for a literal rendering, 'saving energy', but the word may also be regarded as having the connotation of 'increased efficiency', and it is discussed in these terms here.

8. Simmel's son was incarcerated in Dachau, but subsequently released and allowed to emigrate to the United States.

9. Quoted in Rudolph H. Weingartner, 'Theory and Tragedy of Culture', in Lewis Coser (ed.), *Georg Simmel*, Prentice-Hall, Englewood Cliffs, N.J., 1965.

10. Originally published as *Der Krieg und die Geistigen Entscheidungen*, Duncker & Humblot, Leipzig, 1917.

**II**  *Readings from Simmel's Works*

*Reading One*
# The Field of Sociology

The first difficulty which arises if one wants to make a tenable statement about the science of sociology is that its claim to *be* a science is not undisputed. Further, there is a chaotic multitude of opinions concerning its contents and aims. There are so many contradictions and confusions, that one doubts again and again whether one deals with a scientifically justifiable problem at all here. The lack of an undisputed and clear definition would not be so bad if it were made up for by the existence of a certain number of specific problems which are not, or not exhaustively, treated in other disciplines and which contain the fact or concept of 'society' as their common element and point of contact. They might be too different from one another in content, orientation, and method of solution to be treated as if they amounted to a homogeneous field of inquiry. Yet even then, they could at least find a preliminary refuge under the heading of 'sociology'; at least superficially, it would be clear where to look for them. In such a scheme, sociology would resemble technology, a tag quite legitimately attached to an immense range of tasks whose understanding and solution are not too greatly helped by the suggestion (through the name 'technology') that they have some feature in common.

## 1. Society and Knowledge of Society

Such a tenuous tie among heterogeneous problems might hold out the promise of their unity at a deeper level. Yet even this tenuous tie appears impossible because of the problematic character of the only concept that holds these problems together—'society'. In fact, all existing denials of the possibility of sociology as a science arise on the basis of this problematic character. It is remarkable that the denials either minimize or exaggerate this concept. Existence, we hear, is an exclusive attribute of individuals, their qualities and experiences. 'Society', by contrast, is an abstraction. Although indispensable for practical purposes and certainly very useful for a rough and preliminary survey of the phenomena that surround us, it is no real *object*. It does not exist outside and in addition to the individuals and the processes among them. After each of these individuals is investigated in his natural and historical characteristics, nothing is left by way of subject matter for a particular science.

For this sort of critique, 'society', obviously, is too slight a matter to constitute a field of science. For another kind of critique, however, it is too big: for on the other hand it is said all that men are and do occurs within society, is determined by society, and is part of its life; there is no science of man that is not science of society. The science of society thus ought to replace the artificially compartmentalized special disciplines, historical, psychological, and normative. It ought to make it evident that it is *sociation* which synthesizes all human interests, contents, and processes into concrete units. But, obviously, this definition, which wants to give sociology everything, takes as much away from it as did the first conception that left it nothing. For jurisprudence and philology, political science and literary criticism, psychology and theology, and all the other disciplines that have divided up the study of human life among themselves, will certainly continue to exist. Nothing is gained by throwing their sum total into a pot and sticking a new label on it: 'sociology'.

The trouble is that the science of society, in contrast to other sciences that are well established, is in the unfortunate position of still having to prove its right to exist. Yet this is fortunate, too, for sociology's struggle for existence is bound to lead to a clarification of its basic concepts (which is good and necessary in itself) and to the establishment of its specific manner of investigating reality.

Let us grant for the moment that only individuals 'really' exist. Even then, only a false conception of science could infer from this 'fact' that any knowledge which somehow aims at synthesizing these individuals deals with merely speculative abstractions and unrealities. Quite on the contrary, human thought always and everywhere synthesizes the given into units that serve as subject matters of the sciences. They have no counterpart whatever in immediate reality. Nobody, for instance, hesitates to talk of the development of the Gothic style. Yet nowhere is there such a thing as 'Gothic style', whose existence could be shown.

Instead, there are particular works of art which, along with individual elements, also contain stylistic elements; and the two cannot be clearly separated. The Gothic style as a topic of historical knowledge is an *intellectual* phenomenon. It is abstracted from reality; it is not itself a given reality. Innumerable times, we do not even want to know how individual things behave in all detail: we form new units out of them. When we inquire into the Gothic style, its laws, its development, we do not describe any particular cathedral or palace. Yet the *material* that makes up the unit we are investigating—'Gothic style'—we gain only from a study of the details of cathedrals and palaces. Or, we ask how the 'Greeks' and the 'Persians' behaved in the battle of Marathon. If it were true that only individuals are 'real', historical cognition would reach its goal only if it included the behaviour of each individual Greek and each individual Persian. If we knew his whole life history, we could psychologically understand his behaviour during the battle. Yet even if we could manage to satisfy such a fantastic claim, we would not have solved our problem at all. For this problem does not concern this or that individual Greek or Persian; it concerns all of them. The notion, 'the Greeks' and 'the Persians', evidently constitutes a totally different phenomenon, which results from a certain intellectual synthesis, not from the observation of isolated individuals. To be sure, each of these individuals was led to behave as he did by a development which is somehow different from that of every other individual. In reality, none of them behaved precisely like any other. And, in no one individual, is what he shares with others clearly separable from what distinguishes him from others. Both aspects, rather, form the inseparable unity of his personal life. Yet in spite of all this, out of all these individuals we form the more comprehensive units, 'the Greeks' and 'the Persians'.

Even a moment's reflection shows that similar concepts constantly supersede individual existences. If we were to rob our cognition of all such intellectual syntheses because only individuals are 'real', we would deprive human knowledge of its least dubious and most legitimate contents. The stubborn assertion that after all there exist nothing but individuals which alone, therefore, are the concrete objects of science, cannot prevent us from speaking of the histories of Catholicism and Social Democracy, of cities, and of political territories, of the feminist movement, of the conditions of craftsmen, and of thousands of other synthetic events and collective phenomena—and, therefore, of society in general. It certainly is an abstract concept. But each of the innumerable articulations and arrangements covered by it is an object that can be investigated and is worth investigation. And none of them consists of individual existences that are observed in all their details.

This whole consideration, however, might be due, simply, to an imperfect grasp of the matter at issue. It might merely be a (perhaps) necessary preliminary that would, potentially or actually, be overcome by a more intimate knowledge of the individuals as the ultimately concrete elements. Yet if we examine 'individuals' more closely, we realize that they are by no means such ultimate elements or 'atoms' of the human world. For the unit denoted by the concept 'individual' (and which, as a matter of fact, perhaps is insoluble, as we shall see later) is not an object of cognition at all, but only of experience. The way in which each of us, in himself and in others, knows of this unit, cannot be compared to any other way of knowing. What we know about man *scientifically* is only single characteristics. They may exist once, or they may stand in a relation of reciprocal influence to one another; but each of them requires its special investigation and derivation, which leads to innumerable influences of the physical, cultural, personal environment—influences that come from everywhere and extend infinitely in time. Only by isolating and grasping them and by reducing them to increasingly simple, covert and remote elements do we approach what is really 'ultimate', that is, what is real in the rigorous sense of the word. This 'real' alone must form the basis for any higher intellectual synthesis. Colour molecules, letters, particles of water indeed 'exist'; but the painting, the book, the river are syntheses: they are units that do not exist in objective reality but only in the consciousness which constitutes them. But what is more, even *these* so-called elements are highly synthetic phenomena. It is, therefore, not true that reality can be attributed only to properly ultimate units, and not to phenomena in which these units find their forms. Any form (and a form always is a synthesis) is something added by a synthesizing subject. Thus, a conception that considers only individuals as 'real' lets what *should* be considered real get out of hand. It is perfectly arbitrary to stop the reduction, which leads to ultimately real elements, at the individual. For this reduction is interminable. In it, the individual appears as a composite of single qualities, and destinies, forces and historical derivations, which in comparison to the individual himself have the same character of elementary realities as do the individuals in comparison to society.

In other words, the alleged realism that performs this sort of critique of the concept of society, and thus of sociology, actually eliminates all knowable reality. It relegates it into the infinite and looks for it in the realm of the inscrutable. As a matter of fact, cognition must be conceived on the basis of an entirely different structural principle. This principle is the abstraction, from a given complex of phenomena, of a number of heterogeneous objects of cognition that are nevertheless recognized as equally definitive and consistent. The principle may be expressed by the symbol of different *distances* between such a complex of phenomena and the human mind. We obtain different pictures of an object when we see it at a distance of two, or of five, or of ten yards. At each distance, however, the picture is 'correct' in its particular way and only in this way. And the different distance also provides different margins for error. For instance, if the minute detail of a painting that we gain at very close range were injected into a perspective gained at a distance of several yards, this perspective would be utterly confused and falsified. And yet on the basis of a superficial conception, one might assert that the detailed view is 'truer' than the more distant view. But even this detailed perception involves some distance whose lower limit is, in fact, impossible to determine. All we can say is that a view gained at any distance whatever has its own justification. It cannot be replaced or corrected by any other view emerging at another distance.

In a similar way, when we look at human life from a certain distance, we see each individual in his precise differentiation from all others. But if we increase our distance, the single individual disappears, and there emerges, instead, the picture of a 'society' with its own forms and colours—a picture which has its own possibilities of being recognized or missed. It is certainly no less justified than is the other in which the parts, the individuals, are seen in their differentiation. Nor is it by any means a mere preliminary of it. The difference between the two merely consists in the difference between purposes of cognition; and this difference, in turn, corresponds to a difference in distance.

The right to sociological study thus is not in the least endangered by the circumstance that all real happenings only occur in individuals. Yet the independence of sociology from this circumstance can be argued even more radically. For it is not true that the cognition of series of individual occurrences grasps immediate reality. This reality, rather, is given to us as a complex of images, as a surface of contiguous phenomena. We articulate this datum—which is our only truly primary datum—into something like the destinies of individuals. Or we reduce its simple matter-of-factness to single elements that are designed to catch it as if they were its nodal points. Clearly in either case there occurs a process which *we* inject into reality, an *ex post facto* intellectual *transformation* of the immediately given reality. Because of constant habit, we achieve this almost automatically. We almost think it is no transformation at all, but something given in the natural order of things. Actually, this transformation is exactly as subjective—but also, since it yields valid cognition, exactly as objective—as is the synthesis of the given under the category of society. Only the particular purpose of cognition determines whether reality, as it emerges or is experienced in its immediacy, is to be investigated in a personal or in a collective frame of reference. Both frames of reference, equally, are 'stand-points'. Their relation to one another is not that of reality to abstraction. Rather, since both are interpretations, though different ones, both are detached from 'reality', which itself cannot be the immediate subject matter of science. It becomes amenable to cognition only by means of categories such as, for instance, 'individual', or 'society'.

Nor is the concept of society invalidated by the fact that, if we look at it from still another angle, we must admit that human existence is real only in individuals. If the concept 'society' is taken in its most general sense, it refers to the psychological interaction among individual human beings. This definition must not be jeopardized by the difficulties offered by certain marginal phenomena. Thus, two people who for a moment look at one another or who collide in front of a ticket window, should not on these grounds be called sociated. Yet even here, where interaction is so superficial and momentary, one could speak, with some justification, of sociation. One has only to remember that interactions of this sort merely need become more frequent and intensive and join other similar ones to deserve properly the name of sociation. It is only a superficial attachment to linguistic usage (a usage quite adequate for daily practice) which makes us want to reserve the term 'society' for *permanent* interactions only. More specifically, the interactions we have in mind when we talk about 'society' are crystallized as definable, consistent structures such as the state and the family, the guild and the church, social classes and organizations based on common interests.

But in addition to these, there exists an immeasurable number of less conspicuous forms of relationship and kinds of interaction. Taken singly, they may appear negligible. But since in actuality they are inserted into the comprehensive and, as it were, official social formations, they alone produce society as we know it. To confine ourselves to the large social formations resembles the older science of anatomy with its limitation to the major, definitely circumscribed organs such as heart, liver, lungs, and stomach, and with its neglect of the innumerable, popularly unnamed or unknown tissues. Yet without these, the more obvious organs could never constitute a living organism. On the basis of the major social formations—the traditional subject matter of social science—it would be similarly impossible to piece together the real life of society as we encounter it in our experience. Without the interspersed effects of countless minor syntheses, society would break up into a multitude of discontinuous systems. Sociation continuously emerges and ceases and emerges again. Even where its eternal flux and pulsation are not sufficiently strong to form organizations proper, they link individuals together. That people look at one another and are jealous of one another; that they exchange letters or dine together; that irrespective of all tangible interests they strike one another as pleasant or unpleasant; that gratitude for altruistic acts makes for inseparable union; that one asks another man after a certain street, and that people dress and adorn themselves for one another—the whole gamut of relations that play from one person to another and that may be momentary or permanent, conscious or unconscious, ephemeral or of grave consequence (and from which these illustrations are quite casually chosen), all these incessantly tie men together. Here are the interactions among the atoms of society. They account for all the toughness and elasticity, all the colour and consistency of social life, that is so striking and yet so mysterious.

The large systems and the super-individual organizations that customarily come to mind when we think of society, are nothing but immediate interactions that occur among men constantly, every minute, but that have become crystallized as permanent fields, as autonomous phenomena. As they crystallize, they attain their own existence and their own laws, and may even confront or oppose spontaneous interaction itself. At the same time, society, as its life is constantly being realized, always signifies that individuals are connected by mutual influence and determination. It is, hence, something functional, something individuals do and suffer. To be true to this fundamental character of it, one should properly speak, not of society, but of sociation. Society merely is the name for a number of individuals, connected by interaction. It is because of their interaction that they are a unit—just as a system of bodily masses is a unit whose reciprocal effects wholly determine their mutual behaviour. One may, of course, insist that only these masses are true 'realities', and that their mutually stimulated movements and modifications are something intangible, and thus only secondary realities, so to speak, for they have their locus only in the concrete bodies themselves. The so-called unit merely is the synopsis of these materially separated existences: after all, the impulses and formations they receive and produce remain in *them*. In the same sense one may insist that ultimately it is the human individuals that are the true realities. But this adds nothing to our argument. In accordance with it, society certainly is not a 'substance', nothing concrete, but an *event*: it is the function of receiving and effecting the fate and development of one individual by the other. Groping for the tangible, we find only individuals; and between them, only a vacuum, as it were. Later, we shall consider the consequences of this conception. At any rate, if it leaves 'existence' (more strictly speaking) only to individuals, it must nevertheless accept the process and the dynamics of acting and suffering, by which the individuals modify one another, as something 'real' and explorable.

## 2. The Abstract Character of Sociology

Under the guidance of its particular conception, any science extracts only one group or aspect out of the totality or experienced immediacy of phenomena. Sociology does so, too. It acts no less legitimately than does any other science if it analyses individual existences and recomposes them in the light of its own conception. Sociology asks what happens to men and by what rules they behave, not in so far as they unfold their understandable individual existences in their totalities, but in so far as they form groups and are determined by their group existence because of interaction. It treats the history of marriage without analysing particular couples; the principle underlying the organization of offices, without describing a 'typical day' at a particular office; the laws and consequences of the class struggle, without dealing with the development of a particular strike or of particular wage negotiations. The topics of its researches certainly arise in a process of abstraction. But this feature does not distinguish sociology from such sciences as logic or economic theory. They, too, under the guidance of certain conceptions (such as cognition and economics, respectively), produce, out of reality, interrelated phenomena that do not exist as something experienceable but whose laws and evolution they discover.

Sociology thus is founded upon an abstraction from concrete reality, performed under the guidance of the concept of society. We have already noted the invalidity of the accusation of unreality, which was derived from the assertion of the exclusive reality of individuals. But this realization also protects our discipline from the exaggeration that I have mentioned, earlier, as an equally grave danger for its existence as a science. To repeat: since man in all aspects of his life and action is determined by the fact that he is a social being, all sciences of him are reduced to parts of the science of social life. All subject matters of these sciences are nothing more than particular channels, as it were, in which social life, the only bearer of all energy and of all significance, flows. I have shown that all this conception does is to yield a new common name for all the branches of knowledge that will continue to exist anyway, unperturbed and autonomous, with all their specific contents and nomenclatures, tendencies and methods. Nevertheless, this erroneous exaggeration of the concepts 'society' and 'sociology' is based upon a fact of great significance and consequence. For, the recognition that man in his whole nature and in all his manifestations is determined by the circumstance of living in interaction with other men, is bound to lead to a new viewpoint that must make itself felt in all so-called human studies.[1]

As recent a period as the eighteenth century explained the great contents of historical life—language, religion, the formation of states, material culture—essentially, as inventions of single individuals. Where the reason and interests of the individual were not adequate explanations, transcendental forces were resorted to. The 'genius' of the single inventor, incidentally, served as a link between the two explanatory principles: it suggested that the known and understandable forces of the individual did not suffice to produce the phenomenon in question. Thus, language was either the invention of individuals or a divine gift; religion (as a historical event), the invention of shrewd priests or divine will; moral laws were either inculcated into the mass by heroes or bestowed by God, or were given to man by 'nature', a no less mystical hypostasis. These two insufficient alternatives were replaced by the notion of societal production, according to which all these phenomena emerge in interactions among men, or sometimes, indeed, *are* such interactions. They cannot be derived from the individual considered in isolation. In addition to the two earlier possibilities, therefore, we now have a third: the production of phenomena through social life. This production occurs in a twofold manner. In the first place, there is the simultaneity of interacting individuals which in each produces what cannot be explained on the basis of him alone. In the second place, there is the succession of generations. The inheritance and tradition of this succession inseparably fuse with the acquisitions made by the individual himself: social man, in contrast to all subhuman animals, is not only a successor but also an heir.

## 3. Sociology as a Method

The notion of societal production lies, as it were, somewhere between the notions of purely individual and transcendental production. It has provided all human studies with a genetic method, with a new tool for the solution of their problems, whether they concern the state or church organization, language or moral conditions. Sociology thus is not only a science with its own subject matter that is differentiated, by division of labour, from the subject matters of all other sciences. It also has become a *method* of the historical disciplines and of the human studies in general. Yet in order to use it, these sciences by no means need abandon their own particular viewpoints. They need not become mere parts of sociology, as that fantastic exaggeration of its idea, which I mentioned earlier, would make us believe. Rather, sociology adapts itself to each specific discipline—economics, history of culture, ethics, theology, or what not. In this respect, it is essentially like induction. At its time, induction, as a new principle of investigation, penetrated into all kinds of problem areas. It thus contributed new solutions for tasks well established in these areas. The parallel suggests that sociology is no more a special science than induction is (and surely, it is not an all-embracing science). In so far as it is based on the notions that man must be understood as a social animal and that society is the medium of all historical events, sociology contains no subject matter that is not already treated in one of the extant sciences. It only opens up a new avenue for all of them. It supplies them with a scientific method which, precisely because of its applicability to all problems, is not a science with its own content.[2]

In its very generality, this method is apt to form a common basis for problem areas that previously, in the absence of their mutual contact, lacked a certain clarity. The universality of sociation, which makes for the reciprocal shaping of the individuals, has its correspondence in the singleness of the sociological way of cognition. The sociological approach yields possibilities of solution or of deeper study which may be derived from fields of knowledge contentally quite different (perhaps) from the field of the particular problem under investigation. I will mention three examples, which range from the most specific to the most general.

(1) The criminologist may learn much concerning the nature of so-called mass crimes from a sociological investigation of the psychology of the theatre audience. For here, the stimulus of a collective-impulsive behaviour can still be clearly ascertained. Furthermore, this behaviour occurs in the sphere of art which, as it were, is abstract and precisely delimited. Thus here—and this is very important for the problem of guilt in regard to 'mass crimes'—the extent to which the individual can be determined by a mass in physical proximity with him, and the extent to which subjective and objective value judgements can be eliminated under the impact of contagion, may be observed under conditions that are as purely experimental and crucial as scarcely anywhere else.

(2) The student of religion is often inclined to explain the life of the religious community and its readiness to sacrifice in terms of their devotion to an ideal that is common to all members. He may tend to ascribe the conduct of life, inspired as it is by the hope in a perfect state beyond the lives of the existing individuals, to the strength in content of the religious faith. Yet the members of a Social Democratic trade union may exhibit the same traits in their common and mutual behaviour. If the student of religion notes this similarity, he may learn that religious behaviour does not exclusively depend on religious contents, but that it is a generally human form of behaviour which is realized under the stimulus not only of transcendental objects but also of other motivations. He will also gain insight into something even more important to him. This is the fact that, even in its autonomy, religious life contains elements that are not specifically religious, but social. Certainly, these elements—particular kinds of reciprocal attitude and behaviour—are fused organically with the religious mood itself. But only when they are isolated by means of the sociological method, will they show what within the whole complex of religious behaviour may legitimately be considered purely religious, that is, independent of anything social.

(3) I will give one last example of the mutual fertilization of problem areas that is suggested by the common involvement of human sociation in all of them. The contemporary student of political or cultural history is often inclined, for instance, to derive the character of the domestic policy pursued by a given country from its economic conditions and processes as sufficient causes. Suppose he explains the strong individualism of early Italian Renaissance political constitutions as the effect of the liberation of economic life from guild and church ties. Here

it is an observation of the historian of art that may greatly qualify his conception. The observation is that already in the beginning of the epoch under discussion there was an immense spread of naturalistic and individualistic portrait busts. Thus the general attention appears to have shifted from what men have in common (and what therefore can easily be relegated into somewhat more abstract and ideal spheres) to what must be left to the *individual*. Attention is focused on the significance of personal strength; the concrete is preferred to the general law that is valid 'on the whole'. And this discovery suggests that the observed economic individualism is the manifestation of a fundamental sociological change which has found its expression in the fields of art and politics as well. It suggests that none of these immediately caused the other.

Perhaps, in fact, sociological analyses of this sort are apt quite generally to point the way towards a conception of history which is more profound than historical materialism, and which may even supersede it. Historical changes, at their properly effective level, are possibly changes in sociological forms. It is perhaps the way in which individuals and groups behave towards one another; in which the individual behaves towards his group; in which value accents, accumulations, prerogatives, and similar phenomena shift among the elements of society—perhaps it is *these* things which make for truly epochal events. And if economics seems to determine all the other areas of culture, the truth behind this tempting appearance would seem to be that it itself is determined—determined by sociological shifts which similarly shape all other cultural phenomena. Thus, the form of economics, too, is merely a 'superstructure' on top of the conditions and transformations in the purely sociological structure. And this sociological structure is the ultimate historical element which is bound to determine all other contents of life, even if in a certain parallelism with economics.

## 4. The Problem Areas of Sociology
### [a] The Sociological Study of Historical Life ('General Sociology')

These considerations afford a glimpse, beyond the mere concept of sociological *method*, at the first basic *problem area* of sociology. Although it covers almost all of human existence, it does not therefore lose that character of one-sided abstraction that no science can get rid of. For however socially determined and permeated, as it were, each item in the economic and intellectual, political and juridical, even religious and generally cultural spheres may be, nevertheless, in the actuality of concrete life, this social determination is interwoven with other determinations that stem from other sources. Above all, from the circumstance that things also have a purely objective character. It is always some objective content—technical, dogmatic, intellectual, physiological—which channels the development of the social forces and which, by virtue of its own character, logic, and law, keeps it within certain directions and limits. Any social phenomenon, no matter in what material it realize itself, must submit to the natural laws of this material. Any intellectual achievement is tied, in however various ways, to the laws of thought and to the behaviour of objects. Any creation in the fields of art, politics, law, medicine, philosophy, or in any other field of invention, observes a certain order that we can understand in terms of the objective situation of its contents and that is characterized by such relations as intensification, connection, differentiation, combination, etc. No human wish or practice can take arbitrary steps, jump arbitrary distances, perform arbitrary syntheses. They must follow the intrinsic logic of things.

Thus, one could very well construct the history of art, as a perfectly understandable development, by presenting works of art themselves, anonymously, in their temporal sequence and stylistic evolution; or the development of law, as the sequence of particular institutions and laws; or that of science, as the mere series, historical or systematic, of its results; etc. Here, as in the cases of a song that is analysed in terms of its musical value, or of a physical theory in terms of its truth, or of a machine in terms of its efficiency, we realize that all contents of human life, even though they materialize only under the conditions and in the dynamics of social life, nevertheless permit interpretations ignoring it. Objects embody their own ideas; they have significance, laws, value standards which are independent of both the social and the individual life and which make it possible to define and understand them in their own terms. In comparison with full reality, of course, even this understanding involves abstraction, since no objective content is realized by its own logic alone but only through the co-operation of historical and psychological forces. Cognition cannot grasp reality in its total immediacy. What we call objective content is something conceived under a specific category.

Under one of these categories, the history of mankind appears as the behaviour and product of *individuals*. One may look at a work of art only in regard to its artistic significance; one may place it, as if it had fallen from the sky, within a series of artistic products. Yet one may also understand it in terms of the artist's personality and development, his experiences and tendencies. One may interpret it as a pulsation or immediate experience of individual life. Thus viewed, the work of art remains within the bounds of the individual and his continuity. Certain cultural data—above all art and, in general, everything that has the breath of creativity—appear more easily graspable in such a perspective than do other data. Quite generally, to look at the world as something that is carried by the active and receptive, typical or unique subject, is one of the possibilities of translating the unity of all human creation into understandability. The manifestation of the individual strikes us as an active element everywhere. Its laws permit us to form a plane, as it were, on which to project reality in all its fullness.

The purpose of this discussion is to show that there exists *not only* social life as a basis for the life of mankind and as a formula of it. This life may also be derived from the objective significance of its contents, and be interpreted in *these* terms. And it may finally be conceived in the framework of the nature and creativity of the individual. Perhaps there are other interpretive categories that have not yet been clearly developed. At any rate, all these analyses and structuralizations of our immediate life and creativity experience this life as a unity. They lie on the same plane and have the same right to be heard. Therefore—and this is the point—no one of them can claim to be the only or the only adequate manner of cognition. Naturally, neither can such a claim be made by the approach which proceeds in terms of the social form of our existence. It, too, is limited; and it supplements other approaches by which in turn it is supplemented. With this qualification, however, it can, in principle, offer a possibility of cognition in front of the totality of human existence.

The facts of politics, religion, economics, law, culture styles, language and innumerable others can be analysed by asking how they may be understood, not as individual achievements or in their objective significance, but as products and developments of society. Nor would the absence of an exhaustive and undisputed definition of the nature of society render the cognitive value of this approach illusory. For it is a characteristic of the human mind to be capable of erecting solid structures, while their foundations are still insecure. Physical and chemical propositions do not suffer from the obscure and problematical character of the concept of matter; juridical propositions, not from the quarrel over the nature of law and of its first principles; psychological ones, not from the highly questionable 'nature of the soul'. If, therefore, we apply the 'sociological method' to the investigation of the fall of the Roman Empire or of the relation between religion and economics in the great civilizations or of the origin of the idea of the German national state or of the predominance of the Baroque style; if, that is, we view these and similar phenomena as the result of indistinguishable contributions made by the interaction of individuals, or as life stages in the lives of superindividual groups; then we are, in point of fact, conducting our investigations according to the sociological method. And these investigations may be designated as sociology.

Yet from these sociological investigations there emerges a further abstraction that may well be characterized as the result of a highly differentiated scientific culture. This abstraction yields a group of sociological problems in the narrower sense of this term. If we study all kinds of life data in terms of their development within and by means of social groups, we must assume that they have common elements in their materialization (even though different elements, under different circumstances). These common elements emerge if, and only if, social life itself emerges as the origin or the subject of these data. The question thus arises whether perhaps it is possible to find, in the most heterogeneous historical developments that share nothing but the fact that they are exhibited by one particular group, a common law, or a rhythm, that is fully derivable from this one fact.

It has been maintained, for instance, that all historical developments pass through three phases. The first is the undifferentiated unity of manifold elements. The second is the differentiated articulation of these elements, that have become alienated from one another. The third is a new unity, the harmonious interpenetration of the elements that have been preserved, however, in their specific characters. More briefly, the road of all completed developments leads from an undifferentiated unity through a differentiated manifoldness to a differentiated unity. Another conception of historical life sees it as a process which progresses from organic commonness to mechanical simultaneousness. Property, work, and interests originally grow out of the solidarity of the individuals, the carriers of the group life; but later are distributed among egoists, each of whom seeks only his own benefit and, only because of this motive, enters into relations with others. The first stage is the manifestation of an unconscious will which inheres in the very depth of our nature and becomes evident only as a feeling; the second stage, by contrast, is the product of an arbitrary will and of the calculating intellect. According to a still different conception, it is possible to ascertain a definite relation, in any given epoch, between its intellectual world view and its social conditions: both equally are manifestations, in some sense, of biological development. Finally, there is the notion that human cognition, on the whole, must go through three stages. In the first, or theological stage, natural phenomena are explained by recourse to the arbitrary will of all kinds of entities. In the second, metaphysical stage, the supernatural causes are replaced by laws which, however, are mystical and speculative (as, for instance, 'vital force', 'ends of nature', etc.). Finally, the third, or positive stage corresponds to modern experimental and exact science. Each particular branch of knowledge develops by passing through these three stages; and the knowledge of this fact removes the enigmatic character of social development, which pervades areas of all kinds.

A further sociological question under this category is the problem concerning conditions of group *power*, as distinguished from individual power. The conditions for the power of individuals are immediately evident: intelligence, energy, an apt alternation between consistency and elasticity, etc.; but to account for the historical power of such extraordinary phenomena as Jesus, on the one hand, and Napoleon, on the other, there must also exist as yet unexplained forces which are by no means clarified by labels like 'power of suggestion', 'prestige', and so forth. But in the exercise of power by groups, both over their members and over other groups, there operate still other factors. Some of these are the faculty of rigid concentration, as well as of diversion into independent activities by individual group members; conscious faith in leading minds; groping towards expansion; egoism of the individual paralleled by sacrificial devotion to the whole; fanatical dogmatism, as well as thoroughly critical intellectual freedom. All these are effective in the rise (and, negatively, in the decay) not only of political nations but also of countless economic and religious, party-like and family groups. In all investigations of group power, the question, clearly, is not the origin of sociation as such, but the fate of society as something already constituted. And this fate is ascertained inductively.

Another question that arises out of the sociological consideration of conditions and events is that of the *value* relations between collective and individual conduct, action, and thought. Which differences of level, as measured by certain ideal standards, exist between social and individual phenomena? The inner, fundamental structure of society itself here becomes as little the central problem as it did in connection with the preceding question. Again, this structure is already presupposed, and the data are considered on the basis of this presupposition. The question, rather, is: which general principles are revealed in these data if they are considered in this particular perspective? . . .

## [b] The Study of Societal Forms ('Pure, or Formal, Sociology')

Scientific abstraction cuts through the full concreteness of social phenomena from yet a different angle. It thereby connects all that is 'sociological'—'sociological' in a sense that will be discussed presently and that appears to me to be the most decisive sense of the term. In doing this, scientific abstraction produces a consistent manner of cognition. Yet it fully realizes that in actuality, sociological phenomena do not exist in such isolation and recomposition, but that they are factored out of this living reality by means of an added concept. It will be remembered that societal facts are not *only* societal. It is always an objective content (sense-perceived or intellectual, technical or physiological) which is socially embodied, produced, or transmitted, and which only thus produces the totality of social life. Yet this societal formation of contents itself can be investigated by a science. Geometrical abstraction investigates only the spatial forms of bodies, although empirically, these forms are given merely as the forms of some material content. Similarly, if society is conceived as interaction among individuals, the description of the forms of this interaction is the task of the science of society in its strictest and most essential sense.

The first problem area of sociology, it will be remembered, consisted of the whole of historical life in so far as it is formed societally. Its societal character was conceived as an undifferentiated whole. The second problem area now under consideration, consists of the societal forms themselves. These are conceived as constituting society (and societies) out of the mere sum of living men. The study of this second area may be called 'pure sociology', which abstracts the mere element of sociation. It isolates it inductively and psychologically from the heterogeneity of its contents and purposes, which, in themselves, are not societal. It thus proceeds like grammar, which isolates the pure forms of language from their contents through which these forms, nevertheless, come to life. In a comparable manner, social groups which are the most diverse imaginable in purpose and general significance, may nevertheless show identical forms of behaviour towards one another on the part of their individual members. We find

superiority and subordination, competition, division of labour, formation of parties, representation, inner solidarity coupled with exclusiveness towards the outside, and innumerable similar features in the state,
in a religious community, in a band of conspirators, in an economic
association, in an art school, in the family. However diverse the
interests are that give rise to these sociations, the *forms* in which the
interests are realized may yet be identical. And on the other hand, a
contentually identical interest may take on form in very different
sociations. Economic interest is realized both in competition and in the
planned organization of producers, in isolation against other groups as
well as in fusion with them. The religious contents of life, although they
remain identical, sometimes demand an unregulated, sometimes a
centralized form of community. The interests upon which the relations
between the sexes are based are satisfied by an almost innumerable
variety of family forms; etc.

Hence, not only may the form in which the most divergent contents
are realized be identical; but, inversely, the content, too, may persist,
while its medium—the interactions of the individuals—adopts a variety
of forms. We see, then, that the analysis in terms of form and content
transforms the facts—which, in their immediacy, present these two
categories as the indissoluble unity of social life—in such a way as to
justify the sociological problem. This problem demands the indentifica-
tion, the systematic ordering, the psychological explanation, and the
historical development of the pure forms of sociation. Obviously, in
terms of its subject matter, sociology thus seen is not a special science,
as it was in terms of the first problem area. Yet in terms of its clearly
specified way of asking questions, it is a special science even here. The
discussion of 'sociability', in the third chapter of the present sketch (see
Reading 2), will offer an example that may serve to symbolize the total
picture of the investigations in 'pure sociology'.[3]

## [c] The Study of the Epistemological and Metaphysical Aspects of Society ('Philosophical Sociology')

The modern scientific attitude towards facts finally suggests a third
complex of questions concerning the fact 'society'. In so far as these
questions are adjacent (as it were) to the upper and lower limits of this
fact, they are sociological only in a broad sense of the term; more
properly, they are philosophical. Their *content* is constituted by this fact
itself. Similarly, nature and art, out of which we develop their
*immediate* sciences, also supply us with the subject matters of their

philosophies, whose interests and methods lie on a different level. It is the level on which factual details are investigated concerning their significance for the totality of mind, life, and being in general, and concerning their justification in terms of such a totality.

Thus, like every other exact science which aims at the immediate understanding of the given, social science, too, is surrounded by two *philosophical* areas. One of these covers the conditions, fundamental concepts, and presuppositions of concrete research, which cannot be taken care of by research itself since it is based on them. In the other area, this research is carried towards completions, connections, questions, and concepts that have no place in experience and in immediately objective knowledge. The first area is the epistemology, the second, the metaphysics of the particular discipline.

The tasks of the special social sciences—the study of economics and of institutions, the history of morals and of parties, population theory, and the discussion of occupational differentiation—could not be carried out at all if they did not presuppose certain concepts, postulates, and methods as axiomatic. If we did not assume a certain drive towards egoistic gain and pleasure, but at the same time the limitability of this drive through coercion, custom, and morals; if we did not claim the right to speak of the moods of a mass as a unit, although many of the members of this mass are only its superficial followers or even dissenters; if we did not declare the development within a particular sphere of culture understandable by re-creating it as an evolution with a psychological logic—if we did not proceed in this way, we should be utterly unable to cast innumerable facts into a social picture. In all these and in countless other situations, we operate with methods of thinking that use particular events as raw materials from which we derive social-scientific knowledge. Sociology proceeds like physics, which could never have been developed without grasping external phenomena on the basis of certain assumptions concerning space, matter, movement, and enumerability. Every special social science customarily and quite legitimately accepts without question such a basis of itself. Within its own domain, it could not even come to grips with it; for, in order to do so, obviously it would also have to take all other social sciences into consideration. Sociology thus emerges as the epistemology of the special social sciences, as the analysis and systematization of the bases of their forms and norms.

If these problems go beneath the concrete knowledge of social life, others, as it were, go beyond it. They try, by means of hypothesis and speculation, to supplement the unavoidably fragmentary character of the empirical facts (which always are fragmentary) in the direction of a closed system. They order the chaotic and accidental events into series that follow an idea or approach a goal. They ask where the neutral and natural sequences of events might provide these events or their totality with *significance*. They assert or doubt—and both assertion and doubt, equally, derive from a super-empirical world view—that the play of social-historical phenomena contains a religious significance, or a relation (to be known or at least sensed) to the metaphysical ground of being. More particularly, they ask questions such as these: Is society the purpose of human existence, or is it a means for the individual? Does the ultimate value of social development lie in the unfolding of personality or of association? Do meaning and purpose inhere in social phenomena at all, or exclusively in individuals? Do the typical stages of the development of societies show an analogy with cosmic evolutions so that there might be a general formula or rhythm of development in general (as, for instance, the fluctuation between differentiation and integration), which applies to social and material data alike? Are social movements guided by the principle of the conservation of energy? Are they directed by material or by ideological motives?

Evidently, this type of question cannot be answered by the ascertainment of facts. Rather, it must be answered by interpretations of ascertained facts and by efforts to bring the relative and problematical elements of social reality under an over-all view. Such a view does not compete with empirical claims because it serves needs which are quite different from those answered by empirical propositions.

The investigation of such problems, clearly, is more strictly based on differences in world views, individual and party valuations, and ultimate, undemonstrable convictions than is the investigation within the other two, more strictly fact-determined branches of sociology. For this reason, the discussion of a single problem as an example could not be as objective and could not as validly suggest the whole type of similar problems here, as is possible in the case of the other two branches. It therefore seems to me more advisable to trace . . . a line of pertinent theories as they have been developed, in the course of many controversies, during a particular period of general intellectual history.

[Translation taken from Kurt H. Wolff (ed.), *The Sociology of Georg Simmel*, Chapter 1, Collier-Macmillan, New York, 1964 (paperback edition)]

## NOTES AND REFERENCES

1. *Geisteswissenschaften.* Unless otherwise indicated, this term will always be rendered as 'human studies', a usage which follows Hodges (cf. H.A. Hodges, *Wilhelm Dilthey: An Introduction*, Oxford University Press, New York, 1944, esp. p. 157.)—Tr.

2. These last and some later sentences are taken from my larger work, *Soziologie: Untersuchungen über die Formen der Vergesellschaftung* (1908), which treats some of the thoughts sketched here in greater detail and, particularly, with more thorough historical documentation.

3. I may be allowed to call attention to the fact that my above-mentioned *Soziologie* tries to present the 'forms of sociation' in a completeness which is by no means definitive but is the best I can attain at this time.

# Sociability: An Example of Pure, or Formal, Sociology

In the introductory chapter [Reading 1], I mentioned the motive which is responsible for the constitution of 'pure sociology' as a specific problem area. This motive must now be formulated once more before an example of its application is given. For in its capacity of one among many principles of investigating it, it not only determines this example; what is more, the motive itself furnishes the *material* of the application to be described.

## 1. Contents (Materials) v. Forms of Social Life

The motive derives from two propositions. One is that in any human society one can distinguish between its content and its form. The other is that society itself, in general, refers to the interaction among individuals. This interaction always arises on the basis of certain drives or for the sake of certain purposes. Erotic instincts, objective interests, religious impulses, and purposes of defence or attack, of play or gain, of aid or instruction, and countless others cause man to live with other men, to act for them, with them, against them, and thus to arrange their conditions reciprocally—in brief, to influence others and to be influenced by them. The significance of these interactions lies in their causing the individuals who possess those instincts, interests, etc., to form a unit—precisely, a 'society'. Everything present in the individuals (who are the immediate, concrete data of all historical reality) in the form of drive, interest, purpose, inclination, psychic state, movement—everything that is present in them in such a way as to engender or mediate effects upon others or to receive such effects, I designate as the *content*, as the *material*, as it were, of sociation. In themselves, these materials with which life is filled, the motivations by which it is propelled, are not social. Strictly speaking, neither hunger nor love, neither work nor religiosity, neither technology nor the functions and results of intelligence, are social. They are factors in sociation only when they transform the mere aggregation of isolated individuals into specific forms of being with and for one another—forms that are subsumed under the general concept of interaction. Sociation thus is the form (realized in innumerable, different ways) in which individuals grow together into units that satisfy their interests. These interests, whether they are sensuous or ideal, momentary or lasting, conscious or unconscious, causal or teleological, form the basis of human societies.

## 2. The Autonomization of Contents

These facts have very far-reaching consequences. On the basis of practical conditions and necessities, our intelligence, will, creativity, and feeling work on the materials that we wish to wrest from life. In accord with our purposes, we give these materials certain forms and only in these forms operate and use them as elements of our lives. But it happens that these materials, these forces and interests, in a peculiar manner remove themselves from the service of life that originally produced and employed them. They become autonomous in the sense that they are no longer inseparable from the objects which they formed and thereby made available to our purposes. They come to play freely in themselves and for their own sake; they produce or make use of materials that exclusively serve their own operation or realization.

For instance, originally all cognition appears to have been a means in the struggle for existence. Exact knowledge of the behaviour of things is, in fact, of extraordinary utility for the maintenance and promotion of life. Yet cognition is no longer used in the service of this practical achievement: science has become a value in itself. It quite autonomously chooses its objects, shapes them according to its own needs, and is interested in nothing beyond its own perfection. Another example: the interpretation of realities, concrete or abstract, in terms of spatial systems, or of rhythms or sounds, or of significance and organization, certainly had its origins in practical needs. Yet these interpretations have become purposes in themselves, effective on their own strength and in their own right, selective and creative quite independently of their entanglement with practical life, and not because of it. This is the origin of art. Fully established, art is wholly separated from life. It takes from it only what it can use, thus creating itself, as it were, a second time. And yet the forms by means of which it does this and of which it actually consists, were produced by the exigencies and the very dynamics of life.

The same dialectic determines the nature of law. The requirements of social existence compel or legitimate certain types of individual behaviour which thus are valid and followed, precisely because they meet these practical requirements. Yet with the emergence of 'law', this reason for their diffusion recedes into the background: now they are followed simply because they have become the 'law', and quite independently of the life which originally engendered and directed them. The furthest pole of this development is expressed by the idea of *fiat justitia, pereat mundus* ['justice be done, even if the world perish']. In other words, although lawful behaviour has its roots in the purposes of social life, law, properly speaking, has no 'purpose', since it is not a means to an ulterior end. On the contrary, it determines, in its own right and not by legitimation through any higher, extrinsic agency, how the contents of life should be shaped.

This complete turnover, from the determination of the forms by the materials of life to the determination of its materials by forms that have become supreme values, is perhaps most extensively at work in the numerous phenomena that we lump together under the category of *play*. Actual forces, needs, impulses of life produce the forms of our behaviour that are suitable for play. These forms, however, become independent contents and stimuli within play itself or, rather, *as* play. There are, for instance, the hunt; the gain by ruse; the proving of physical and intellectual strength; competition; and the dependence on chance and on the favour of powers that cannot be influenced. All these forms are lifted out of the flux of life and freed of their material with its inherent gravity. On their own decision, they choose or create the objects in which they prove or embody themselves in their purity. This is what gives play both its gaiety and the symbolic significance by which it is distinguished from mere joke. Here lies whatever may justify the analogy between art and play. In both art and play, forms that were originally developed by the realities of life, have created spheres that preserve their autonomy in the face of these realities. It is from their origin, which keeps them permeated with life, that they draw their depth and strength. Where they are emptied of life, they become artifice and 'empty play', respectively. Yet their significance and their very nature derive from that fundamental change through which the forms engendered by the purposes and materials of life, are separated from them, and themselves become the purpose and the material of their own existence. From the realities of life they take only what they can adapt to their own nature, only what they can absorb in their autonomous existence.

## 3. Sociability as the Autonomous Form, or Play-Form, of Sociation

This process also is at work in the separation of what I have called content and form in societal existence. Here, 'society', properly speaking, is that being with one another, for one another, against one another which, through the vehicle of drives or purposes, forms and develops material or individual contents and interests. The forms in which this process results gain their own life. It is freed from all ties with contents. It exists for its own sake and for the sake of the fascination which, in its own liberation from these ties, it diffuses. It is precisely the phenomenon that we call sociability.

Certainly, specific needs and interests make men band together in economic associations, blood brotherhoods, religious societies, hordes of bandits. Yet in addition to their specific contents, all these sociations are also characterized, precisely, by a feeling, among their members, of being sociated and by the satisfaction derived from this. Sociates feel that the formation of a society as such is a value; they are driven towards this form of existence. In fact, it sometimes is only this drive itself that suggests the concrete contents of a particular sociation. What may be called the art drive, extracts out of the totality of phenomena their mere form, in order to shape it into specific structures that correspond to this drive. In similar fashion, out of the realities of social life, the 'sociability drive' extracts the pure process of sociation as a cherished value; and thereby it constitutes sociability in the stricter sense of the word. It is no mere accident of linguistic usage that even the most primitive sociability, if it is of any significance and duration at all, places so much emphasis on *form*, on 'good form'. For form is the mutual determination and interaction of the elements of the association. It is form by means of which they create a unit. The actual, life-conditioned motivations of sociation are of no significance to sociability. It is, therefore, understandable that the pure form, the individuals' suspended, interacting interrelatedness (we might say), is emphasized the more strongly and effectively.

Sociability is spared the frictions with reality by its merely formal relation to it. Yet just because of this, it derives from reality, even to the mind of the more sensitive person, a significance and a symbolic, playful richness of life that are the greater, the more perfect it is. A superficial rationalism always looks for this richness among concrete *contents* only. Since it does not find it there, it dispenses with sociability as a shallow foolishness. Yet it cannot be without significance that in many, perhaps in all European languages, 'society' simply designates a *sociable* gathering. Certainly, the political, economic, the purposive society of whatever description, is a 'society'. But only the 'sociable society' is 'a society' without qualifying adjectives.[1] It is this, precisely because it represents the pure form that is raised above all contents such as characterize those more 'concrete' 'societies'. It gives us an abstract image in which all contents are dissolved in the mere play of form.

## [a] Unreality, Tact, Impersonality

As a sociological category, I thus designate sociability as the *play-form of sociation*. Its relation to content-determined, concrete sociation is similar to that of the work of art to reality. The great, perhaps the greatest, problem of society finds in it a solution which is possible nowhere else. This problem is the question concerning the proportions of significance and weight that, in the total life of the individual, are properly his, and properly those of his social sphere's. Inasmuch as in the purity of its manifestations, sociability has no objective purpose, no content, no extrinsic results, it entirely depends on the personalities among whom it occurs. Its aim is nothing but the success of the sociable moment and, at most, a memory of it. Hence the conditions and results of the process of sociability are exclusively the persons who find themselves at a social gathering. Its character is determined by such personal qualities as amiability, refinement, cordiality, and many other sources of attraction. But precisely because everything depends on their personalities, the participants are not permitted to stress them too conspicuously. Where specific interests (in co-operation or collision) determine the social form, it is these interests that prevent the individual from presenting his peculiarity and uniqueness in too unlimited and independent a manner. Where there are no such interests, their function must be taken over by other conditions. In sociability, these derive from the mere form of the gathering. Without the reduction of personal poignancy and autonomy brought about by this form, the gathering itself would not be possible. *Tact*, therefore, is here of such a peculiar significance: where no external or immediate egoistic interests direct the self-regulation of the individual in his personal relations with others, it is tact that fulfils this regulatory function. Perhaps its most essential task is to draw the limits, which result from the claims of others, of the individual's impulses, ego-stresses, and intellectual and material desires.

Sociability emerges as a very peculiar sociological structure. The fact is that whatever the participants in the gathering may possess in terms of objective attributes—attributes that are centred outside the particular gathering in question—must not enter it. Wealth, social position, erudition, fame, exceptional capabilities and merits, may not play any part in sociability. At most they may perform the role of mere nuances of that immaterial character with which reality alone, in general, is allowed to enter the social work of art called sociability. But in addition to these objective elements that, as it were, surround the personality, the purely and deeply personal traits of one's life, character, mood, and fate must likewise be eliminated as factors in sociability. It is tactless, because it militates against *interaction* which monopolizes sociability, to display merely personal moods of depression, excitement, despondency—in brief, the light and the darkness of one's most intimate life. This exclusion of the most personal element extends even to certain external features of behaviour. Thus, for instance, at an intimately personal and friendly meeting with one or several men, a lady would not appear in as low-cut a dress as she wears without any embarrassment at a larger party. The reason is that at the party she does not feel involved as an individual to the same extent as she does at the more intimate gathering, and that she can therefore afford to abandon herself as if in the impersonal freedom of a mask: although being *only* herself she is yet not *wholly* herself, but only an element in a group that is held together *formally.*

## [b] 'Sociability Thresholds'

Man in his totality is a dynamic complex of ideas, forces, and possibilities. According to the motivations and relations of life and its changes, he makes of himself a differentiated and clearly defined phenomenon. As an economic and political man, as a family member, and as the representative of an occupation he is, as it were, an elaboration constructed *ad hoc.* In each of these capacities, the material of his life is determined by a particular idea and is cast into a particular form. Yet, the relative autonomy of his roles feeds on a common source of his energy, which is difficult to label. Sociable man, too, is a peculiar phenomenon; it exists nowhere except in sociable relations. On the one hand, man has here cast off all objective qualifications of his personality. He enters the form of sociability equipped only with the capacities, attractions, and interests with which his pure human-ness provides him. On the other hand, however, sociability also shies away from the entirely subjective and purely inwardly spheres of his personality. Discretion, which is the first condition of sociability in regard to one's behaviour towards others, is equally much required in regard to one's dealing with oneself: in both cases, its violation causes the sociological art form of sociability to degenerate into a sociological naturalism. One thus may speak of the individual's upper and lower *sociability thresholds*. These thresholds are passed both when individuals interact from motives of objective content and purpose and when their entirely personal and subjective aspects make themselves felt. In both cases, sociability ceases to be the central and formative principle of their sociation and becomes, at best, a formalistic, superficially mediating connection.

## [c] The 'Sociability Drive' and the Democratic Nature of Sociability

Perhaps it is possible, however, to find the positive formal motive of sociability which corresponds to its negative determination by limits and thresholds. As the foundation of law, Kant posited the axiom that each individual should possess freedom to the extent which is compatible with the freedom of every other individual. If we apply this principle to the sociability drive (as the source or substance of sociability itself), we might say that each individual ought to have as much satisfaction of this drive as is compatible with its satisfaction on the part of all others. We can also express this thought not in terms of the sociability drive itself but in terms of its results. We then formulate the principle of sociability as the axiom that each individual should *offer* the maximum of sociable values (of joy, relief, liveliness, etc.) that is compatible with the maximum of values he himself *receives*.

Just as Kant's law is thoroughly democratic, this principle, too, shows the democratic structure of all sociability. Yet, this democratic character can be realized only within a given social stratum: sociability among members of very different social strata often is inconsistent and painful. Equality, as we have seen, results from the elimination of both the wholly personal and the wholly objective, that is, from the elimination of the very material of sociation from which sociation is freed when it takes on the form of sociability. Yet the democracy of sociability even among social equals is only something *played*. Sociability, if one will, creates an ideal sociological world in which the pleasure of the individual is closely tied up with the pleasure of the others. In principle, nobody can find satisfaction here if it has to be at the cost of diametrically opposed feelings which the other may have. This possibility, to be sure, is excluded by many social forms other than sociability. In all of these, however, it is excluded through some superimposed ethical imperative. In sociability alone is it excluded by the intrinsic principle of the social form itself.

## [d] The Artificial World of Sociability

Yet, this world of sociability—the only world in which a democracy of the equally privileged is possible without frictions—is an *artificial* world. It is composed of individuals who have no other desire than to create wholly pure interaction with others which is not disbalanced by a stress of anything material. We may have the erroneous notion that we enter sociability purely 'as men', as what we really are, without all the burdens, conflicts, all the too-much and too-little which in actual life disturb the purity of our images. We may get this notion because modern life is overburdened with objective contents and exigencies. And forgetting these daily encumbrances at a social gathering, we fancy ourselves to return to our natural-personal existence. But under this impression we also forget that sociable man is constituted by this personal aspect, not in its specific character and in its naturalistic completeness, but only in a certain reservedness and stylization. In earlier periods of history, sociable man did not have to be wrested from so many objective and contentual claims. His form, therefore, emerged more fully and distinctly in contrast with his *personal* existence: behaviour at a social gathering was much stiffer, more ceremonial, and more severely regulated super-individually than it is today. This reduction of the personal character which homogeneous interaction with others imposes on the individual may even make him lean over backwards, if we may say so: a characteristically sociable behaviour trait is the courtesy with which the strong and extraordinary individual not only makes himself the equal of the weaker, but even acts as if the weaker were the more valuable and superior.

If sociation itself is interaction, its purest and most stylized expression occurs among equals—as symmetry and balance are the most plausible forms of artistic stylization. Inasmuch as it is abstracted from sociation through art or play, sociability thus calls for the purest, most transparent, and most casually appealing kind of interaction, *that among equals*. Because of its very nature, it must create human beings who give up so much of their objective contents and who so modify their external and internal significance as to become sociable equals. Each of them must gain for himself sociability values only if the others with whom he interacts also gain them. Sociability is the game in which one 'does as if' all were equal, and at the same time, as if one honoured each of them in particular. And to 'do as if' is no more a lie than play or art are lies because of their deviation from reality. The game becomes a lie only when sociable action and speech are made into mere instruments of the intentions and events of practical reality—just as a painting becomes a lie when it tries, in a panoramic effect, to simulate reality. What is perfectly correct and in order if practised within the autonomous life of sociability with its self-contained play of forms, becomes a deceptive lie when it is guided by non-sociable purposes or is designed to disguise such purposes. The actual entanglement of sociability with the events of real life surely makes such a deception often very tempting.

## [e] Social Games

The connection between sociability and play explains why sociability should cover all phenomena that already by themselves may be considered sociological play-forms. This refers above all to games proper, which in the sociability of all times have played a conspicuous role. The expression '*social* game' is significant in the deeper sense to which I have already called attention. All the forms of interaction or sociation among men—the wish to outdo, exchange, the formation of parties, the desire to wrest something from the other, the hazards of accidental meetings and separations, the change between enmity and co-operation, the overpowering by ruse and revenge—in the seriousness of reality, all of these are imbued with purposive contents. In the game, they lead their own lives; they are propelled exclusively by their own attraction. For even where the game involves a monetary stake, it is not the money (after all, it could be acquired in many ways other than gambling) that is the specific characteristic of the game. To the person who really enjoys it, its attraction rather lies in the dynamics and hazards of the sociologically significant forms of activity themselves. The more profound, double sense of 'social game' is that not only the game is played in a society (as its external medium) but that, with its help, people actually 'play' 'society'.

## [f] Coquetry

In the sociology of sex, we find a play-form: the play-form of eroticism is coquetry. In sociability, it finds its most facile, playful, and widely diffused realization.[2] Generally speaking, the erotic question between the sexes is that of offer and refusal. Its objects are, of course, infinitely varied and graduated, and by no means mere either-ors, much less exclusively physiological. The nature of feminine coquetry is to play up, alternately, allusive promises and allusive withdrawals—to attract the male but always to stop short of a decision, and to reject him but never to deprive him of all hope. The coquettish woman enormously enhances her attractiveness if she shows her consent as an almost immediate possibility but is ultimately not serious about it. Her behaviour swings back and forth between 'yes' and 'no' without stopping at either. She playfully exhibits the pure and simple form of erotic decisions and manages to embody their polar opposites in a perfectly consistent behaviour: its decisive, well-understood content, that would commit her to one of the two opposites, does not even enter.

This freedom from all gravity of immutable contents and permanent realities gives coquetry the character of suspension, distance, ideality, that has led one to speak, with a certain right, of its 'art', not only of its 'artifices'. Yet in order for coquetry to grow on the soil of sociability, as we know from experience it does, it must meet with a specific behaviour on the part of the male. As long as he rejects its attractions or, inversely, is its mere victim that without any will of his own is dragged along by its vacillations between a half 'yes' and a half 'no', coquetry has not yet assumed for him the form that is commensurate with sociability. For it lacks the free interaction and equivalence of elements that are the fundamental traits of sociability. It does not attain these until he asks for no more than this freely suspended play which only dimly reflects the erotically definitive as a remote symbol; until he is no longer attracted by the lust for the erotic element or by the fear of it which is all he can see in the coquettish allusions and preliminaries. Coquetry that unfolds its charms precisely at the height of sociable civilization has left far behind the reality of erotic desire, consent, or refusal; it is embodied in the interaction of the mere silhouettes, as it were, of their serious imports. Where they themselves enter or are constantly present in the background, the whole process becomes a private affair between two individuals: it takes place on the plane of reality. But under the sociological sign of sociability from which the centre of the personality's concrete and complete life is barred, coquetry is the flirtatious, perhaps ironical play, in which eroticism has freed the bare outline of its interactions from their materials and contents and personal features. As sociability plays with the forms of society, so coquetry plays with those of eroticism, and this affinity of their natures predestines coquetry as an element of sociability.

## [g] Conversation

Outside sociability, the sociological forms of interaction are significant in terms of their contents. Sociability abstracts these forms and supplies them—which circle around themselves, as it were—with shadowy bodies. The extent to which it attains this aim—becomes evident, finally, in *conversation*, the most general vehicle for all that men have in common. The decisive point here can be introduced by stressing the very trivial experience that people talk seriously because of some content they want to communicate or come to an understanding about, while at a social gathering they talk for the sake of talking. There, talk becomes its own purpose; but not in the naturalistic sense that would make it mere chatter, but as the *art* of conversation that has its own, artistic laws. In purely sociable conversation, the topic is merely the indispensable medium through which the lively exchange of speech itself unfolds its attractions. All the forms in which this exchange is realized—quarrel, appeal to norms recognized by both parties, pacification by compromise and by discovery of common convictions, grateful acceptance of the new, and covering up of anything on which no understanding can be hoped for—all these forms usually are in the service of the countless contents and purposes of human life. But here, they derive their significance from themselves, from the fascinating play of relations which they create among the participants, joining and loosening, winning and succumbing, giving and taking. The double sense of *sich unterhalten*[3] becomes understandable. For conversation to remain satisfied with mere form it cannot allow any content to become significant in its own right. As soon as the discussion becomes objective, as soon as it makes the ascertainment of a truth its *purpose* (it may very well be its *content*), it ceases to be sociable and thus becomes untrue to its own nature—as much as if it degenerated into a serious quarrel. The *form* of the ascertainment of a truth or of a quarrel may exist, but the seriousness of their contents may as little become the focus of sociable conversation as a perspectivistic painting may contain a piece of the actual, three-dimensional reality of its object.

This does not imply that the content of sociable conversation is indifferent. On the contrary, it must be interesting, fascinating, even important. But it may not become the purpose of the conversation, which must never be after an objective result. The objective result leads an ideal existence, as it were, outside of it. Therefore, of two externally similar conversations, only that is (properly speaking) sociable, in which the topic, in spite of all its value and attraction, finds its right, place, and purpose only in the functional play of the conversation itself that sets its own norms and has its own peculiar significance. The ability to change topics easily and quickly is therefore part of the nature of social conversation. For since the topic is merely a means, it exhibits all the fortuitousness and exchangeability that characterize all means as compared with fixed ends. As has already been mentioned, sociability presents perhaps the only case in which talk is its own legitimate purpose. Talk presupposes two parties; it is two-way. In fact, among all sociological phenomena whatever, with the possible exception of looking at one another, talk is the purest and most sublimated form of two-way-ness. It thus is the fulfilment of a relation that wants to be nothing but relation—in which that is, what usually is the mere form of interaction becomes its self-sufficient content. Hence even the telling of stories, jokes, and anecdotes, though often only a pastime if not a testimonial of intellectual poverty, can show all the subtle tact that reflects the elements of sociability. It keeps the conversation away from individual intimacy and from all purely personal elements that cannot be adapted to sociable requirements. And yet, objectivity is cultivated not for the sake of any particular content but only in the interest of sociability itself. The telling and reception of stories, etc., is not an end in itself but only a means for the liveliness, harmony, and common consciousness of the 'party'. It not only provides a content in which all can participate alike; it also is a particular individual's gift to the group—but a gift behind which its giver becomes invisible: the subtlest and best-told stories are those from which the narrator's personality has completely vanished. The perfect anecdote attains a happy equilibrium of sociable ethics, as it were, with its complete absorption of both subjective-individual and objective-contentual elements in the service of pure sociable form.

## [h] Sociability as the Play-Form of Ethical Problems and of Their Solution

Thus sociability also emerges as the play-form of the ethical forces in concrete society. In particular, there are two problems that must be solved by these forces. One is the fact that the individual has to function as part of a collective for which he lives; but that, in turn, he derives his own values and improvements from this collective. The other is the fact that the life of the individual is a roundabout route for the purposes of the whole; but that the life of the whole, in turn, has this same function for the purposes of the individual. Sociability transfers the serious, often tragic character of these problems into the symbolic play of its shadowy realm which knows no frictions, since shadows, being what they are, cannot collide. Another ethical task of sociation is to make the joining and breaking-up of sociated individuals the exact reflection of the relations among these individuals, although these relations are spontaneously determined by life in its totality. In sociability, this freedom to form relations and this adequacy of their expression are relieved of any concrete contentual determinants. The ways in which groups form and split up and in which conversations, called forth by mere impulse and occasion, begin, deepen, loosen, and terminate at a social gathering give a miniature picture of the societal ideal that might be called the freedom to be tied down. If all convergence and divergence are strictly commensurate with inner realities, at a 'party' they exist in the absence of these realities. There is left nothing but a phenomenon whose play obeys the laws of its own form and whose charm is contained in itself. It shows *aesthetically* that same commensurateness which those inner realities require as *ethical* commensurateness.

## [i] Historical Illustrations

Our general conception of sociability is well illustrated by certain historical developments. In the early German Middle Ages, there existed brotherhoods of knights. They consisted of patrician families that entertained friendly relations with one another. The originally religious and practical purposes of these groups seem to have been lost fairly early. By the fourteenth century, *knightly* interests and ways of behaviour alone were left as their contentual characteristics. Soon afterwards, however, even they disappeared, and there remained nothing but purely sociable aristocratic associations. Here then, evidently, is a case where sociability developed as the residuum of a society that had been determined by its content. It is a residuum which, since all content was lost, could consist only of the form and forms of reciprocal behaviour.

The fact that the autonomy of such forms is bound to exhibit the nature of play or, more deeply, of art, becomes even more striking in the courtly society of the *Ancien Régime*. Here, the disappearance of any concrete content of life—which royalty, so to speak, had sucked out of French aristocracy—resulted in the emergence of certain freely suspended forms. The consciousness of the nobility became crystallized in them. Their forces, characteristics, and relations were purely sociable. They were by no means symbols or functions of any real significances or intensities of persons and institutions. The etiquette of courtly society had become a value in itself. It no longer referred to any content; it had developed its own, intrinsic laws, which were comparable to the laws of art. The laws of art are valid only in terms of art: by no means have they the purpose of imitating the reality of the models, of things outside of art itself.

## [j] The 'Superficial' character of Sociability

In the *Ancien Régime*, sociability attained perhaps its most sovereign expression. At the same time, however, this expression came close to being its own caricature. Certainly, it is the nature of sociability to free concrete interactions from any reality and to erect its airy realm according to the form-laws of these relations, which come to move in themselves and to recognize no purpose extraneous to them. Yet the deep spring which feeds this realm and its play does not lie in these forms, but exclusively in the vitality of concrete individuals, with all their feelings and attractions, convictions and impulses. Sociability is a *symbol* of life as life emerges in the flux of a facile and happy play; yet it also is a symbol of *life*. It does not change the image of life beyond the point required by its own distance to it. In like manner, if it is not to strike one as hollow and false, even the freest and most fantastic art, however far it is from any copying of reality, nevertheless feeds on a deep and loyal relation to this reality. Art, too, is *above* life, but it is also above *life*. If sociability entirely cuts its ties with the reality of life out of which it makes its own fabric (of however different a style), it ceases to be a play and becomes a desultory playing around with empty forms, a lifeless schematism which is even proud of its lifelessness.

Our discussion shows that people both rightly and wrongly lament the *superficiality* of sociable intercourse. To account for this, we must remember and appreciate one of the most impressive characteristics of intellectual life. This is the fact that if certain elements are taken out of the totality of existence and united into a whole that lives by its own laws and not by those of the totality, it shows, if it is completely severed from the life of the totality, a hollow and rootless nature, in spite of all intrinsic perfection. And yet, and often only by an imponderable change, this same whole, in its very distance from immediate reality, may more completely, consistently, and realistically reveal the deepest nature of this reality than could any attempt at grasping it more directly. Applying this consideration to the phenomenon of sociability, we understand that we may have two different reactions to it. Accordingly, the independent and self-regulated life, which the superficial aspects of social interaction attain in sociability, will strike us as a formula-like and irrelevant lifelessness, or as a symbolic play whose aesthetic charms embody the finest and subtlest dynamics of broad, rich social existence.

In regard to art, in regard to all the symbolism of religious and church life, and to a large extent even in regard to the formulations of science, we depend on a certain faith, or feeling, which assures us that the intrinsic norms of fragments or the combinations of superficial elements do possess a connection with the depth and wholeness of reality. Although it can often not be formulated, it nevertheless is this connection which makes of fragments embodiments and representations of the immediately real and fundamental life. It accounts for the redeeming and relieving effect that some of the realms, constructed of mere forms of life, have on us: although in them we are unburdened of life, we nevertheless *have* it. Thus, the view of the sea frees us internally, not in spite, but because of the fact that the swelling and ebbing and the play and counterplay of the waves stylize life into the simplest expression of its dynamics. This expression is quite free from all experienceable reality and from all the gravity of individual fate, whose ultimate significance seems yet to flow into this picture of the sea. Art similarly seems to reveal the mystery of life, the fact, that is, that we cannot be relieved of life by merely looking away from it, but only by shaping and experiencing the sense and the forces of its deepest reality in the unreal and seemingly quite autonomous play of its forms.

To so many serious persons who are constantly exposed to the pressures of life, sociability could not offer any liberating, relieving, or serene aspects if it really were nothing but an escape from life or a merely momentary suspension of life's seriousness. Perhaps it often *is* no more than a negative conventionalism, an essentially lifeless exchange of formulas. Perhaps it frequently was·this in the *Ancien Régime* when the numb fear of a threatening reality forced men merely to look away and to sever all relations with it. Yet it is precisely the more serious person who derives from sociability a feeling of liberation and relief. He can do so because he enjoys here, as if in an art play, a concentration and exchange of effects that present all the tasks and all the seriousness of life in a sublimation and, at the same time, dilution, in which the content-laden forces of reality reverberate only dimly, since their gravity has evaporated into mere attractiveness.

[Translation taken from Kurt H. Wolff (ed.), *The Sociology of Georg Simmel*, Chapter 3, Collier-Macmillan, New York, 1964 (paperback edition)]

NOTES AND REFERENCES

1. *Gesellschaft* is both 'society' and 'party' (in the sense of 'social, or sociable, gathering').—Tr.

2. I have treated coquetry extensively in my book, *Philosophische Kultur* [Philosophic Culture].

3. This double sense is not obvious in English. *Unterhalten* literally is 'to hold under', 'to sustain'. Customarily, however, *sich unterhalten* is 'to entertain or enjoy oneself', as well as 'to converse'. This is the double sense Simmel emphasizes.—Tr.

# Part Two: The Persistence of Society

## Reading Three
# The Intersection of Social Spheres

The difference between advanced and more primitive thought can be seen in the different factors governing the association of ideas. At the early stage, fortuitous spatial or temporal proximity is sufficient to establish a psychological association. The combination of properties constituting a concrete object is perceived, at this stage, as a unified whole, and a close associative connection is felt to exist between each of these qualities and all the others, which are the only environment in which it has been encountered. The mind only becomes conscious of the separate existence of such properties when they occur in a number of different combinations. The manifestations of the property common to all these combinations are thereby illuminated; at the same time, they form a group of their own as they become increasingly detached from the other properties, with which they were associated solely by virtue of fortuitous proximity in the same object. Thus association triggered by immediate perception gives way to association arising from the content of ideas. This is the basis both for the formation of higher concepts and for the disentanglement of recurrent elements from the most diverse phenomena.

This development in the sphere of ideas is paralleled in the interrelationships of individuals. The individual finds himself initially in an environment which is relatively indifferent to him as an individual, but to whose destiny he is chained, and which imposes on him a close proximity with those people with whom he is associated by the accident of birth. 'Initially' refers to the commencement of both phylogenetic and ontogenetic development. Further development, however, is towards the goal of associative relationships of homogeneous members of heterogeneous spheres. Thus the family comprises a number of diverse individuals who are initially dependent to the highest degree on this association. But as he develops, each individual member of the family establishes links with people outside this original sphere of association, whose relationship to him is based instead on objective similarity of character, inclination and activity, etc. Association arising from external proximity is progressively replaced by that arising from internal affinity. Just as higher concepts unify what is common to many disparate complexes of perception, so higher expediency brings together similar individuals from altogether alien and unconnected groups. This creates new spheres of contact which cut across at very many points the former spheres, which were, relatively speaking, more the product of nature, and whose cohesion was more a matter of direct physical relationships.

One of the simplest examples is that cited above: the original cohesion of the family sphere is modified when the individual's particular nature leads him into other spheres. One of the most elevated examples is the 'republic of letters', that semi-ideal, semi-real association of all the people with a common aim of the most universal nature: the aim of knowledge. These people belong, in other respects, to the most disparate groups, as regards nationality, specific personal interests, social position, etc. During the Renaissance one could see more clearly and characteristically than at the present time the power of intellectual and cultural interests to differentiate people of a homogeneous nature from the most diverse spheres and to join them in a new community. Humanist interests broke down the medieval separation of spheres and classes. People from the most diverse walks of life, who often moreover kept their allegiance to the most diverse callings, were united in the active or passive pursuit of ideas and understanding, a pursuit which in a great variety of ways cut across the previous forms and groupings of life. The prevailing idea was the affinity of excellence. We can see this in the collections of biographies which begin to appear in the fourteenth century, which brought together in one volume descriptions of eminent people as such, whether they were theologians or artists, statesmen or philologists. Only thus could a mighty monarch, Robert of Naples, be the friend of the poet Petrarch, to whom he made a gift of his own purple cloak. Only thus could purely intellectual eminence be divorced from all other respected qualities, so that the Venetian Senate, when handing Giordano Bruno over to the Curia, could write that Bruno was one of the worst of heretics, had committed the most abominable acts and led a loose and positively diabolical life—but that otherwise he was one of the most outstanding intellects imaginable, with the rarest erudition and loftiness of spirit. The humanists' desire for travel and adventure—indeed, in some cases their volatile and unreliable character—was in keeping with the fact that the intellectual sphere which was the centre of their existence was independent of all the usual claims of human life; it was bound to make them indifferent to such claims. The individual humanist, traversing the motley variety of life, enacted the destiny of humanism as a whole, which united the poor scholar and monk, the mighty general and the brilliant princess within common intellectual interests.

The number of different spheres to which an individual belongs is one of the yardsticks of culture. Modern man belongs first to his parental family, then, to the family which he himself founds (and thus also his wife's family), then to his profession. The latter will itself often take him into a number of spheres of common interest: for example, in any profession where there are superiors and subordinates each individual belongs both to the sphere of his particular business, department, office, etc., which in each case comprises people of higher and lower rank, and also to the sphere comprising those of equal rank in various businesses, etc. If he is conscious of his nationality and of his membership of a particular social class, and if on top of this he is also an officer in the Reserve, belongs to a few clubs and leads an active social life involving contact with a variety of spheres, then all in all it adds up to a very wide variety of groups. Some of these are, of course, co-ordinated, but others can be arranged to show one of them as the more primary association, from which the individual moves to a more distant sphere as a result of those special attributes which distinguish him from the other members of the first sphere. The connection with the first sphere may continue, just as one aspect of a complex idea, even when it has long since acquired purely objective psychological associations, will not by any means necessarily lose its association with the complex in whose spatial-temporal environment it exists.

A number of different consequences arise from this. The groups to which an individual belongs constitute, as it were, a system of co-ordinates, such that each new association defines him more precisely and unmistakably. Membership of any single group by itself leaves wide scope to the individual personality; but the more groups that are added, the more improbable it becomes that anyone else will have the same combination of groups, that all these spheres will intersect again at a single point. A concrete object loses its epistemological individuality when it is grouped under a general concept by virtue of one quality, but regains that individuality progressively as other concepts are highlighted to which it belongs by virtue of its other qualities. Thus, in a Platonic sense, any object is associated with as many ideas as it has properties; and this is what gives it its individual character. The personality has exactly the same relationship to the spheres to which it belongs. There is an exact parallel to this in the field of theoretical psychology. What in our image of the world we call the objective element, in apparent contrast to the subjectivity of individual impressions, is, in fact, only a subjective element which has accumulated by repetition. Likewise causality (concrete cause and effect) is, according to Hume, only the frequent repetition of a temporal sequence of sense impressions, and the substantive object exists for us only as a synthesis of sense impressions. Thus from these objectified elements we create subjectivity *par excellence*: personality, with its individual combination of the elements of culture. First the synthesis of the subjective created the objective, now the synthesis of the objective in its turn creates a new and higher subjectivity. In just the same way the personality is absorbed and submerged in one social sphere, but subsequently, through its individual combination of spheres, regains its individuality. Moreover, the purposive constitution of the personality is in a way the mirror image of its causal constitution: personality originates at the point of intersection of innumerable social threads, it is the hereditary product of the very diverse spheres and processes of adaptation, and it acquires individuality by virtue of its particular degrees and combinations of generic elements. When the personality, with its diverse impulses and interests, then enters into association with social groups, it discharges, it gives back, as it were, what it once received, in an analogous but now conscious and heightened form.

The personality will be more closely defined if the majority of the defining spheres are contiguous rather than concentric. That is to say, progressively narrowing spheres such as nation, social position, occupation and any special group within the latter, the narrowest of which entails membership of the others anyway, will not give as much individuality to their members as a man will have if, for example, apart from his professional position, he also belongs to a scholarly association, is on the supervisory board of a joint-stock company and holds an honorary civic office. The less indication membership of one sphere gives of membership of another, the more clearly the individual is characterized by being at their point of intersection. I wish here only to point out in passing the vast scope for individual differentiation arising from the fact that the same person may simultaneously occupy quite different relative positions within various spheres. Every new association of like-minded people immediately creates its own degrees of difference between leaders and followers. When a common interest, such as the humanist interest mentioned above, created a bond between persons of high and low rank overriding their other differences, then within this community, in accordance with its own criteria, new distinctions between superiors and inferiors arose which were entirely unaffected by differences of rank within the other spheres. This complete independence of one person's different status within different groups sometimes produces odd combinations. For example, in countries with universal military service a man of the highest social and intellectual standing may be subordinate to a sergeant. Likewise the Paris Beggars' Guild has an elected 'king'; though originally only a beggar like the rest of them (which, as far as I know, he remains), he is given veritably regal honours and privileges—perhaps the strangest and most unique individual combination of low status in one social position and eminence in another. Here one must also remember the complications which arise from competition within a single group. A tradesman is on the one hand associated with other tradesmen in a sphere with a large number of common interests. Economic legislation, the prestige of the trading community, its political representation, solidarity *vis-à-vis* the consumer for the sake of price maintenance, and many other issues all concern the entire world of commerce as such, thus giving it an appearance of unity by contrast with outsiders. But, on the other hand, each tradesman is in competition with a number of others. Entry into this occupation brings him simultaneously association and isolation, a common interest and a special interest. He protects his interests by the most cut-throat competition with those very people with whom he must often collaborate most closely when their common interest is at stake. This internal paradox is of course at its most extreme in the area of trade, but it exists to some degree in all other areas right down to the ephemeral socialization of a dinner party. Considering the importance for the personality of the degree of contact or opposition which it encounters in its social spheres, we can see that membership of a large variety of spheres with widely varying proportions of competition and co-operation provides incalculable scope for individual permutations. And since everyone needs a certain degree of gregariousness, the mixture of gregariousness and isolation offered by any sphere provides a new rational criterion for the individual's choice of spheres. Where there is strong competition within one sphere, its members will tend to seek other spheres which are as uncompetitive as possible. Thus among trades people there is a decided preference for social clubs, whereas the aristocrat's class consciousness more or less rules out competition within his own sphere, so that he has little need of that sort of compensation and is more likely to prefer groups with a greater element of competition, such as those based on sporting interests.

Finally, I should like to mention here the intersections of incompatible spheres which often arise when an individual or group is governed by contrary interests and hence belongs simultaneously to opposing factions. For individuals, such a course is very likely in a highly diversified culture with an intense political life. What tends to happen is that, even in matters quite unconnected with politics, the different attitudes become divided between the political parties so that a particular trend in literature, art, religious life, etc., becomes associated with one party and the opposite trends with the other party. Eventually the line separating the parties cuts through every sphere of life. The individual who does not wish to be entirely governed by party allegiance is then, quite likely, as regards his aesthetic preferences or religious convictions for example, to join a group which is associated with his political opponents. He will then be at the point of intersection of two groups which are in general opposed to each other. Vast numbers of people were forced into such an equivocal position during the cruel suppression of the Irish Catholics by the English. One moment Protestants in both England and Ireland felt themselves united against the common religious enemy regardless of nationality, the next moment Irish Protestants and Catholics were united against the oppressor of their common motherland regardless of religious differences.

The evolution of a communal intellectual life is to be seen in the existence of enough spheres with some degree of objective form and organization to provide every aspect of a versatile personality with an opportunity for fellowship and communal activity. This constitutes an approach equally to the ideals of both collectivism and individualism. On the one hand, for every inclination and aspiration the individual finds an association which facilitates their fulfilment and provides his activities with the form which experience has shown to be most suitable, along with all the advantages of group membership. But, at the same time, his specific individuality is preserved by the *combination* of groups which can be different in each individual case. Advanced culture increasingly enlarges the social sphere to which we belong with our entire personality, but at the same time it makes the individual increasingly self-dependent and deprives him of much of the support and advantage of a close-knit sphere. But the formation of spheres and associations as meeting-points for any number of people with common interests and goals compensates for this personal isolation resulting from the rejection of the constrictions of earlier ways of life.

How close-knit such groups are can be measured by whether and to what extent they have evolved a particular sense of 'honour', either in the sense that the loss or violation of one member's honour is felt by every other member as a slight to his own honour, or that the group has a collective code of honour whose evolution is reflected in the sense of honour of each of its members. By creating this specific concept of honour (family honour, officers' honour, tradesmen's honour, etc.) such groups ensure desirable behaviour on the part of their members, especially in their specific province inasmuch as this is not covered by the rules of behaviour imposed by the broadest social sphere, viz. the laws of the state. One of the greatest advances in social ethics comes about in this way. In earlier forms of society with their close, strict ties, individual behaviour in the most diverse spheres is regulated by the social group as a whole, or its central authority. But this control becomes increasingly limited to the vital general interests of the group, leaving more and more areas to individual discretion. These areas are then taken over by new group formations, but in such a way that group membership is now a matter of free individual choice. As a result, no external compulsion is necessary; the individual's sense of honour suffices to ensure his allegiance to the norms necessary to preserve the group. This development is, moreover, not restricted to the power of the state. Wherever a group power (including the family, the guild, or the religious community) begins by regulating many aspects of individual life which have no actual relevance to its aims, authority and solidarity regarding such aspects of life are eventually taken over by particular groups, membership of which is a matter of personal freedom. The task of socialization can then be performed much more satisfactorily than by the former group which tended rather to neglect the individual personality.

Furthermore, where men are ruled exclusively by a single social power, however extensive and stringent that power may be, it invariably ignores, indeed cannot but ignore, a number of aspects of life. The greater the compulsion exercised in other respects, the more readily these aspects are left to purely arbitrary and unregulated personal choice. Thus, in Ancient Greece, and even more so in Ancient Rome, the citizen had to comply unconditionally with the norms and purposes of his native community in all matters at all connected with politics. But, as master of his household, he enjoyed an equally unconditional autocratic authority. Likewise, the most close-knit social organizations, such as can be observed in primitive peoples that live in small groups, leave the individual complete freedom to act entirely as he sees fit towards anybody outside the tribe. Thus despotism often finds its counterpart, and, indeed, a source of support, in absolute freedom and even licentiousness in those few areas of personal life which it considers of no importance. This inexpedient distribution of collective compulsion and individual arbitrariness is followed by an arrangement that is both more efficacious and more just, by which people's actual habits and inclinations determine the formation of associations. Collective authority can then more easily influence even such activities as have hitherto been of a purely individual and unregulated kind. As the personality as a whole attains freedom, it seeks social association for the satisfaction of its separate needs and will voluntarily restrict the arbitrary individualism which formerly compensated for undifferentiated bondage to a collective power. Thus, for example, in countries with a high degree of political freedom we find that clubs and associations are especially popular and widespread. In religious communities without a strong ecclesiastical authority hierarchically exercised, we find extensive sectarianism. In a word, freedom and restriction are more evenly distributed when socialization, instead of forcing the heterogeneous components of personality into one unified sphere, allows the association of homogeneous elements from heterogeneous spheres.

This is one of the most important directions of development. Differentiation and division of labour are, to begin with, quantitative, so to speak: spheres of activity are distributed in such a way that different individuals or groups are allocated different spheres, but each sphere comprises a number of qualitatively distinct aspects. But later these different aspects are differentiated out of all these spheres and reorganized in new, qualitatively unified spheres of activity. Public administration often develops in such a way that a number of areas are separated off from the centre of administration, which initially was wholly undifferentiated, and put under the charge of separate authorities or personalities. To begin with, however, these areas are of a spatial character. For example, the French Council of State sends a government official to a province in order to perform all the various functions there which are normally performed by the Council of State itself over the whole country. This is a quantitative division, unlike the later functional division whereby, for example, various ministries are formed from the Council of State covering the whole country, but only with regard to one qualitatively defined aspect. Even in Ancient Egypt, medical specialization produced different doctors for the arm and the leg; this was likewise a spatial differentiation. In modern medicine, by contrast, one specialist is responsible for the same pathological conditions regardless of what part of the body they affect: again, functional similarity determines the allocation of duties, replacing fortuitous external factors. The same new mode of distribution transcending former differentiations and associations is to be seen in those businesses which supply all the various raw materials for the manufacture of complex objects, e.g. all railway building materials, all articles required by innkeepers, dentists, or shoemakers, or shops that sell all domestic and kitchen articles, and so on. Here, the common factor governing the association of objects from the most disparate manufacturing spheres is that they all serve a single purpose, the *terminus ad quem*; whereas division of labour is usually determined by a single *terminus a quo*, viz. the method of manufacture. Such businesses (which, of course, presuppose the existence of the latter division of labour) constitute an enhanced division of labour, one raised, as it were, to a higher power: from wholly heterogenous areas, which are themselves highly labour divided, they take articles which belong together by virtue of a particular common aspect and unite them in a new harmony.

An interesting case of association creating a common social consciousness—interesting because of its high degree of abstraction from the individual and particular—is the solidarity of wage-earners as such. No matter what work the individual does, be it the manufacture of guns or of toys, the very fact that he works for a wage at all links him with others in the same situation. The identical relationship to capital constitutes, as it were, the exponential factor which produces the differentiation of the common element from such diverse activities and unites all those who share that element. The incalculable significance of the psychological differentiation of the concept of 'worker' *qua* worker from that of weaver, machine-builder, miner, etc., had already become clear to the English reactionaries at the beginning of this century. By means of the Corresponding Societies Act, they managed to prohibit all written communication between different workers' associations, along with all associations comprising members from different industrial fields. They obviously realized that once working men ceased to identify their general situation with their specific activity, once the comradeship of workers from different fields were to override their differences and open their eyes to their common lot, a new social sphere would thus be defined and promoted, whose relationship to the previous spheres would create unpredictable complications. First the differentiation of labour creates its various spheres, then a more abstract consciousness rediscovers their common element and unifies this element in a new social sphere. A similar association creates the tradesman class as such, and produces actual collective institutions.

Before division of labour reaches an advanced stage, while a fair number of related tasks are performed by the same individual or occupational group, i.e. where there are only a small number of such groups, it is easy for far-reaching psychological identification of two kinds to occur (or rather, a unity of elements which is seen as identification when viewed in the light of later differentiation; the word is imprecise, however, since it appears to suggest a foregoing distinction between elements which are only later identified). First, the higher concept common to a number of diverse activities is insufficiently distinct from the individual activities to engender common action and institutions. Thus, for example, it is only in the most recent period of our culture that large numbers of women have joined forces to agitate for social and political rights or to make collective arrangements for economic support and other purposes which concern only women as such. We may suppose that hitherto every woman identified the general concept of 'woman' too closely with the particular variety that she herself embodied. It makes no difference here, of course, whether the establishment of this general concept was the starting-point for practical measures, or whether, vice versa, it was itself necessitated by external circumstances. Women's activities were, and still are, too similar in general for a general concept with any real practical content to come into being. People only ever become conscious of such general concepts as a result of *different* individual manifestations. If there were only one kind of tree, the general concept of 'tree' would never have arisen. Likewise, people who are highly differentiated within themselves, with a broad education and range of activities, are more prone to cosmopolitan sentiments and convictions than one-sided personalities, for whom common humanity exists only in their own limited particular form, who are incapable of empathizing with other people and therefore cannot become aware of what is common to all men. The more areas economic production diversifies into, the more precisely the general norms of commerce are kept separate from the special regulations required for any one area. By contrast, in industrial towns, for example, which are basically limited to one field of production, one can see that the concept of 'industrialist' is as yet scarcely distinct from that of the iron, textile, or toy manufacturer, and even in other fields commercial practice follows that of the field of which people are chiefly conscious.

As has been suggested, the practical consequences of the emergence of higher general concepts do not always appear chronologically as such; on the contrary, they also frequently provide in their turn the stimulus which helps to create the consciousness of a common social situation. Thus, for example, the artisan class becomes aware of its homogeneity through the apprentice system. When excessive employment of apprentices leads to reduction in both price and quality of work, to curb this abuse in one craft would only mean that the apprentices forced out of that craft would flock into another; hence only a concerted campaign can help. This consequence is, of course, possible only because of the variety of crafts involved, but the people concerned can only become aware of it through their unity over and above their specific differences.

Secondly, whereas differentiation here brings about the emergence of the more general sphere from the more individual one in which it was hitherto only latent, it also has the function of separating more equally co-ordinated spheres from one another. The guilds, for example, controlled the entire personality inasmuch as all behaviour had to be regulated in the interests of the craft. A person who was taken on as an apprentice by a master-craftsman thereby also became a member of his family, etc. In brief, a man's occupation became the centre of his entire life, often including its political and emotional aspects, in the most far-reaching way. Of the various factors which led to the breakdown of this identification, we are concerned here with the factor inherent in the division of labour. For anybody whose life is influenced in all its various aspects by one single sphere of interest, the influence of this sphere will decrease with its magnitude. The restricted range of consciousness has the effect that a multi-facetted occupation with a wide variety of associated ideas casts its shadow over the rest of mental life also. There need be no actual objective connections between the two. The relatively rapid succession of different mental images required in any occupation that is not the product of the division of labour, consumes so much mental energy that the cultivation of other interests suffers. The interests thus impaired are all the more likely to become associatively or otherwise dependent on the centre of mental life. A man who is filled with a great passion will connect anything that passes through his mind, even the remotest things that have no real connection with it at all, with that passion in some way. All the fluctuations of his inner life are governed by it. A similar mental unity will be created by any occupation which leaves only a relatively slight degree of consciousness for other aspects of life. This is the key to one of the most important inner consequences of the division of labour, which arises from the psychological fact mentioned above that in any given time, other things being equal, the more frequently the mind changes from one idea to another, the more mental energy is consumed. This alternation of ideas has the same result as the intensity of passion. That is why an occupation that is not the result of the division of labour will be much more likely than a highly specialized occupation, other things again being equal, to assume a central, all-absorbing position in a man's life. This is especially so in periods when the other aspects of life lacked the stimulus of excitement and variety of the modern age. And inasmuch as a more one-sided and hence more mechanical occupation leaves more room in the mind for those other aspects of life, their value and independence is bound to increase. This separation and co-ordination of interests which were formerly subsumed in one central interest is also encouraged by a further consequence of the division of labour, one connected with the abstraction, discussed above, of a higher social concept from more specifically defined spheres. Associations, arising from purely psychological or historical factors, between central and peripheral ideas and spheres of interest, are usually regarded as objectively necessary until experience shows us personalities with the same centre but a quite different periphery, or the same periphery and a different centre. So when other aspects of life were dependent on a man's occupation, this dependence was bound to diminish as the number of occupations increased, because despite differences between them, many similarities in all other areas became visible. Likewise, in the subtlest aspects of inner life we gain many kinds of inner and outer freedom when we realize that, for other people, morally necessary behaviour and sentiments are dependent on quite different preconditions than have been associated with such behaviour in our own case. This applies very much, for example, to the ethical aspects of religion. Some people feel committed to religion because long-standing psychological habit has invariably linked their moral impulses to religious impulses. Only the discovery that people of a quite different religious cast of mind are not a whit less moral liberates them from that centralization of ethical life and gives independent validity to ethical impulses.

Thus with the increasing differentiation of occupations the individual was bound to realize that difference of occupation was compatible with the closest similarity in other aspects of life, and that the latter must therefore be substantially independent of occupation. The increasing differentiation of those other aspects of life has the same result as culture progresses. Difference of occupation combined with similarity of other interests (and vice versa) was bound to lead in the same way to the psychological and concrete separation of the two. Examination of the development from differentiation and association according to external schematic criteria, to those according to objective homogeneity, reveals a marked parallel to the realm of scientific theory: it used to be thought that the chief task of research with regard to living creatures was fulfilled when they were categorized in large groups according to external indications of affinity. But a deeper and truer understanding was achieved only by the discovery of morphological and physiological similarities in creatures that were apparently very different and which had accordingly been grouped under very different generic categories. This led to the discovery of laws of organic life which were manifested at widely separated points in the series of organic entities, a discovery which unified phenomena which had been divided in accordance with the earlier external criteria into wholly unconnected species. Here too the unification of what is objectively homogeneous from heterogeneous spheres marks the higher stage of development.

Thus the victory of the principle of rational objectivity over that of superficial schematism goes hand in hand with the general progress of culture. But this is not an *a priori* connection, and therefore it can break down in some cases. Though the solidarity of the family seems to be an external mechanical principle when compared with association according to objective factors, it seems objectively well-founded when compared with purely arithmetical systems of association such as the groupings of ten or a hundred men in ancient Peru, China and a large part of earlier Europe. The social-political unity of the family and its responsibility as a whole for each member is meaningful, and the more we learn about the effects of heredity, the more rational it appears. The idea of forming a permanent group from a fixed number of men and then treating them as a single unit as regards organization, military obligation, taxation and criminal responsibility, etc., is by comparison devoid of any rational basis. But, for all that, it originates, in those cases of which we possess evidence, as a substitute for the principle of consanguinity and serves a higher stage of culture. Here also the justification lies not in the *terminus a quo*—in this respect the family principle is superior to all others as a basis for differentiation and integration—but in the *terminus ad quem*. The higher political purpose is clearly better served by this grouping—which, precisely because of its schematic nature, facilitates organization and control—than by the older grouping. We have here a peculiar manifestation of cultural life: meaningful, profoundly significant institutions and modes of behaviour are replaced by others which *per se* appear utterly mechanical, external and mindless. Only the higher purpose which lies beyond the earlier stage lends to their combined effect or later consequences a spiritual significance, which each individual element in itself entirely lacks. This is true of the modern soldier by comparison with the medieval knight, of machine work by comparison with manual crafts, and of the modern uniformity and levelling of so many aspects of life which in earlier times were left to individual initiative. On the one hand, the world is now too vast and complex for each of its elements to embody, as it were, a complete idea. In themselves, they can only be mechanical and meaningless. Only as parts of a whole can they contribute to the embodiment of an idea. On the other hand, the differentiation which separates out the intellectual element of an activity has the widespread effect that the mechanical and intellectual aspects come to exist separately. For example, a woman working at an embroidering machine is engaged in a much more mindless activity than an embroideress; the intellectual element of the activity has been taken over by the machine and objectified in it. Thus social institutions, gradations, and associations can become more mechanical and external and yet serve the progress of culture, if a higher social aim arises to which they simply have to be subordinated and which no longer permits them to preserve for themselves the purpose and intellectual element with which an earlier way of life brought the teleological series to a conclusion. This, too, is the explanation for the transition from the principle of social grouping by consanguinity to the principle of groups of ten, although the latter actually appears to be a grouping of what is objectively heterogeneous as opposed to the natural homogeneity of the family.

Furthermore, primitive societies, especially those which are formed from a combination of basic, self-contained groups, very often elect their chieftain initially as a leader in war, but then also as a permanent ruler. He is spontaneously invested with this position as a result of his virtues. In other places he attains the same position by the same virtues, but by way of usurpation. But in both cases his chieftaincy ends when he dies, if not before, and some other similarly qualified person takes over leadership in one way or the other. Social progress, however, requires the rejection of this procedure based on personal virtue and the establishment of hereditary chieftainship. The comparatively mechanical and external principle of heredity gives the power of kingship to children, idiots and people unsuitable in every respect, but the political security and continuity thus attained outweigh all the advantages of the more rational principle of deciding who shall rule on the basis of personal qualities. The sequence of rulers is determined by the external hazard of birth instead of by objective selection, but this is nevertheless conducive to cultural progress. One can only say that this exception confirms the rule inasmuch as it shows that it is subordinate to itself: that is to say, not even this rule, not even the rejection of external and schematic considerations in favour of internal and rational criteria, can be allowed to become itself a schematic norm. And, finally, I should like to cite the more or less analogous process that has made monogamy preferable to sexual promiscuity. If the parents' health, strength and beauty ensure the best chance of sturdy offspring, then one can expect a degeneration of the species where its ageing and declining members are guaranteed the opportunity of procreation. But this is precisely the case with life-long marriage. If after every fertile union both partners were again to have active and passive freedom of choice with regard to the other sex, then those members of the species who had by then lost their health, strength, and attractiveness would no longer be able to procreate; furthermore, individuals who were really suited to each other would be more likely to come together. Such renewal of selection would do justice every time to the rational reason and purpose of sexual union. The sanctity of marriage, by comparison, its continuance even after the complete disappearance of the reasons which once determined it (even when this disappearance applies only to the existing relationship, whereas a union of each partner with somebody else would still be entirely rational) is to a certain extent a mechanical and external arrangement. Just as it is schematic to base leadership on heredity rather than personal qualities, so marriage for life makes a couple's entire future subject to a schematic relationship. At a particular time that relationship is the fitting expression of an inner bond, but it precludes the possibility of change, which, it would appear, society as a whole ought to desire in the interest of better-endowed offspring—cf. the popular belief that illegitimate children are the more well-endowed and talented. But just as in the former case stability with its secondary consequences far outweighs all the advantages of decision based on objective factors, so the externally regulated transition, the bequea- thing, so to speak, of the form of one period of life to the next, is for the relationship of the sexes a blessing which needs no elaboration. For the species it outweighs any advantages to be derived from the continual differentiation of personal unions. Here, to join what is really homogeneous from previous heterogeneous associations would not be to the benefit of culture.

[New translation. From Georg Simmel, *Über Soziale Differenzierung*, Chapter 5, Leipzig, 1890]

NOTE

1. In this translation it has been decided to translate the key term *Kreis* as 'sphere'. Other translators, when dealing with the concept in Simmel's later work, have rendered it as 'circle'.—Tr.

# Differentiation and the Principle of Saving Energy

All upward development in the series of organisms can be regarded as governed by the impulse to save energy. The more highly developed being differs from the less developed in that, in the first place, it is capable of performing the same functions as the latter, and others in addition. This will, of course, be possible if such a being has greater resources of energy at its disposal. But if such resources are equal, the increase in purposive activity will be achieved by performing the lower functions with less expenditure of energy and thus gaining energy for the additional functions. Saving of energy is the precondition of its expenditure. Any being is superior to the extent that it achieves the same end with less energy. All culture aspires not only to harness more and more natural energy to our ends, but also to achieve all such ends in ways that save more and more energy.

There are, I believe, three categories of obstacle to purposive activity, by avoiding which energy is saved: friction, indirectness and superfluous co-ordination of means. Indirectness is in consecutive form what co-ordination of means is in concurrent form. Perhaps, in order to achieve some end, I could perform an action leading directly to it, but instead I adopt a more remote procedure, which then triggers off the direct purposive action, perhaps even by way of involving some third element. The equivalent behaviour in concurrent form would be to perform a number of other actions in addition to the single action sufficient to achieve my end. This might be because they were, although superfluous at that moment, inseparably associated with the first action; or because they did in fact serve the same end, though this could be adequately achieved by just one such action.

The evolutionary advantage of differentiation can be interpreted as a saving of energy in almost all the ways indicated here. I will begin with a field which is not directly a social one. In the evolution of language, differentiation has led to the elaboration of the few vowel sounds of ancient languages into a great variety of them in modern languages. The earlier vowels show clear and abrupt phonological differences, whereas the modern ones provide transitions and gradations, breaking the old vowels down into parts, as it were, and reassembling them in a wide variety of ways. This has probably been correctly explained as a means of facilitating the operations of the organs of speech. To glide easily through hybrid sounds and indeterminate, flexible gradations was a saving of energy by comparison with abrupt alternation between very different vowels, each requiring a completely different innervation. Perhaps, in the purely intellectual sphere, the blurring of precise boundaries between concepts brought about by the doctrine of evolution and the philosophy of monism in general, is likewise a saving of mental energy. To create a mental image of the world requires a greater effort the more heterogeneous are its components and the more remote the idea of one of them is from the ideas of the others. More complex, energy-consuming legislation is necessary where the classes of the group differ by virtue of special rights or legal standing; it is easier for the mind to grasp the latter when the rigidity of absolute legal distinctions gives way to those fluid variations which remain even in legislation that is absolutely uniform and applies to everybody equally, because of differences of property and social position. Likewise all mental tasks are perhaps made easier to the extent that the rigidity of stringently demarcated concepts is replaced by intermediate gradations and transitions. This can be regarded as differentiation inasmuch as the schematic linking of a large number of individual entities thereby breaks down, and in place of shared collective qualities the individuality of an entity determines how it is conceived. Whereas sharply demarcated conceptual groupings are always subjective—as Kant put it definitively: no synthesis can exist in things, but only in the mind—reversion to the individual *qua* individual is realistic. Reality always plays a mediatory role *vis-à-vis* our concepts, it is always a compromise between them, for they are only aspects of reality that have become detached and independent in our minds, but which, in reality, coexist with many other aspects. That is why differentiation, though it appears to be a principle of separation, is so often in fact one of conciliation and reunification, and hence a saving of energy for the mind which operates with it in theory or practice.

Here differentiation again reveals its relationship to monism. As soon as sharp demarcation of separate groups and concepts ceases, mediation and gradual transitions become possible, as well as individualization; one has a coherent series of minimal differences and thus the whole abundance of phenomena as a unified whole. But all monism has been described as a principle of saving mental energy. There is certainly much truth in this, though I take leave to doubt whether it is either an absolute truth or such an immediate truth as it appears. Even if the monist view of things follows reality more closely than, for example, the dogma of separate acts of creation and its epistemological corollaries, it also requires, for all that, an act of synthesis, indeed perhaps one of a more laborious and comprehensive kind than if one is content to regard as genetically homogenous any number of series of phenomena, depending on whether one happens to be struck by similarities between them. It surely requires a higher thought process to derive the sum total of physical events from a single source of energy and its overlapping conversions than to postulate a different cause for every different phenomenon: a special thermal energy for heat, a special vital force for life, or, with typical exaggeration, a special *vis dormitiva* for opium. It is surely more difficult, finally, to recognize mental life, which appears as broken down into the interaction of individual ideas, as a unified whole, than to postulate special mental faculties and to imagine that one can explain the reproduction of ideas in terms of 'memory' or the ability to think logically in terms of 'reason'.

True, where philosophical monism does not have differentiation and individualization as its correlates, it does in many cases effect a saving of energy, not in the sense of enhancing activity in other spheres or in general, but rather in the sense of producing inertia. Thus, to remain in the realm of theory, it is by no means always intellectual vigour which rises to such lofty and universal abstractions as, for example, the Indian notion of Brahma. It is, on the contrary, often a flabby debility, which flees the sharp edges and glaring reality of things. Unable to cope with the mysteries of individuality, the mind is impelled higher and higher until it arrives at the metaphysical notion of the All-One, where all real thinking ceases. Instead of descending into the dark mineshaft of concrete reality, where alone the gold of true knowledge is to be obtained, a more easy-going, less energetic way of thinking disregards the tensions of existence which it ought rather to strive to resolve, and basks in the ether of the all-benevolent cosmic principle. But where, as in the cases mentioned above, monism based on differentiation consumes more energy than pluralism, this is a temporary rather than a final situation. The results obtained are all the richer, so that measured by them, less energy is consumed. In a roughly similar way, a locomotive consumes far more energy than a mail coach, but much less energy when measured against the effect achieved. Likewise, a large state with a centralized administration needs a large civil service, organized by division of labour right down to the smallest units. But with the substantial amount of energy required by its centralization and differentiation, it achieves, relatively speaking, much more than if the same territory were broken down into many small political units, each of which would in itself of course require no great differentiation of its administrative body.

Greater difficulties arise over the question of whether energy is saved where differentiation involves a split into hostile opposites, for example, in the case mentioned earlier of an originally unified body producing a variety of opposing factions. This can be considered as a division of labour, for the pressures which give rise to factions are basic impulses of human nature which are to be found in any individual, even if in greatly varying degrees. One can imagine that the diverse elements which were formerly pondered and more or less reconciled in each individual's mind are then distributed between different personalities who cultivate them in a more specialized fashion, while there is reconciliation only if they are all considered together. Any faction, which as such only embodies a one-sided idea, suppresses in its members (to the extent that they are members) all divergent impulses—from which they are unlikely to be entirely free from the outset. If we trace the psychological factors determining individual allegiance to factions, we find that in the great majority of cases they are impelled not by an irreversible natural constitution, but by fortuitous circumstances and influences to which the individual has been exposed and which have allowed just one of his various potential dispositions or energies to develop, leaving the others at a rudimentary stage. This factor—the cessation of those internal conflicts which, before joining a one-sided faction, robbed our thought and volition of some of its energy—explains the power of the faction over the individual. This power can be seen *inter alia* in the way that the most moral and conscientious men will go along with all the ruthless policies of vested interest considered necessary by the faction, which is almost as indifferent to the scruples of individual morality as nations are in their dealings with one another. Its strength lies in its one-sidedness. This is particularly evident from the way factional passions retain all their intensity even when the faction no longer has any purpose or significance—indeed, this intensity often develops only *after* this point, when there is no longer any struggle for positive goals, but membership of one faction, though no longer based on any objective reasons, itself creates antagonism towards the opposing faction. The most striking example is perhaps that of the circus parties of Rome and Byzantium. There was not the slightest actual difference between the white party and the red, or the blue and the green, especially as not even the horses and charioteers belonged to the parties but were kept by entrepreneurs who hired them out to any party. But for all that, if someone decided, for no particular reason, to support one of them, this was enough to make the opponent a mortal enemy. Innumerable family feuds of former times were of exactly the same kind by the time they had been perpetuated through several generations. The bone of contention had often long since disappeared, but the fact of belonging to one family put a member in a position of extreme hostility towards the other family. In the fourteenth and fifteenth centuries when the tyrants came to power in Italy, depriving political factions of any significance at all, the struggles between Guelphs and Ghibellines continued nonetheless, despite the fact that there was nothing for them to struggle over. Factional conflict as such had acquired a significance quite independent of any real point. In brief, the formation of factions is a differentiation which unleashes energies whose extent can be seen precisely in the way they can jettison any particular content and merely keep to the form of the faction as such without any real meaning, but often without suffering any diminution. All social association arises, of course, from the weakness and vulnerability of the individual, and blind, senseless devotion to a faction as in the above cases is especially widespread in periods when nations or groups are defeated or powerless, and the individual has lost the secure sense of his individual powers, at least as regards their previous modes of expression. After all, energies can still be perceived in this form which would otherwise have been left undeveloped. Even if much energy may be pointlessly consumed and squandered by such formation of factions, this is merely a case of the abuse and excess which are liable to befall any human impulse. On the whole, it is clear that the formation of factions creates focal points of association through which the individual can be spared inner conflict and enabled to develop his energies to great effect by channelling them in a single direction which provides them with an outlet free from psychological obstacles. As faction struggles against faction, each embodying a concentration of many personal energies, as different attitudes and their associated energies test their strength against each other, the outcome is bound to be more clear-cut, swift and decisive than if the battle were fought within one individual's mind or between separate individuals.

There is a peculiar relationship between consumption of energy and differentiation in that division of labour which might be called quantitative. Whereas division of labour usually means that different people perform different tasks, i.e. is of a qualitative nature, the kind of division of labour where one person does more work than another is also important. This quantitative division of labour is, it is true, beneficial to culture only inasmuch as it becomes a means of qualitative division: different quantities of a work which is basically the same in kind for everybody produces personalities and activities that are different in kind. Slavery and capitalist economy demonstrate the cultural value of this quantitative division of labour. Its conversion to qualitative division began with the differentiation of physical and mental activity. Merely to be freed from the burden of the former was bound to lead to an automatic enhancement of the latter, as mental activity occurs more spontaneously than physical activity, often without the aid of conscious stimulus or effort. Here, too, we see that saving of energy by differentiation enables that energy to be put to much more effective use. For the essence of mental as opposed to physical work can surely be seen in the fact that it achieves greater effects with less expenditure of energy.

This polarity is, of course, not an absolute one. There is neither any physical activity of the kind relevant here which is not in some way controlled by consciousness and will, nor any mental activity which is entirely without any physical agency or effect. One can only say that the relative preponderance of the mental element in any activity has the effect of saving energy. This relationship between work of a more physical and a more mental nature may be compared to that between lower and higher mental activities. Mental processes that do not rise above the sphere of the particular and concrete are less strenuous than abstract rational processes, but their theoretical and practical results are also that much slighter. Thinking in accordance with the principles and laws of logic saves energy inasmuch as its generalizing approach replaces the need to analyse each individual phenomenon. The law which summarizes an infinite number of individual phenomena in a single formula constitutes the greatest saving of mental energy. Anyone who is familiar with the law is as superior to anyone who knows only its individual manifestation, as is a man who owns a machine to a man who works by hand. But if higher thinking is thus generalization and concentration, it begins, for all that, as differentiation. Every concrete phenomenon is only one individual manifestation of a particular law, but even so it is also a point of intersection of an extraordinary number of forces and laws. These must first be psychologically analysed to isolate the particular aspect which, when collated with the same aspect of other phenomena, will provide the basis and the province of the higher law. Only by way of differentiation of all the elements whose fortuitous combination constitutes the individual phenomenon can a higher norm come into being. Mental activity obviously bears the same relationship to physical activity as, within the sphere of the former, higher activity bears to lower activity. For, as mentioned above, the difference between physical and mental activity is only a matter of there being quantitatively more or less of either element in the activity. Thought interposes itself between mechanical activities just as money does between real economic values and processes: concentrating, mediating, removing obstacles. Money also came into being by a process of differentiation. The exchange-value of things, a quality or function which they acquire in addition to their other properties, had to be detached from them and made independent in people's minds before this quality, which is common to the most disparate things, could be integrated in one overriding concept and symbol. The saving of energy achieved by this differentiation and subsequent integration is likewise to be found in the progress to higher concepts and norms, similarly derived. How much energy is saved by concentration, i.e. combination of individual functions in one central power, needs no elaboration. But it is not immediately evident that such centralization is always based on differentiation, that energy is saved by combining only selected aspects, not the totality of complex phenomena. The history of human thought, like that of social evolution, can be conceived as the history of this dynamic process, whereby the motley chaos of phenomena is differentiated in certain ways and the results of differentiation are re-integrated in a higher structure. The balance between dissolution and integration is, however, never stable, but always volatile. The higher unity is never final, either it is itself re-differentiated into elements which in their turn become the constituents of new, higher central structures, or the former complexes are differentiated in different ways, creating new integrations and rendering the earlier one obsolete.

This entire process can be thought of as governed by the impulse to save energy, initially by way of reducing friction. I have elaborated this idea in an earlier section from a different point of view, with regard to the relationship of ecclesiastical interests to state and scientific interests. Immeasurable energy is lost where division of labour has not yet allocated a special area to everyone and competition is unleashed by conflicting claims to the same undivided area. For much as competition is in many cases beneficial to the end product and provides an incentive to increased objective achievement, in many other cases it means that a good deal of energy has to be spent at first in eliminating competitors, before work is begun or while it is in progress. In innumerable cases, victory in this battle is decided by concentrating all energies not on the work but on more or less subjective extraneous factors. These energies are wasted, they are lost as regards the purpose they ought to serve. They are employed only to remove an obstacle which exists for one party because it exists for the other, which would vanish for both if they set themselves more appropriate goals. It is doubly inexpedient that energies should be consumed in order to paralyse other energies. If the ideal of culture is that human energies should be devoted to the conquest of the objective world, i.e. nature, rather than of one's fellow-men, then the distribution of spheres of work is the greatest furtherance of this ideal. The Greek political thinkers regarded the merchant profession as such as socially pernicious, and were willing to acknowledge only agriculture as a proper and just way of earning a living on the grounds that it did not profit from men and their exploitation. There is no doubt that this verdict was justified by the absence of division of labour. The approval of agriculture shows that they realized that only concern with the object of work can defeat the competition which they feared would destroy the fabric of the state, and that as things were then, with no division of labour, such concern was impossible except in a field as inaccessible to competition as agriculture. Only increasing differentiation can eliminate the friction created by shared goals which divert energies away from the goal to the personal defeat of the competitor.

Consideration of the individual demonstrates this from another point of view. If an individual's thoughts and volitional acts, taken as a whole, are highly differentiated from his group, and thus highly unified in themselves, this avoids the adjustments and changes of innervation which are necessitated by greater variety of thoughts and impulses. We can observe in our mental make-up something at least analogous to physical inertia: an urge to linger on the thought that is upmost at any particular time, to continue in one's present desires, to remain within one's current sphere of interests. When change becomes necessary, this inertia must first be overcome by a special impulse. The new innervation must be stronger than the purpose *per se* requires, because initially it is diverted by an impulse of a different kind whose effect can only be offset by increased energy. This psycho-physical parallel with the *vis inertiae* may perhaps be explained by the fact that we can never calculate with complete accuracy how much energy must be converted from a latent to an active state for any particular internal or external purpose. But since it would very soon be apparent if the necessary amount were not fully activated, we obviously err more often and to a greater extent in the direction of mobilizing too much energy, and the kinetic energy thus activated takes effect beyond the point to which it is rationally directed. If a new volitional impulse then comes into being at this point, it is impeded to a certain extent by encountering this surplus of counter-effective energy which it must first overcome by being intensified accordingly.

Here one must also recall processes within the individual which can be understood, at least symbolically, as friction and competition. The more diversified a man's activities and the less uniform and clearly defined his personality, the more frequently will the available energy be claimed by different aspirations which will not divide the energy up amicably between themselves any more than individuals would. On the contrary, each will demand as much energy as possible for itself to the detriment of all the others. The form that this very often clearly takes is that energy is directly devoted to eliminating the competing impulse, and thus brings us no nearer our actual goal. All that happens is that opposing energies cancel each other out, the end result being zero rather than any positive achievement. Only by two kinds of differentiation can the individual prevent this squandering of energy. Either he can differentiate himself as a whole, i.e. harmonize his impulses as closely as possible in one single basic direction with which they are all compatible, so that their similarity or parallelity preclude competition. Or he can differentiate his separate aspects and impulses, i.e. allocate to each of them a sufficiently separate sphere (either concurrently or—a point to be elaborated later—consecutively), a sufficiently clearly defined goal, and sufficiently independent paths to that goal, that do not cross any other paths so that there is no contact at all between them and thus no friction and competition. Differentiation of the whole and of the parts are both equally energy-saving. If one wishes to find a place for this fact in a cosmological metaphysics (which can, of course, never pretend to be more than vague intuition and suggestive symbolism), one might refer to Zöllner's hypothesis: viz. the energies inherent in the elements of matter must be such that the motions occurring under their influence aspire to minimize the number of collisions occurring in a confined space. According to this hypothesis, the motions, for example, in a cubic vessel filled with gas molecules would in time divide into three groups, each of which would proceed parallel to two surfaces. There would then be no collisions of gas molecules with one another, but only with two opposite walls, thus minimizing the number of collisions. We can see an exact parallel in the way collision, or rather friction, is within more composite organizations reduced by as far as possible keeping the orbits of individual elements separate. The chaotic confusion which brings them together every moment at a single point, where there is therefore friction, repulsion and dissipation of energy, develops into the establishment of separate orbits. The physical tendency can just as appositely be described as differentiation as the psychological and social tendency can be described as a reduction of collisions. Zöllner himself, for epistemological reasons, elaborates his hypothesis in the idea that external collisions of objects entail a sensation of pain, and hence puts the above physical hypothesis in the following metaphysical form: all work performed by natural creatures is determined by the sensations of pleasure and pain. Thus motions within a confined area of phenomena act as if they were pursuing the unconscious goal of minimizing the number of sensations of pain.

It is obvious how the impulse towards differentiation accords with this principle. But perhaps one can go a stage further in abstraction and regard the saving of energy as the most universal formal impulse in the natural world. This would replace the old principle (whose formulation at least is most misleading) that nature always *takes* the shortest path, by the maxim that it *seeks* the shortest path. The goals to which this path leads are then a matter of empirical circumstances, and there is perhaps no common formula for them. Obtaining pleasure and avoiding pain would then be either one of these goals, or, for certain creatures, a sign of successful saving of energy, or an acquired psychological incentive and aid to this end.

If, then, differentiation is subordinated to the principle of saving energy, it is *a priori* probable that processes and restrictions that run counter to differentiation will occasionally be harnessed to this supreme end. Human affairs being as manifold and heterogeneous as they are, no supreme principle will always and everywhere be served by the same individual processes. Because of the variety of raw material and because different objects need different influences to achieve the same effects, the intermediate stages leading up to the supreme unity will of necessity vary in proportion to their distance from that unity in the teleological chain. Failure to realize this—the illusion of monism which the unity of the supreme principle psychologically lends also to the stages leading to that unity—explains innumerable cases of delusion and one-sidedness in both behaviour and understanding.

The dangers of excessive individualization and division of labour are too well-known to need more than a passing reference here. I would like to mention only one fact, viz. that the energy devoted to specialized activity is initially maximized by forgoing other activities, but is reduced again if this condition is very pronounced and of long duration. For lack of exercise weakens the other groups of muscles or ideas and causes them to atrophy, which of course affects the entire organism in the same way. And since the only part that has a function draws nourishment and energy from the whole, its efficiency is bound to be impaired if the whole suffers. Thus one-sided exertion weakens the very organ it was originally intended to strengthen, because it affects the constitution of the entire organism, which is weakened by the neglect of other organs necessitated by such exertion.

Furthermore, the division of labour which consists in transferring functions to public institutions, and which in general effects a very substantial saving of energy, often reverts to individuals or smaller groups as a way of saving energy. What happens is as follows. A number of functions are detached from individuals and taken over by a common central body, e.g. the State. Then, within this unified central body, interrelationships and interdependencies arise, so that any modification of one function also affects all the others. Each individual function is thereby burdened with the need to take others into account, to restore a constantly threatened balance. This entails a greater expenditure of energy than would *per se* be necessary for the particular goal. As soon as the transferred functions constitute a new organism with multiple activities, the viability of this organism is dependent on a new nexus of conditions. These conditions are bound up with the totality of concerns and hence involve for each individual function a more extensive organization than its expediency would demand in isolation. The following are only a few of these burdens which affect any function that is transferred to the State: budgeting of expenditure; the need to take even tiny items into account when balancing enormous overall sums; the multiple checks which, though necessary in general, are often superfluous in particular cases; the vested interests of political factions and public criticism which, on the one hand, often enforce pointless experiments while on the other they suppress useful ones; the special privileges enjoyed by state officials: pensions, social prestige and many more besides. In a word, the principle of saving energy which produces the separation of functions from individuals and their transfer to a central body will often equally impose restrictions on this separation.

The alternating expediency of differentiation and its opposite can be clearly seen in the religious and military spheres. The evolution of the Christian Church led at a very early stage to the distinction between perfect men and ordinary men, between an intellectual and spiritual élite and the *misera contribuens plebs*. The Catholic priesthood, which mediates the relationships of the faithful with Heaven, is merely a result of the same division of labour which, for instance, has constituted the Post Office as a special social institution for mediating the relationships of citizens to distant places. This differentiation was abolished by the Reformation, which restored to the individual his relationship to his God which Catholicism had detached from him and unified in a central structure. The benefits of religion again became accessible to everyone, and earthly things such as hearth and home, family and civic occupation were given a religious aura, at least potentially, which the previous differentiation had detached from them. The most thorough-going abolition of this differentiation is to be seen in those communities which no longer have any special priesthood as such at all, but where anybody preaches as the spirit moves him.

The extent to which the earlier arrangement complies with the energy-saving principle will, however, become evident from the following reflections. Three pillars of Catholicism, celibacy, monasticism and the dogmatic hierarchy which culminated in the Inquisition, were extremely effective and comprehensive devices for the monopolization of all intellectual life by one particular class which absorbed all the progressive elements from the most disparate social spheres. In the most barbarous periods, this was a way of preserving what spiritual energies existed, which without such support by a particular class and particular focal points would have been dissipated without effect. But, in due course, it produced a negative natural selection. For any more profound or spiritual man there was no other calling than the monastic life, and since this demanded celibacy, the hereditary transmission of higher spiritual potential was severely impeded. Thus the baser, more primitive elements gained ground for themselves and their offspring. This has always and everywhere been the curse of the ideal of chastity. If chastity is regarded as a moral challenge and a moral achievement, it will only win over such people as are susceptible to the influence of ideals, that is to say, precisely the more refined, superior, ethically inclined individuals, and for such individuals to forgo reproduction is bound to give preponderance to poor genetic material. We have here an example of the pattern described above, where concentration of energy on one component, determined by division of labour, initially strengthens it, but then, by affecting the overall constitution of the organism, weakens that same component. The clear-cut differentiation between institutions concerned with sacred and profane interests meant at first that the former were preserved and enhanced. But by completely repudiating the profane sphere, they prevented the great mass of people from being permeated with hereditary superior qualities. And since they could recruit their own numbers only from these masses, their own material was bound to degenerate. To this was added doctrinal dogmatism which impeded spiritual progress, first by directly influencing men's minds, then also indirectly by the persecution of heretics, which has also been compared to a process of natural selection whereby the boldest and most open-minded men were selected with the utmost care in order to render them powerless in one way or another. But in all of this there was perhaps even so a profoundly beneficial saving of energy. Perhaps in that age the spiritual powers were too exhausted in the older racial elements and too barbaric in the younger for complete freedom of development for every spiritual impulse to create viable forms. On the contrary, it was a good thing that they were prevented from germinating, or pruned away in order to concentrate the vital essences. Thus the Middle Ages were a period for husbanding the energies of the racial soul. Its stultifying religiosity played the part of the gardener who cuts away untimely shoots until, by concentrating the sap that would have been wasted on them, a genuinely viable branch is formed. It is obvious how much energy was then, on the other hand, saved directly and indirectly by the abolition of that division of labour at the Reformation. Priestly mediation and elaborate ritual were no longer necessary for religious sentiment and activity. Pilgrimages to particular places were no longer needed, but the shortest of routes led directly from every humble chamber to the ear of God. Prayer no longer had to proceed via the authority of interceding saints in order to be answered. Individual conscience was permitted to become directly aware of the moral value of actions, without having to consult the priest and thereby burden both him and oneself with discussion, doubts and mediation. In this way, religion in its entirety, both internal and external, was simplified, and by restoring to the individual those qualities which had been detached by differentiation, the energy which had been consumed by the necessary indirect route via the central authority was saved.

Finally there is the following form of energy-saving reversal of differentiation, especially in the religious sphere. Two factions, starting from a common basis, have, because of doctrinal differences, established themselves as definitely separate, independent groups. Now a reunion is to be effected. But this will not often be made possible by one faction or the other abandoning the source of difference, but only by leaving the matter to the personal conviction of each individual member. The elements common to both groups existed hitherto only in such close connection with their specific difference that, in a sense, each faction possessed them separately; they were not common elements in the sense of a unifying force. But now, by disregarding the differences, they again become genuine common elements. The differences, on the other hand, lose their constitutive power and are transferred from the group to the individual. In the attempts at reconciliation with the Lutherans to which Paul III showed himself disposed, the intention on both sides was obviously to work out ways of formulating dogmas which would restore some common ground to both factions, while in other respects leaving it to each individual to add in his own mind whatever special or divergent elements he personally felt a need for. In the Prussian Protestant Union likewise, the idea was not at all that previous doctrinal differences should vanish, but only that they should be made a private matter for the individual instead of being embodied in a specially differentiated denominational structure. According to this idea, the Unionists would have been free to conceive of freedom of the will in a Lutheran fashion and communion in the fashion of the Reformed Church. The issues which divided the factions were no longer decisive; they had reverted to individual conscience, thereby enabling common fundamental ideas to revoke the previous differentiation. This complies, incidentally, with the formula . . . that development leads on the one hand from the smaller group to the larger, but on the other hand leads simultaneously to individualization. There is a saving of energy here inasmuch as the central religious body is freed from the burden of such questions and issues as the individual can best decide for himself unaided, and likewise the individual is no longer compelled by ecclesiastical authority to accept not only what he considers right but also a number of secondary articles of faith which are superfluous to him personally.

The evolution of the warrior class shows, if not an exact parallel, a partial formal affinity with the above. Originally every male member of a tribe is also a warrior. Wherever there is property and the desire to increase it, a direct result is that it is fought for and defended: the bearing of arms is the automatic consequence of someone having something to gain or lose. It is a high degree of differentiation and a particularly substantial saving of energy for such a universal natural activity—a concomitant of any vested interest—to be detached from the individual as such and made independent in a special structure. The more cultural the pursuits evolved, the more of an impediment the need to take up arms at any moment was bound to become, and the more energy could be saved by arranging for part of the group to devote itself entirely to the pursuit of war, leaving the others free to develop their energies in other vital spheres of interest with a minimum of disturbance. This division of labour culminated in the mercenaries, who were divorced from any non-military interest to the extent of offering their services to any warring faction. The first reversal of this differentiation came about when armies ceased to be international and non-political and did at least come from the country they were fighting for. Thus the fighter, even if he was this and nothing else, could at least be a patriot at the same time. This means, however, that the underlying state of mind of a man going into battle, his courage, energy and martial efficiency, are enhanced to a degree that the unpatriotic mercenary could achieve only artificially, by a conscious effort of will entailing a correspondingly greater consumption of energy. There is always a substantial saving of energy when a necessary activity is performed willingly and with spontaneous emotional involvement. The obstacles of apathy, cowardice and all manner of disinclination then automatically disappear, whereas if our heart is not in what we are doing, special effort is required to overcome them. The energy saved in this way is maximized in modern national armies where the differentiation of the warrior class has been completely reversed. Every citizen is now liable to conscription, the entire motherland with its innumerable members now depends on the support of each individual citizen, and the most diverse interests require military protection. This unleashes a maximum of inner energy of this kind, and neither money nor compulsion nor artificial effort are needed to achieve the same, or rather a much greater, military efficiency than was brought about by the differentiation of the warrior class.

This widespread pattern of development, where the last stage formally resembles the first, is to be seen in the important matter of the ability of differentiated bodies to substitute for one another. In physical life such substitution is quite frequent, and it is immediately evident that the more primitive and undifferentiated a creature's physical structure is, the more readily its organs can substitute for one another. If a fresh-water hydra is turned inside out so that its internal section, hitherto the digestive section, takes the place of the skin, and vice versa, then soon afterwards a corresponding change of functions occurs: the former skin becomes the digestive organ and vice versa. The more complex a creature's individual organs become, the more restricted each one becomes to its own particular function, which no other organ can perform. But at the pinnacle of evolution—the brain—substitution of parts again occurs to a quite considerable extent. The partial paralysis of the foot suffered by a rabbit as a result of partial destruction of the cerebral cortex disappears after a while. Aphasia resulting from brain damage is to some extent remediable, evidently by other parts of the brain taking over the functions of the damaged parts. Quantitative substitution also occurs: the loss of one sense tends to be followed by sufficient sharpening of the other senses to offset, as far as possible, the difficulties caused by the loss in the pursuit of vital goals. An exact parallel can be seen in society. In the lowest strata, lack of differentiation between its members means that most of the activities which occur there can be performed by anyone; anyone can substitute for anyone else. Further development rules out such substitution by equipping each individual for a special function beyond the abilities of others. But here again we find that the most superior, intelligent individuals have an outstanding capacity to adapt to any situation and take on any manner of functions. Here, differentiation has been transferred from the whole, where it requires specialization of the parts, to the part itself. Thus the part itself is so versatile that it has all the abilities appropriate to any external challenge that may arise. The evolutionary spiral here reaches a point vertically above its starting-point; at this level of development, the relationship of the individual to the whole is the same as at the primitive stage, except that in the latter neither was differentiated, but now both are. What appears to be a reversal of differentiation in these phenomena is, in fact, its further evolution: it has reverted to the microcosm.

Likewise the military development outlined above must be regarded not as a reversal of the process of differentiation, but rather as a change of its form and object. In the age of the mercenaries only a fraction of the population were soldiers, but they were so for more or less their whole lifetime. Now, by contrast, the entire population bears arms, but only for a certain period. Differentiation has changed from being concurrent within the group to being consecutive within the individual life. Consecutive differentiation is of great general importance. What occurs is not simultaneous transference of different functions to different elements; instead, the whole takes on different functions at different times. In synchronic differentiation, one part restricts itself to one function, cutting itself off from others. Here, a period of life does the same thing. The parallelism of concurrent and consecutive aspects of phenomena that can be observed in so many fields exists here also. In the course of evolution, clearly distinguished elements with different functions emerge from undifferentiated organizations. Individualized personalities with specialized training emerge by differentiation from a homogenous multitude of group members. But evolution also leads to the progressive breakdown of the uniform, more consistently unchanging course of life at more primitive stages, into clearly defined and sharply distinguished periods of life. Even if the life of the individual, taken as a whole, is relatively speaking more specialized, it comprises for all that an increasing number of distinct stages of development. This is suggested by the very fact that the more superior a being is, the longer it takes to reach the pinnacle of its development. An animal fully develops all its powers in a very short time, and the rest of its life consists in the exercise of those powers; but man needs an incomparably longer time and thus passes through many more different stages of development. This difference is clearly bound to apply also if superior and inferior human beings are compared. The lives of the most superior specimens of the human race are often one continuous development right into old age. (Goethe based his belief in immortality on the fact that he had insufficient time here below to complete his development.) In many cases, it even seems not so much that the later stage constitutes an advance beyond all earlier ones, making them only preliminary phases that have to be outgrown in order to reach the final stage, as that these various modes of conviction and activity represent aspects of human nature that are all *per se* of equal validity. It is as if those men who most completely represent our species in its entirety go through these stages consecutively because it is logically and psychologically impossible for them to exist concurrently. It will be recalled that Kant went through a rationalist-dogmatic, a sceptical and a critical period; these all constitute universal and relatively valid aspects of human development, which usually occur concurrently, distributed among various individuals. One may also think of stylistic changes within an artist's development, or changes in non-professional interests—ranging from circles of acquaintance to sport—the alternation of realistic and idealistic, theoretical and pragmatic periods of life, or the changes of conviction in many outstanding political careers. Every political stance adopted at a particular period of such a career arises from a deep-rooted aspect of human nature. As society as a whole develops, circumstances arise which favour collectivism as well as individualism, conservative as well as progressive measures, authoritarianism as well as liberalism—though not always in equal degrees. The increasing vigour of party-political life demonstrates at least that all these trends have great psychological weight, even if not that they are all justified. If an individual is able to absorb every aspect of social life and thus become a point of intersection of all its threads, he may do so either concurrently or consecutively. Here the energy-saving factor comes into operation once again. If opposing impulses make simultaneous claims on our awareness, they will create countless friction, obstruction and wastage of energy. Therefore natural expediency differentiates them by distribution over different periods of time. In very many cases, the energy of specialized personalities is definitely not to be explained as the result of having more than the normal amount of energy from the outset, but rather of being spared the useless obstruction and wastage of energy that arise from diversity of interests and aspirations. Likewise it is easy to see that, given an equal range of dispositions and susceptibilities, the lowest inner resistance, and thus the lowest consumption of energy, will occur in the person who, during any one period of his life, devotes himself one-sidedly to either one *or* the other, and, since it is impossible to distribute his interests, etc., concurrently to different faculties, at least differentiates them consecutively into separate periods. Conflict of incompatible aspirations, with the resulting deadlock of energies, will then occur only in comparatively brief periods of transition, when the old is not yet quite dead and the new not yet quite alive; such periods are always marked by reduced development of energies.

One arrives at the same answer to the question of what kind of activity will save or develop a maximum of energy, if one stresses not, as hitherto, the consecutive sequence of different elements, but the diversity within a consecutive sequence. If the problem is to arrange many diverse aspirations in such a way that they can all be fulfilled as completely and vigorously as possible, then we have established that this necessitates their temporal differentiation. If, conversely, temporal development is taken as the starting-point so that the question becomes: what is the most suitable content for such development in order to achieve maximum effect with minimum energy?—then the answer must be: a content with maximum internal differentiation. There is a very obvious parallel here with the advantages of rotation of crops over two-crop farming. If a field is always planted with the same crop, then in a relatively short time all the elements needed for its growth will have been extracted from the soil, which will then need a period of rest to recover. But if a different crop is planted, it needs different elements of the soil which were not used up by the former crop, but makes no demands on those already exhausted. Thus the same field enables two different crops to develop, but not two similar ones. It is the same with demands made on human energies. A new demand extracts from the soil of life nourishment which would not have been available for the same unchanged demand, for it would require elements which were needed previously and thus had been more or less exhausted. Personal relationships are also easily exhausted if we always make the same demands, whereas they remain fruitful if we activate different aspects of the other person's personality by alternating our demands. With regard to the senses, man is change-orientated, i.e. he only feels and perceives changes from his foregoing state. It is the same with his kinetic aspects: the energy required by a movement flags extremely rapidly if no change is involved. The saving of energy in this form of differentiation of action can be described as follows. If we take two different forms of activity, $a$ and $b$, which can produce the same effect, or two quantitatively equal effects $e$, and if we have just been performing $a$, or have done so continuously for some time, then to achieve $e$ by means of $a$ will require greater effort than by means of $b$, which constitutes a change from the foregoing activity. A sensory nerve requires a greater centripetal stimulus to repeat an excitation that has just previously occurred than does a different nerve that has not previously been stimulated, or has been stimulated in a different way, requires to produce the same excitation. In exactly the same way, a greater centrifugal stimulus, i.e. a greater overall expenditure of energy by the organism, is necessary for the immediate repetition of an effect than for a new effect for which the specific energy has not yet been consumed. One cannot say that a being whose activities are not consecutively differentiated therefore consumes more energy than a differentiated being, but what one can say is that it needs more energy to achieve equal results with the latter.

If we survey our findings thus far, a fundamental contradiction appears to run through them, which, rather than recapitulate previous material, I propose to describe directly. The fact is that differentiation of the social group is evidently directly opposed to that of the individual. The former requires that the individual must be as specialized as possible, that some single task must absorb all his energies and that all his impulses, abilities and interests must be made compatible with this one task, because this specialization of the individual makes it both possible and necessary to the highest degree for him to be different from all other specialized individuals. Thus the economic set-up of society forces the individual for life into the most monotonous work, the most extreme specialization, because in this way he will acquire the skill which makes possible the desired quality and cheapness of the product. Thus public interest often requires a one-sided political stance which is often very uncongenial to the individual; cf. Solon's ordinance prohibiting neutrality during civil strife. Thus the community intensifies its demands on those to whom it gives a position of responsibility, often to the extent that they can only be met by the utmost concentration on one special field to the exclusion of all other intellectual interests. The differentiation of the individual, by contrast, entails precisely the rejection of specialization. It breaks down the interwoven capacities of will and thought and develops each of them into an independent quality. By duplicating within itself the destiny of the species, the individual places himself in opposition to that destiny. The part which aspires to develop in the manner of the whole thereby rejects its role as a part of that whole. The variety of clearly distinguished aspects demanded by the whole is only possible if the individual forgoes such variety. One cannot build a house out of houses.

The incompatibility of these two impulses is obviously not absolute but limited in various ways, because the impulse towards differentiation is itself not unbounded, but necessarily stops short, in any individual or collective organism, at the point where the opposing impulse comes into its own. Thus, as has been emphasized several times, there comes a point in the individualization of members of a group where either they can no longer function even in their specialized occupations, or the group disintegrates for lack of inter-relationships. Also, the individual will himself forgo the complete satisfaction of all his diverse impulses because it would entail intolerable fragmentation. Up to a point, therefore, the interest of the individual in his own differentiation as a whole will coincide with the interest of society in his differentiation as a part. But as to where this point lies, where exactly the individual's desire for inner variety or more specialized concentration coincide with those same claims made on him by society—the only people who think that this question can be definitively answered will be those who believe that the demands arising from the situation of the moment can only be supported by presenting them as absolute demands arising from the nature of things. Be that as it may, the task of culture is to push that point further and further back and progressively to give to social and individual tasks a form that will demand the same degree of differentiation from both of them.

What militates against further progress towards this goal is above all the fact that opposing demands are increasing on both sides. When the whole is highly differentiated and encompasses an abundance of widely differing activities and personalities, the impulses and potential inherited by the individual will likewise be very numerous and disparate. These will struggle for expression in all their motley variety to precisely the same degree that differentiation in the outside world (which produced them in the first place) will deny them the opportunity for any diversified fulfilment. Wherever the differentiation of the social whole affects whole sub-divisions of society rather than individuals, e.g. in the caste system, the system of hereditary crafts, the patriarchal form of the family, the guild, or wherever class distinctions are strictly upheld, this internal evolutionary paradox will be less pronounced. The hereditary transmission of characteristics will be substantially restricted to the same sphere, i.e. to such persons as are able to develop their hereditary impulses and potential. But when social spheres begin to intersect, whether the individual belongs to a number of spheres or inherits an accumulation of characteristics from a variety of sources, then if this intersection persists through a number of generations, eventually every individual will become aware of a number of unsatisfiable needs within himself. The more extensively the various elements of society intersect, the greater will be the variety of characteristics embodied in its offspring, and the more completely he will appear its potential microcosm. But it will also be the more impossible for him to fulfil all his potential in the way it demands. For only the substantial growth of the social macrocosm brings about the intermingling of its elements, and it is precisely this growth that obliges it to demand increasing specialization of its members. The increased frequency of so-called problematic characters in the modern age may be connected with this dilemma. Goethe described as problematic people who can neither give nor obtain satisfaction in any situation. The coexistence of a great number of impulses and characteristics, which, of course, also occur in the form of desires, can easily cause frustration in many areas of life. Reality can gratify only one specific desire or another, and if at first it sometimes appears that some destiny, some vocation, some human relationship has given us complete fulfilment, in more complex persons this tends soon to become narrowed down to a partial satisfaction. Even if psychological association initially permits the warmth of this satisfaction to suffuse the entire personality, it soon becomes restricted to its original source. The sympathetic oscillations die away, and this situation also fails to give a sense that the problem of all-round satisfaction has been solved. Circumstances, for their part, demand the whole man for specific situations, but the whole man can only devote himself to the task if all his potential can to some extent be focused on it. This is precisely what is increasingly unlikely in view of the great diversity of inherited characteristics. Only people of very strong character can avoid becoming problematic in periods when situations become more and more specialized and human potential more and more diversified. On the one hand, they curb such impulses as are not appropriate to the task in hand, and on the other hand they themselves have the energy to make that task compatible with their own desires. The term 'problematic character' has thus rightly become almost synonymous with 'weak character', even though weakness of character is not the real, basic cause of such a temperament. This cause is to be found, on the contrary, solely in the factors of individual and social differentiation. Weakness is a cause only inasmuch as it can be said that pronounced strength of character would have offset these factors.

Thus because the impulse towards differentiation applies to both the whole and its parts, it gives rise to a paradox which is anything but energy-saving. In exactly the same way, we also see a conflict within the individual between the consecutive and concurrent differentiation described earlier. Integrated personality, strength of character and decisiveness in action and interests, the ability to persist in a chosen direction of development—all these qualities are demanded by powerful impulses of our nature, even at the cost of specialization, thus effecting the primary saving of energy which lies in the simple rejection of all multiplicity. Against this there is the desire for diversified self-expression and all-round development, which effects the secondary saving of energy which lies in flexibility, versatility and the ability to move easily from one challenge of life to another. Here, too, one can see the effect of the major principles which govern all organic life: heredity and adaptation. The stable unity of life, the similarity of different periods of life are the individual equivalents of the results of heredity in the species, while active and passive diversity can be seen as adaptation, as modification of innate character under the influence of circumstances which we encounter in unpredictable abundance and complexity. Then we see the conflict of these impulses, which run through the whole of life, recurring within the very impulse towards differentiation itself—as, in general, in organic entities the interrelationships of the various parts of a whole often recur in the interrelationships of the sub-divisions of one part. Wherever there is a tendency towards differentiation, a paradox becomes apparent: on the one hand, any particular shorter period is filled with some content, which is cultivated as intensively as possible but in one direction only; after a while this is followed by another period with different content in the same form; this is consecutive differentiation. On the other hand, any particular segment of time demands a content that is as varied and internally, i.e. concurrently, differentiated as possible. This dichotomy is of the utmost importance in innumerable fields. For example, the selection of an educational curriculum for the young must almost compromise between the two impulses: one unified section of the syllabus is first taken and learned one-sidedly, but all the more reliably; it is then followed by another section which is treated in the same way. But, on the other hand, there must also be concurrent learning which, although it does not achieve thorough command so quickly, does keep the mind alert and adaptable by means of variety. Temperament, character, all the diversity of human nature, ranging from the externals of occupation to a man's metaphysical philosophy, are distinguished by the fact that some people develop or master a variety of things more consecutively, others more concurrently. It might perhaps be said that the proportion between the two will vary somewhat from one individual to the next, and that to strike the right balance is one of the ultimate goals of practical wisdom. An extraordinary amount of energy tends to be wasted through friction between the two impulses before they are distributed between the various tasks of life in a way that obeys the principle of maximum saving of energy.

One must, however, not forget that here, too, the difference is ultimately more one of degree than of kind. The restricted capacity of consciousness limits it at any given moment to one or at most a small number of ideas; hence what we call concurrency of various inner and outer activities and developments is itself strictly speaking a consecutive series. It is, after all, purely arbitrary to mark off a particular period of time as a unit and describe what happens within it as concurrent. We disregard the small differences in time between the emergence of different aspects of development in one period and treat them as simultaneous; but there is no objective boundary to the degree of difference thus disregarded. Thus, in the above-mentioned educational instance, several subjects are taught concurrently, but this is strictly speaking not concurrence, it is consecutive teaching, but at shorter intervals than in the narrower usage of the term. Thus concurrence has only two specific meanings. First: consecutive alternation. Two developmental series are described as simultaneous if a step in one is always followed by a step in the other and then another step in the first. Thus, taken as a whole, they occur within the same period of time, even if their sections always occupy different sub-divisions of that period. Secondly: abilities and characteristics acquired by consecutive activities actually exist concurrently, so that a stimulus can activate any of them. Consecutive acquisition and exercise of abilities coexist with concurrent latent energies. These being the two forms of concurrent differentiation properly defined, the rivalry between them and the consecutive pattern will take the following form. Where it consists in alternation of activities, the question is how long either element is to be given priority before being replaced by the other. The difference between this and the simple conflict between the inertia of one activity and the attraction of another, is that here the cessation of any activity is associated with the idea of its resumption. On the one hand this can make such cessation easier, but it can also make it more difficult. Wherever the transition from one activity to the other is at all difficult, the awareness that the first change always also brings the second change nearer can easily make one delay for as long as possible. A clear counter-impulse can be seen, for instance, in the organization of the functions of civil servants and private administrative employees. The superior, or manager, will often have an interest in seeing that the activity of his subordinates encompasses a certain range of alternating duties. This extends competence and, especially, makes it easier for employees to deputize and help out when necessary. But this will often run counter to the employee's own interest: he will prefer to organize the duties that lie within his scope sequentially, so that when a new duty begins, the old one is definitely left behind. This is much more likely to bring him promotion, for it is very often not so much the case that the higher and better-paid function comes later, as that the function which is customarily allocated later in due course acquires the status and reward of a higher function. This can be observed as particularly in the hierarchy of junior officials as it can in the highest positions bordering on sinecure. But where one position comprises an alternating sequence of diverse higher and lower functions, promotion will be more difficult, because the differentiation usually entailed or demanded by consecutive distribution already exists in concurrent form.

Other conflicts arise from concurrent differentiation of the individual in its second proper sense, in which latent energies and abilities are taken into account. Intellectual and moral differences between individuals will be evident from the fact that some will perform a number of activities in order to store up, as it were, as many different skills as possible, whereas others will desire only a fluid sequence of changing current activities. The same kind of difference can be seen also, for example, in two men of private means, one of whom invests his capital in a number of different ways—property, mortgages, stocks and shares, etc.—while the other invests his entire capital now in one way that seems promising, now in another. If capital is differentiated into a number of either concurrent or consecutive investments, the former are more productive of security, the latter more of high return. Possession of capital, especially possession of money, might be generally regarded as latent differentiation. For its essence is that it can be used to produce an unlimited diversity of effects. Although entirely unvarying in character (for, as a mere medium of exchange, it has no character of its own), it permeates the entire range of activity and consumption. It embodies, in potential form, the entire rich diversity of economic life, just as the colour white contains in itself all the colours of the spectrum. It distils, as it were, both the potential and the results of innumerable functions. It encompasses this diversity not only in advance but also in retrospect: this medium of exchange, which transcends, so to speak, all factions, could only emerge from the greatest abundance of intersecting interests and disparate activities. The differentiation of economic life in general is the origin of money, and for the individual its ownership is the opportunity for any economic differentiation. Money is thus the most thoroughgoing form of potential concurrent differentiation. Compared with the possession of money, all activity is consecutive differentiation, or at least it divides the available amount of energy into a number of different segments, even if it takes the same form in all of them. But the moment in which money is possessed must be regarded as the outstanding 'pregnant moment', a momentary conjunction of innumerable threads, which immediately diverge again in equally innumerable effects.

It is obvious what multiple and profound conflicts the dichotomy of these impulses is bound to produce both in the individual and in society, and that we have here nothing less than one particular aspect of the struggle between capital and labour. And here we return to the question of the saving of energy. Capital is objectified saving of energy, in the dual sense that previously created energy is stored up rather than immediately consumed, and that future effects are achieved with this all-embracing, all-purpose instrument. Money is clearly the instrument whose use entails less loss of energy through friction than any other. It is produced from work and differentiation, and it is converted into work and differentiation without anything being lost in the process of conversion. But consequently it also necessitates the separate existence of work and differentiation; for otherwise it is simply the general without the particular, function devoid of raw material, a meaningless word. Thus simultaneous differentiation, in the sense that we have attributed it to capital, necessarily implies consecutive differentiation. One of the greatest problems for both the individual and the community is to determine the proportion of the two so as to effect a maximum overall saving of energy; and both often differ very radically, sometimes allowing the concurrent differentiation constituted by property to preponderate, sometimes the consecutive differentiation involved in work. Both are indispensible in any more highly developed society.

Where, as here, two elements or impulses reinforce but also limit each other, the mind easily falls into the trap of a double error. First, there is the idea that the proportions in which the elements should be combined to create a desirable state of affairs can be determined by the trivial formula: not too much and not too little. This is a purely analytical, indeed tautological proposition, for the very use of the word 'too' indicates an incorrect proportion, and its negation gives no indication whatsoever of the correct proportion. The whole question is precisely at what point of increase or diminution this 'too much' or 'too little' begins. This danger of thinking that merely to have formulated a problem is to have solved it is especially acute where the proportion of one element is a function, albeit an unstable one, of the other, as is the case with capital and labour. Consecutive deployment of energies such as that of labour can easily appear to be determined by the proportion in which its potential concurrent differentiation, capital, exists or is desirable; the correct proportion for the latter is then determined according to the quantity of existing or required work.

The second widespread error has more palpable consequences: that of thinking that the volatile balance between the two elements is a stable one, both in reality and ideally. The so-called iron law of wages is such an attempt to perceive a constant relationship between current differentiation of labour and latent differentiation of capital. The same applies to Carey's explanation of the harmony of interests between capital and labour: as the progress of civilization is steadily reducing the quantity of work necessary to manufacture any product, the worker is receiving more and more, relatively speaking, for the same product; but since, at the same time, consumption is also on the increase to an extraordinary degree, the capitalist's profit is also increasing; he has a relatively smaller stake in any individual product, but as a result of mass production he has greater absolute profit than he would with lower production. Here, at least, there is thought to be a constant relationship between the development of current differentiation inherent in labour under the conditions of civilization, and the development of its storage in the form of capital—a relationship determined not by fortuitous historical factors, but by the objective logical relationship between the two elements. On the other hand, Utopian socialists attempt to construct such a relationship, for the future at least, based on the naïve assumption that one can in principle be devised which could be universally applied and which—to interpret the socialist ideal for the moment within the context of these reflections—would constitute a maximum saving of social energy. I am thinking here, for example, of the proposals of Louis Blanc, who hopes to avoid the wastage of energy arising from competition by not employing labour (which produces profit, and is latent in it) in an individualistic fashion, but dividing up one third of it in exactly equal proportions, and employing the remaining two thirds for improvement and augmentation of machinery, etc.

I believe that all attempts to define an unvarying relationship between capital and labour, either in theory or in practice, will suffer the fate of the 'mental faculties' of older psychology. Here, too, constant relationships were postulated between intellect and reason, volition and emotion, memory and imagination; until it was realized that these are only crude linguistic formulae for very complex mental events, which can only be understood by eschewing all such hypostasizations and returning to basic mental processes in order to discover the rules governing the interaction and integration of individual ideas in the higher structures which constitute the immediate contents of consciousness. Similarly, understanding of such universal and complex structures as capital and labour and their interrelationship will not be achieved by direct extrapolation under the illusion that the one is directly determined by the other, but rather by returning to the original processes of differentiation of which both capital and labour are merely different combinations or stages of development.

[New translation. From Georg Simmel, *Über Soziale Differenzierung*, Chapter 6, Leipzig, 1890]

*Reading Five*
# Conflict

## Antagonism as an Element in Sociation

While antagonism by itself does not produce sociation, it is a sociological element almost never absent in it. Its role can increase to infinity, that is, to the point of suppressing all convergent elements. In considering sociological phenomena, we thus find a hierarchy of relationships. This hierarchy can also be constructed from the viewpoint of ethical categories, although ethical categories are generally not very suitable points of departure for the convenient and complete isolation of sociological elements. The value-feelings with which we accompany the actions of individual wills fall into certain series. But the relation between these series, on the one hand, and constructs of forms of social relation according to objective-conceptual viewpoints, on the other, is completely fortuitous. Ethics conceived of as a kind of sociology is robbed of its deepest and finest content. This is the behaviour of the individual soul in and to itself, which does not enter at all into its external relations: its religious movements, which exclusively serve its own salvation or damnation; its devotion to the objective values of knowledge, beauty, significance, which transcend all connections with other people. The intermingling of harmonious and hostile relations, however, presents a case where the sociological and the ethical series coincide. It begins with A's action for B's benefit, moves on to A's own benefit by means of B without benefiting B but also without damaging him, and finally becomes A's egoistic action at B's cost. Inasmuch as all this is repeated by B, though hardly ever in the same way and in the same proportions, the innumerable mixtures of convergence and divergence in human relations emerge.

To be sure, there are conflicts which seem to exclude all other elements—for instance, between the robber or thug and his victim. If such a fight simply aims at annihilation, it does approach the marginal case of assassination in which the admixture of unifying elements is almost zero. If, however, there is any consideration, any limit to violence, there already exists a socializing factor, even though only as the qualification of violence. Kant said that every war in which the belligerents do not impose some restrictions in the use of possible means upon one another, necessarily, if only for psychological reasons, becomes a war of extermination. For where the parties do not abstain at least from assassination, breach of word, and instigation to treason, they destroy that confidence in the thought of the enemy which alone permits the materialization of a peace treaty following the end of the war. It is almost inevitable that an element of commonness injects itself into the enmity once the stage of open violence yields to any other relationship, even though this new relation may contain a completely undiminished sum of animosity between the two parties. After conquering Italy in the sixth century, the Lombards imposed on the conquered a tribute of one third on the ground yield, and they did so in such a fashion that every single individual among the conquerors depended upon the tribute paid him by particular individuals among the conquered. In this situation, the conquered's hatred of their oppressors may be as strong as it is during the war itself, if not stronger, and it may be countered no less intensely by the conquerors—either because the hatred against those who hate us is an instinctive protective measure, or because, as is well known, we usually hate those whom we have caused to suffer. Nevertheless, the situation had an element of community. The very circumstance which had engendered the animosity—the enforced participation of the Lombards in the enterprises of the natives—at the same time made for an undeniable convergence of interests. Divergence and harmony became inextricably interwoven, and the content of the animosity actually developed into the germ of future commonness.

This formal type of relationship is most widely realized in the enslavement—instead of the extermination—of the imprisoned enemy. Even though slavery very often represents the extreme of absolute inner hostility, its occasion nevertheless produces a sociological condition and thus, quite frequently, its own attenuation. The sharpening of contrasts may be provoked directly for the sake of its own diminution, and by no means only as a violent measure, in the expectation that the antagonism, once it reaches a certain limit, will end because of exhaustion or the realization of its futility. It may also happen for the reason which sometimes makes monarchies give their own opposition princes as leaders—as did, for instance, Gustavus Vasa. To be sure, opposition is strengthened by this policy; elements which would otherwise stay away from it are brought to it by the new equilibrium; but at the same time, opposition is thus kept within certain limits. In apparently strengthening it on purpose, government actually blunts it by this conciliating measure.

Another borderline case appears to be the fight engendered exclusively by the lust to fight. If the conflict is caused by an object, by the will to have or control something, by rage or revenge, such a desired object or state of affairs make for conditions which subject the fight to norms or restrictions applying to both warring parties. Moreover, since the fight is centred in a purpose outside itself, it is qualified by the fact that, in principle, every end can be attained by more than one means. The desire for possession or subjugation, even for the annihilation of the enemy, can be satisfied through combinations and events other than fight. Where conflict is merely a means determined by a superior purpose, there is no reason not to restrict or even avoid it, provided it can be replaced by other measures which have the same promise of success. Where, on the other hand, it is exclusively determined by subjective feelings, where there are inner energies which *can* be satisfied only through fight, its substitution by other means is impossible; it is its own purpose and content and hence wholly free from the admixture of other forms of relation. Such a fight for its own sake seems to be suggested by a certain formal hostility drive which sometimes urges itself upon psychological observation . . .

## The Socializing and Civilizing Function of Competition

The progress of its content which competition achieves by means of its peculiarly interwoven form of interaction[1] is not so important here as is its immediately sociological process. The aim for which competition occurs within a society is presumably always the favour of one or more third persons. Each of the competing parties therefore tries to come as close to that third one as possible. Usually, the poisonous, divisive, destructive effects of competition are stressed, and for the rest it is merely admitted that it creates certain values as its product. But in addition, it has, after all, this immense sociating effect. Competition compels the wooer who has a co-wooer, and often in this way alone comes to be a wooer properly speaking, to go out to the wooed, come close to him, establish ties with him, find his strengths and weaknesses and adjust to them, find all bridges, or cast new ones, which might connect the competitor's own being and doing with his.

To be sure, this often happens at the price of the competitor's own dignity and of the objective value of his product. Competition, above all competition among the makers of the highest intellectual products, makes those who are destined to guide the mass subordinate themselves to it. In order to permit the effective exercise of their function as teachers, party leaders, artists, or journalists, they must obey the instincts or moods of the mass once the mass can choose among them, which it can because of their competition. As far as *content* is concerned, this certainly makes for a reversal of the hierarchy of social life-values; but this does not detract from the *formal* significance of competition for the synthesis of society. Innumerable times, it achieves what usually only love can do: the divination of the innermost wishes of the other, even before he himself becomes aware of them. Antagonistic tension with his competitor sharpens the businessman's sensitivity to the tendencies of the public, even to the point of clairvoyance, in respect to future changes in the public's tastes, fashions, interests—not only the businessman's, but also the journalist's, artist's, bookseller's, parliamentarian's. Modern competition is described as the fight of all against all, but at the same time it is the fight of all *for* all. Nobody will deny the tragedy of social elements working against one another, instead of for; of the squandering of innumerable forces in the struggle against the competitor—forces which could be used for positive achievements; or, finally, of the discarding of the positive and valuable achievement, unused and unrewarded, as soon as a more valuable or at least a more appealing one competes with it.

But all these liabilities of competition in the social balance sheet must only be added to the immense synthetic force of the fact that, in society, competition is competition for man, a wrestling for applause and effort, exemption and devotion of all kinds, a wrestling of the few for the many, as well as of the many for the few. In short, it is a web of a thousand sociological threads by means of conscious concentration on the will and feeling and thinking of fellow men, of the adaptation of the producers to the consumers, of the delicately multiplied possibilities of gaining favour and connection. Once the narrow and naïve solidarity of primitive social conditions yielded to decentralization (which was bound to have been the immediate result of the quantitative enlargement of the group), man's effort towards man, his adaptation to the other, seems possible only at the price of competition, that is, of the simultaneous fight *against* a fellow man *for* a third one—*against* whom, for that matter, he may well compete in some other relationship *for* the former. Given the breadth and individualization of society, many kinds of interest, which eventually hold the group together throughout its members, seem to come alive and stay alive only when the urgency and requirements of the competitive struggle force them upon the individual.

The socializing power of competition shows itself not only in these coarser, so-to-speak public, cases. We find two parties competing for a third in numberless combinations of family and love relationships, of social small talk and discussions over convictions, of friendship and satisfactions of one's vanity; sometimes, of course, only in allusions, beginnings which are dropped, side phenomena and partial phenomena of an over-all process. Wherever it occurs, however, the antagonism of the competitors is paralleled by some offering, coaxing, promising, imposing, which sets each of them in relation to the third party. For the victor in particular, this relation often attains an intensity which it would not have without the excitement by the chances of competition and without the peculiar, continuous comparison of his own achievement with the achievement of the other, which is possible only through competition. The more liberalism penetrates not only economic and political conditions but also those of the family, sociability, the church, friendship, stratification, and general social intercourse—that is, the less these conditions are predetermined and regulated by broad, historical norms and the more they are left to shifting forces or to an unstable equilibrium which must be attained from case to case—the more will their shape depend on continual competitions. And the result of these competitions will in turn depend in most cases upon the interest, love, hope which the competitors know to arouse in different degrees in these or those third parties, the centres of the competitive movements.

Man's most valuable object is man, directly and indirectly. Indirectly, because in him are stored the energies of sub-human nature, as in the animal we eat or make work for us, are stored those of the vegetable kingdom; and in plants, those of sun and earth, air and water. Man is the most condensed, most fruitfully exploitable phenomenon; and the necessity of psychologically winning him over grows in the measure in which slavery, that is, his mechanical appropriation, weakens. The fight against man, which was a fight for him and his enslavement, thus changes into the more complex phenomenon of competition. To be sure, in it too, a man fights another man, but *for* a third one. And the winning over of that third one can be achieved in a thousand ways only through the sociological means of persuasion or conviction, surpassing or underselling, suggestion or threat, in short, through psychological connection. But just as often, this winning over also means in its effect such a psychological connection, the founding of a relationship—from the momentary relation established by a purchase in a store to marriage. As the intensity and condensation of life-contents increases culturally, the struggle for the most condensed of all goods, the human soul, must take on ever larger proportions and must multiply and deepen interactions which bring men together and which are both the means and the ends of that struggle. . .

## Conflict and the Structure of the Group

The discussion up to this point has shown numerous regularities among parties to a conflict—mixtures of antithesis and synthesis, superordination of one over the other, mutual restrictions as well as intensifications. But conflict has another sociological significance: not for the reciprocal relation of the parties to it, but for the inner structure of each party itself.

Daily experience shows how easily a quarrel between two individuals changes each of them not only in his relation to the other but also in himself. There are first of all the distorting and purifying, weakening or strengthening *consequences* of the conflict for the individual. In addition, there are the conditions of it, the inner changes and adaptations which it breeds because of their usefulness in carrying it out. Our language offers an extraordinarily telling formula of the essence of these changes: the fighter must 'pull himself together' [*sich zusammennehmen*]. That is, all his energies must be, as it were, concentrated in one point so that they can be employed at any moment in any required direction. In peace, the individual may 'let himself go'—'himself' referring to the various forces and interests of his nature: they may be allowed to develop in various directions and independently of one another. In times of attack and defence, however, this would entail a loss of strength because of the counter-strivings of parts of his nature; and a loss of time because of the continual need for bringing them together and organizing them. The whole individual must therefore take on, as his inner position of conflict and chance of victory, the form of concentration.

# Conflict and the Centralization of the Group

The formally same behaviour in the same situation is required of the group. This need for centralization, for the tight pulling together of all elements, which alone guarantees their use, without loss of energy and time, for whatever the requirements of the moment may be, is obvious in the case of conflict. It is so obvious that there are innumerable historical examples where such centralization supersedes even the most perfect peacetime democracy. Take, for instance, the well-known differences between the peacetime organization and the wartime organization of the North American Indians. Or take the London tailors who in the first quarter of the nineteenth century had a very different organization, one for peace and one for war with their employers. In quiet times, it consisted in small, autonomous, general assemblies in some thirty inns. In times of war, each inn had a representative; these representatives formed a committee which in turn elected a very small committee from which all commands issued and which was obeyed unconditionally. At that time, workers' organizations generally followed the principle of the interests of all to be decided by all. Here, however, necessity led to the formation of an organ of the strictest efficiency. It had a wholly autocratic effect, and its benefit was recognized by the workers without contradiction.

The well-known reciprocal relation between a despotic orientation and the warlike tendencies of a group rests on this formal basis: war needs a centralistic intensification of the group form, and this is guaranteed best by despotism. And vice versa: once despotism exists and that centralized form has materialized, the energies thus accumulated and pushed close together very easily strive after a natural relief, war with the outside. An example of the reverse of this connection may be mentioned because of its striking character. The Greenland Eskimos are one of the most anarchistic peoples, with no chieftainship whatever. When they fish, they like to follow the most experienced among them; but he has no authority, and there are no means of coercing an individual who isolates himself from the common undertaking of the group. It is reported of these people that the only way of fighting out quarrels among them is the singing contest. The person who believes himself harmed by another thinks up mocking verses against him and recites them at a tribal gathering especially called for the purpose; whereupon the adversary answers in similar fashion. The absolute lack of any warlike impulse is thus paralleled by the equally absolute lack of political centralization.

For this reason, the organization of the army is the most centralized among all organizations of the total group—with the exception, perhaps, of the fire service, which operates on the basis of formally parallel requirements. The army is the organization in which the unconditional rule of the central authority excludes any independent movement of the elements. Hence every impulse issuing from that authority is translated into the movement of the whole without any dynamic loss. On the other hand, that which characterizes a federation of states is its unit as a war-conducting power. In all other respects, the individual states may preserve their autonomies; in this one not, if there is to be a federation at all. The perfect federation of states may well be described as one which in its relations to other states (at bottom openly or latently warlike) forms an absolute unit, while in their relations to one another its members possess absolute independence.

## The Behaviour of the Centralized Group in Conflict

In view of the incomparable utility of unified organization for purposes of fight, one would suppose every party to be extremely interested in the opposed party's lack of such unity.[2] Nevertheless, there are some contrary cases. The centralized form into which the party is pushed by the situation of conflict grows beyond the party itself and causes it to prefer that the opponent, too, take on this form. In the struggles of the last decades between workers and employers, this has been most unmistakably the case. The Royal Labour Commission in England passed the decision in 1894 that the firm organization of the workers was favourable for the entrepreneurs in a given industry, and likewise that of the entrepreneurs for the workers. For, although the result of such organization was that an incipient strike could rapidly spread and last a long time, this was still more advantageous and economical for both parties than were the many local quarrels, work stoppages, and petty conflicts which could not be arrested in the absence of a strict organization of the employers and workers. This parallels war between modern states which, no matter how destructive and expensive, nevertheless results in a better over-all balance than do the incessant small conflicts and frictions characteristic of periods during which governments are less strongly centralized. In Germany, too, workers had realized that a tight and effective organization of the employers, especially for the fighting out of interest conflicts, is of benefit to the workers themselves. For only an organization of this type can supply representatives with whom one can negotiate with full certainty. Only if there is such an organization can the workers in a given industry be sure that the success achieved is not at once put in jeopardy by disagreeing employers.

The disadvantage a party suffers from the unified organization of its opponent—because this is an advantage for the opponent—is more than compensated for by the fact that if both parties are thus organized, their conflict itself can be concentrated, stay within their purview, and lead to a truly general peace for both. By contrast, if one finds oneself up against a diffuse multitude of enemies, one gains more often particular victories, but has great difficulty in achieving decisive actions which definitely fix the mutual relationship of the forces. This case is so deeply instructive in regard to the interdependence between the unitary form of the group and its behaviour in conflict because it lets the efficacy of this interdependence triumph even over the immediate advantage of the enemy. It shows the objectively ideal form of organization for conflict to be that centripetality which the actual result of the fight brings out in the surest and fastest way. This teleology which, as it were, transcends the parties, allows each of them to find its advantage and achieves the seeming paradox that each of them makes the opponent's advantage its own.

## The Effect of Inter-Group Conflict on the Group

For the sociological meaning of the formation of groups and group constellations, it makes an essential difference whether one or the other of the following two alternatives is the case. On the one hand, the group as a whole may enter into an antagonistic relation with a power outside of it, and it is because of this that the tightening of the relations among its members and the intensification of its unity, in consciousness and in action, occur. On the other hand, each element in a plurality may have its own opponent, but because this opponent is the same for all elements, they all unite—and in this case, they may, prior to that, not have had anything to do with each other; or they may have had, but now new groups emerge among them.

In respect to the first alternative, it must be emphasized that while the conflict or war of a group may let it overcome certain discrepancies and individual alienations within it, it often brings out these intra-group relationships with a clarity and decisiveness not otherwise reached. This can be observed particularly well in smaller groups which have not yet attained the degree of objectification characteristic of the modern state. If a political party which unifies many different directions of interest is pushed into a decisive and one-sided position of conflict, an occasion for secession results. In such situations, there are only two alternatives—either to forget internal counter-currents or to bring them to unadulterated expression by expelling certain members. If a family contains personalities among whom there are strong though latent discrepancies, then the moment when danger or attack pushes the family towards its tightest closing of ranks is that very moment which either secures its unity for a long time or destroys it permanently. It is the moment which decides with keen precision whether co-operation among such personalities is possible. If a school class plans a prank on the teacher or a fist fight with another class, all kinds of inner enmities are silenced; but on the other hand, certain students find themselves forced to separate from the rest not only because of objective motives but also because in such decisive attacks they do not wish to join certain others with whom they nevertheless do not hesitate to co-operate in other respects within the framework of the class. In short: the group in a state of peace can permit antagonistic members within it to live with one another in an undecided situation because each of them can go his own way and can avoid collisions. A state of conflict, however, pulls the members so tightly together and subjects them to such a uniform impulse that they either must completely get along with, or completely repel, one another. This is the reason why war with the outside is sometimes the last chance for a state ridden with inner antagonisms to overcome these antagonisms, or else to break up definitely.

[Translation taken from Georg Simmel, *Conflict and the Web of Group Affiliations*, translated by Kurt H. Wolff and Reinhard Bendix, Collier-Macmillan, New York, 1964 (paperback edition)].

NOTE AND REFERENCE

1. '*Wechselwirkungsform.*' '*Wechselwirkung*' itself is translated as 'interaction'. On the term and its various renditions, see Kurt H. Wolff, *The Sociology of Georg Simmel*, Free Press of Glencoe, Ill., p. lxiv.—Tr.

2. cf. the earlier discussion of *Divide et impera* [see *The Sociology of Georg Simmel, loc. cit.*, Part Two, Chapter IV, Section 4, pp. 162-9].

*Reading Six*
# Individual Freedom

The evolution of any human destiny can be presented as a continual alternation of commitment and release, obligation and freedom. However, this preliminary approximation constitutes a drastic separation which is tempered by closer scrutiny. For what we perceive as freedom is in fact often no more than a change of obligations: when a previous obligation is replaced by a new one, what we are primarily conscious of is the disappearance of the old pressure. Because we are free of this we feel, at first, completely free. At first we bear the new obligation, so to speak, with muscles that, having been spared hitherto, are particularly strong—until it, too, makes its pressure felt as these muscles gradually grow tired. Then the process of liberation begins in relation to this new burden, just as it had formerly ended with it. This pattern of events does not occur with equal degree for all commitments: certain commitments entail a more lasting, intense and conscious sense of freedom than others. Some kinds of work, which are no less rigorously required than others and which make equally great overall demands on the powers of the personality, appear for all that to give that personality a particularly high measure of freedom. The difference of obligation which produces this difference of freedom compatible with it is of the following type: any obligation towards something other than an idea arises from a legitimate demand by another person—which is why moral philosophy always identifies moral freedom with those *obligations* which are either self-imposed or are imposed upon us by a social or ideal imperative. Another person's demand may concern the personal activity and contribution of the person bound by obligation; or it may concern at least the direct result of personal work; or, finally, it may concern merely a particular commodity which the other person is legitimately entitled to enjoy while no longer having any influence over the manner in which that commodity is provided by the person under obligation. This gradation also indicates the degrees of freedom compatible with fulfilment of the obligation. Of course, all obligations are basically fulfilled by way of personal action on the part of the individual concerned: but it makes a great difference whether an obligation is directly related to the person who fulfils it or only to the product of his work, or solely to the product *per se*, regardless of the work involved in its provision or even of whether the person concerned carries out that work himself. Even if the advantages to the person exercising his rights are objectively equal, the first of the cases described above will minimize the freedom of the person under obligation, the second will allow this freedom somewhat greater scope, while the third will entail very substantial freedom. The most extreme instance of the first case is slavery, where the obligation does not concern any specified activity but extends to the person himself and encompasses the exercise of all his powers. Under modern conditions, such obligations as relate to a person's total working capacity rather than the specified result of his work (as is the case with certain groups of workers, civil servants and domestics) do not, for all that, greatly diminish that person's freedom. This is either because work is restricted to certain times or because there is the possibility of choice between the persons towards whom one proposes to enter into obligations, or because of the magnitude of the reward, which creates the feeling that one has rights as well as obligations. Serfs also belong to this first category wherever they and their entire working capacity are wholly the property of the master, or wherever their services are unquantified. The transition of the second stage occurs when services are restricted to fixed times. This is not to say that this stage has historically always been the later one; on the contrary, the deterioration of peasant freedom very often takes them out of the second category into the first. This second stage is fully attained when a particular product is required instead of a particular working time and capacity. Within this category, a difference of degree can be discerned: the peasant vassal has to supply either a specific proportion of his natural produce, for example, a tithe of corn, or a permanently fixed quantity of corn, livestock, honey, etc. Although this latter arrangement can in some circumstances be the harsher and more difficult of the two, it does on the other hand give the peasant greater individual freedom, for it makes the lord of the manor less concerned with the peasant's method of cultivation. Provided that he

produces enough to cover the fixed tribute, then his master has no
interest in the total yield, whereas in the case of a proportional tribute he
does have a considerable interest therein, which is bound to entail
supervision, coercion and harrassment. The fixing of tributes as an
absolute rather than a relative quantity is a transitional phenomenon
which anticipates their replacement by money. In principle, of course,
complete freedom and personal emancipation from obligation is
possible throughout this entire category, for all that the person enjoying
rights is interested in is that he should receive the particular material
tribute, regardless of how the person under obligation obtains it. But, in
fact, given this form of husbandry, he cannot obtain it in any other way
than by his own labour; this is indeed the basis of the master–peasant
relationship. The person's activity is specifically determined by his
obligations. And this is typical wherever in an agricultural economy one
service entails another as an obligation: the obligation and the person
soon diverge to the extent that the person would in principle be entitled
to withdraw personally altogether from the relationship and fulfil his
obligation in a purely objective form, e.g. with the product of another
person's labour; but, in practice, the economic set-up makes this
virtually impossible. The individual himself remains bound and his
personal energies restricted to fixed activities by virtue of the
commodity he is obliged to provide. The extent to which, for all that,
the commodity principle as opposed to the personal principle constitutes
a move towards freedom is shown by, for example, the great advance in
the feudal entitlement of ministers in the thirteenth century. For it was
through this change that their vassalage, which had hitherto been of a
personal nature, was transformed into a purely material commitment,
and they thus became subject to the law of the land, i.e. free, in all
matters other than those relating to their vassalage. Exactly the same
thing happens today when gifted people who are compelled to earn a
living prefer to work for a joint-stock company with its strictly objective
organization rather than for an individual entrepreneur, or when a
shortage of servants arises because young girls prefer to work in a
factory rather than go into domestic service, where, although materially
better off, they feel less free through being subordinated to individual
persons.

The third stage, where the person is actually divorced from the
commodity and no longer included in the obligation, is reached when
tribute in kind is replaced by monetary tribute. For this reason a *magna
carta* of personal freedom in the sphere of civil law has been seen in the

provision of classical Roman law that any material obligation whatsoever could be met with money, and its fulfilment in kind be refused, i.e. the right to pay off any personal obligation with money. The landlord who is entitled to a certain quantity of beer, poultry or honey from his peasants thereby restricts the peasant to a particular activity. As soon as he levies only a sum of money, the peasant is completely free to choose whether to keep bees, livestock or whatever. In the sphere of personal work, the formally identical process occurs when the person becomes entitled to provide a substitute who must be accepted by the other party provided that there are no concrete grounds for objection. This entitlement, which gives the relationship an entirely new basis and significance, often has to be struggled for, like the substitution of money, because it is clearly felt that, like the substitution of money, it will lead to the dissolution of the obligation itself. Typically, the compilers of the Domesday survey, for those peasants who made regular payments of money in lieu of their statute labour, chose terms intended to indicate that they were neither entirely free nor entirely subject. Only the descriptions of the payments continued for a long time to indicate that they were originally payments in kind: they were levied as kitchen tax, barrel tax, hostel money (in lieu of provision of accommodation for the travelling gentry and their officers), honey tax, etc. A transitional stage is often that the original payment in kind is calculated as a sum of money, and this sum of money is then demanded in its place. This intermediate stage also occurs in circumstances very remote from the example quoted above: in Japan in 1877 all taxes and interest payments were still being either paid in rice or *calculated* in rice and paid in *money*, just as when, under Queen Elizabeth [I], certain lands belonging to the universities were leased out and the rent was agreed in corn, although it is clear that it was paid in silver. This at least continues to emphasize the identity of the value-quantity of an obligation, whereas any personal commitment entailed by a material specification has by this stage disappeared. If the *ius primae noctis* ever actually existed anywhere, then it developed in analogous stages: the original right of the lord of the manor pertained to the entirety of the subject person, the surrender of her most fundamental possession, indeed of her inmost being; this was the price to be paid by the female subject for the right to marry. The next stage is that this permission to marry, which can be refused at any time, is granted on payment of a sum of money; the third stage comes when the lord of the manor's right to withhold permission is removed and the subject is free to marry as soon as he has paid his master a fixed sum of money: bridal tax, marriage fee or some such. Thus, by the second stage, personal emancipation is based on money, but not exclusively so, as the master's consent still has to be obtained and cannot be demanded as of right. The relationship only becomes completely depersonalized when the matter is decided solely by the payment of money and no other factor. Until such time as all such seigneurial rights are abolished, personal freedom can rise no higher than the transmutation of the bondman's obligation into a monetary payment which the master must accept. This is why in many cases the reduction and eventual complete abolition of statute labour and tributes proceeded via transmutation into money payments. This connection between money payment and emancipation may sometimes be felt by the master to be so strong that it outweighs even the keenest desire for cash payment. In Germany, the substitution of money payments for state labour and tribute in kind had begun in the twelfth century, but the process was interrupted in the fourteenth and fifteenth centuries when even the manorial lords were infected by capitalism. For they realized that payments in kind were very much more flexible and could be arbitrarily increased to a far greater degree than could money levies whose numerically fixed quantities could not be altered. This advantage of payment in kind seemed to them sufficient for them greedily to hold on to it even at the very moment when in other respects they were governed by interest in money. For the same reason, it is felt generally undesirable that peasants should acquire money. The English tenant farmer was not allowed to sell any livestock at all without his master's special permission, for by selling livestock he came into possession of money with which he could buy land elsewhere and thus escape from his obligations towards his previous master. The ultimate stage in the process of liberation is reached by way of a development with regard to the money payment itself, viz. the substitution of a single capital payment for period payments. Even if the objective value is identical in both cases, the implications for the person concerned are quite different. True, each individual periodic payment does allow the individual, as we have emphasized, complete freedom of activity provided he earns the required amount of money; but the regularity of the payments forces this activity into a particular pattern, imposed by an outside agency.

Thus only capitalization of payments gives any obligation the form which is compatible with the greatest personal freedom. Through capital payment, the obligation is completely transmuted into a money payment, whereas regular periodic payment retains at least a formal element of restriction over and above the particular amount involved. This distinction can be seen, for example, in the following case: in the thirteenth century, and even later, the English Parliament decreed on a number of occasions that the Shires were to provide a certain number of soldiers or workmen for the king; but the representative assemblies of the Shires regularly substituted a payment of money for the provision of men. But however much personal freedom was rescued in this way, it is still fundamentally different from those rights and freedoms which the English people purchased from their monarchs by one-time payments of money. While the recipient of the capital payment is relieved of all the uncertainties entailed by periodic payments, the corresponding advantage to the payer is that his freedom has now changed from the unstable form associated with continually repeated payments to a stable form. The freedom of the English people *vis-à-vis* its monarchs is based partly on the fact that by means of capital payments it has reached agreement with them once and for all regarding certain rights: from *pro hac concessione*, we read for example in a document of Henry II, *dederunt nobis quintam deciman partem omnium mobilium suorum*. Not in spite of but precisely *because* of the somewhat brutal, external, mechanical character of such a transaction concerning popular freedoms, it constitutes a clear mutual agreement, in complete contrast to the feeling of the king that 'no piece of paper should come between him and his people'. For this reason, it also constitutes a radical elimination of all the imponderable elements of more emotive relationships which often provide the means of revoking or rendering illusory liberties which have been achieved by a less businesslike process. A good example of the gradual development whereby the liberation of the individual is based on the substitution of money for payment in kind is to be found in the duty of subjects, citizens and tenant farmers to provide accommodation and food for the sovereign rulers or their officials, baillifs or magistrates when travelling. This duty originated in the ancient royal service and grew in the Middle Ages to very substantial dimensions. The first step towards the depersonalization and objectification of this duty was its strict demarcation: at an early stage, we find precise regulations laying down how many knights and grooms must be accommodated, how many horses and dogs can be included, how much bread, wine, meat, crockery, table-linen, etc., is to be provided. Even so, wherever food and accommodation were actually provided, on the one hand the limits of obligation were bound to become blurred, while on the other hand the obligation very definitely took the form of a personal relationship. A comparatively more advanced stage was reached when goods alone were provided without actual accommodation: the quantities could then be more exactly laid down than when people had to be fed and accommodated to their own satisfaction. Thus we are told that Count von Riesec was to receive a certain payment of corn, and 'from this corn bread is to be baked for his retinue when he is in the village of Crotzenburg so that he may not inflict any further burden or hardship on the village poor'. This development leads on to the stipulation of fixed payments of money when the nobility are present in the course of journeys and assizes. Finally the variable and personal factors still present in this arrangement were removed by making the payments into *permanent* payments, which were levied as food tax, assizes tax or baillif's travel tax, even when the old-style official journeys of judges, etc., were replaced by quite different organizational forms. By this process, such payments were eventually abolished altogether and subsumed in the general taxes payable by subjects, which lack, so to speak, any specific form and which are thus the correlate of the personal freedom of modern times.

   In such cases of substitution of money payments for payment in kind, the advantage tends to be mutual. This is a very remarkable fact which challenges one to set it in a wider context. If one presupposes that the quantity of goods available for consumption is limited, and that it does not satisfy existing demands, and that, finally, 'the world has been given away', i.e. in general all goods have an owner, then it follows from this that anything that is given to one person must be taken away from another. If one excludes all the cases where this is obviously not so, there still remain innumerable instances where satisfaction of one person's needs is possible only at another person's expense. If this were regarded as the foundation, or the characteristic, or one characteristic of our economic life, this would accord with all those philosophies of life which regard the quantity of values allotted to mankind (e.g. in morality, happiness or knowledge) as fundamentally unchangeable because of the nature either of the values or of mankind, so that only the forms and the representatives of these values can change. Schopenhauer is inclined to suppose that the quantity of any man's suffering and happiness is predetermined by his nature and can neither be increased nor reduced, and that all the external circumstances to which we customarily ascribe our degree of well-being constitute only a difference in the form in which we experience that constant quantity of joy and sorrow. If this conception of the individual is applied to the entire human race, then all our striving for happiness, all evolution of material conditions, all struggle for possession and existence seem a mere juggling with values whose total quantity cannot thereby be altered. Thus any change in distribution only illustrates the fundamental phenomenon that one person now possesses what another has voluntarily or otherwise relinquished. This preservation of value clearly accords with a pessimistic, quietist philosophy of life, for the lower we rate our ability really to create new values, the more important it is to ensure that no value is really lost. We see this in India, in the widespread paradoxical idea that if a holy ascetic yields to temptation his merit passes to his tempter.

But the exact opposite can also be observed. All those emotional states where happiness lies not only in gain but equally in self-surrender and where both parties are mutually and equally enriched, give rise to a value which is not obtained by depriving another person of anything. Likewise, when ideas are communicated, what is enjoyed by one person is not in any way taken away from another; at least, only a well-nigh pathological subtlety of feeling can make a man really feel deprived when some objective intellectual idea ceases to be his exclusive personal property and is shared by others. By and large it can be said of intellectual property (at least as long as it is not extended into economic property) that it is not obtained at anyone else's expense, because it is not taken from any existing *stock*. For all that, its content pre-exists, it must be produced from the consciousness of whoever acquires it. This reconciliation of interests, arising here from the nature of the case, ought obviously to be brought about also in those economic spheres where competition for the satisfaction of individual needs can enrich one person only at another's expense. There are two ways of turning this latter state of affairs into that other, more perfect state: the most obvious way is to re-channel the struggle against one's fellow men into a struggle against nature. As additional material and energy are extracted from hitherto unclaimed natural stocks and put at the disposal of man, those already claimed are freed from competition. Unfortunately the principle of conservation of energy and matter apply only to nature in its absolute entirety, not to that sector to which human purposiveness stakes its claim. This relative whole can, of course, be expanded indefinitely as we succeed in shaping more and more matter and energy to our purposes, in, as it were, annexing them. Technological advances enable us to extract increased utility even from areas already claimed: the transition from extensive to intensive economy is by no means restricted to agriculture; it occurs with any material which is broken down into ever smaller parts for increasingly specialised utilization, or whose latent energies are more and more completely released. This extension of human power in various spheres refutes the idea that the world is 'given away' and does not make the satisfaction of human needs conditional on deprivation of any kind; it could be described as the substantive progress of culture. In addition to this, there is also the progress that could be described as functional. This is a matter of finding for change of ownership of particular objects the forms which will make it advantageous to both parties: such forms can only have originally arisen when the first owner had the physical power to withhold the desired object until offered an appropriate reward; otherwise the object would simply be taken away from him. Robbery (and perhaps also the giving of gifts) appear to be the most rudimentary form of change of ownership: all the advantage is on one side, all the disadvantage on the other. When this stage was transcended by exchange as a form of change of ownership—initially, as said, merely as a result of the equal power of the parties—this was one of the greatest steps forward possible for the human race. Faced with the mere differences of degree which in so many respects are all that distinguishes man from the brutes, men have often tried, as we know, to establish the specific difference which would unmistakably and unquestionably set man apart from other animal species: man has been defined as the political animal, the tool-making animal, the goal-pursuing animal; the hierarchic, even (by one serious philosopher) as the megalomaniacal animal. One could perhaps add to this list man as the *bartering* animal, which is, in fact, only one aspect or form of the very general characteristic which appears to be specifically human: man is the *objective* animal. Nowhere in the animal world do we find even the beginnings of what we call objectivity, the contemplation and handling of things independently of subjective feeling and desire.

I have already suggested how this alleviates the human tragedy of competitiveness. This is the true process of moral refinement through culture: the objectification of more and more of the contents of life in a supra-individual form: books, art, ideal constructs such as the fatherland, general culture, the shaping of experience in conceptual and aesthetic images, knowledge of a multitude of interesting and significant things—all these can be enjoyed without one person taking them away from another. The more objective a form values assume, the more room there is in them, as in the house of God, for each and every soul. Perhaps the savagery and bitterness of modern competition would be intolerable were it not accompanied by this increasing objectification of experiences making them immune to the struggle for power. It is surely profoundly significant that the same faculty which on the purely factual, psychological plane distinguishes man from the lower animals, the faculty of objective contemplation, of disregarding personal states and impulses in favour of pure objectivity, that this very faculty enables the historical process to achieve what is perhaps its loftiest and most ennobling result, the construction of a world that can be acquired without strife or suppression. Whoever possesses and enjoys this world does not thereby exclude anybody else from it, but rather thereby makes it accessible to innumerable other people. The solution of this problem, achieved substantively, as it were, by the world of objectivity, is approached on the functional level by exchange. By contrast with the simple act of taking or giving away resulting from a purely objective impulse, exchange, as we have seen, presupposes objective evaluation, reflection and mutual acknowledgement, a withholding of direct subjective desire. It is irrelevant whether this was originally not voluntary but enforced by the equal power of the other partner; for what is decisively and specifically human is that this equality of power leads not to mutual robbery and struggle, but to considered exchange in which unilateral personal possession and desire for possession become elements in an objective transaction which transcends the interaction of the parties involved. Exchange, which we take for granted, is the first way (and in its simplicity a truly wonderful way) to combine change of ownership with justice. The taker is at the same time the giver, thus eliminating any one-sided advantage such as characterizes a change of ownership determined by purely impulsive egoism or altruism—a form which, incidentally, is by no means always historically the first stage of development.

However, the mere justice effected by exchange is after all only formal and relative: the one party is to have no more and no less than the other. But over and above this it increases the absolute quantity of perceived value. Since in the act of exchange each party gives only what for him is relatively expendable, and receives what for him is relatively necessary, it enables those values which have been extracted from nature at any given moment of time to be put to increasingly profitable use. Supposing the world really were 'given away', and all activity really were no more than juggling within an objectively unchangeable value quantum, then even so the form of exchange would produce, as it were, an intercellular growth of value through the more efficacious distribution resulting from exchange. An objectively identical quantity of value is subjectively increased to a higher degree of perceived utility. This is the great cultural task whenever rights and duties are redistributed, a process which always involves an exchange. Even where it might appear that the transfer of advantage is entirely one-sided, any procedure that is truly socially progressive will not neglect this task. Thus, for example, in the peasant liberation of the eighteenth and nineteenth centuries the task was not simply to make the landlords forfeit what was gained by the peasants, but to devise a mode of distribution of property and rights which would also increase the totality of advantage.

In this connection, there are two properties of money which make its exchange for goods or services seem the most perfect form of exchange: its divisibility and its unrestricted utilizability. Without the former quality, no objective equivalence of service and reward would be generally possible. Natural commodities can rarely be valued and graded in such a way that their exchange cannot but be recognized by both parties as absolutely fair. Only money, because it itself represents merely the value of *other* objects and because it can be added and divided almost without limit, makes it technically possible to equate exchange values precisely.

But, as I have emphasized, only the first stage is thereby reached in the evolution away from one-sided change of ownership. The second stage arises out of the fact that exchange of goods rarely puts both parties in possession of goods that are really equally desired, or takes from them goods that are equally expendable. As a rule, one party will desire the exchange more strongly, and the other will consent to it only under compulsion or for a disproportionately high reward. When, on the other hand, goods are exchanged for money, one party receives the commodity he specifically requires, while the other receives something which is universally required. By being unlimitedly utilizable and therefore permanently desirable, money can, in principle at least, make every exchange equally advantageous to both parties. The party taking the commodity does so, we may be sure, because it is precisely what he requires at that particular time; the other party, who takes the money, likewise requires it at that time because he requires it at all times. Thus exchange for money enables both parties to raise their level of satisfaction, whereas with exchange of goods very often only one party will have a specific interest in acquiring or disposing of the goods concerned. It is therefore the most perfect method hitherto devised of solving the great cultural problem arising out of the unilateral advantage of change of ownership; how to increase the objective quantity of value to a higher quantity of subjectively perceived value by merely changing its bearer. This, along with the original creation of values, is clearly *the* task of purposive social action, that part of the general human task which falls to it: to derive a maximum of latent value from the content of life by means of the form given to it. Thus the cases where money is seen to serve this task illustrate the technical role of money in making exchange the fundamental social solution of this problem: they show the concept of exchange itself embodied in money.

The increased quantity of enjoyment made fundamentally possible by the exchange of goods for money (for all its eudemonistic devaluation by virtue of its results in other areas) is based not only on the subjective condition of the two parties. For it is evident that objective economic productivity, the future intensive and extensive growth of goods themselves, also depends on how any given quantity of goods is distributed in the present. It will produce very widely divergent economic results, depending on its various owners. The mere change of ownership of goods can substantially increase or diminish their subsequent quantitative development. One can go so far as to say that the same quantity of goods in different hands signifies a different quantity of goods, as if it were the same seed in different soil. This consequence of variable distribution appears to be greatest in the case of money. However much the economic significance of an estate or a factory may vary with their owners, any fluctuations of return (in excess, that is, of negligible quantities) are fortuitous and abnormal. But it is quite normal for the same sum of money in the hands of a stock exchange speculator or of a rentier, of the state or of an industrial tycoon, to yield extremely varied returns. This follows from the fact that the possession of money offers incomparable scope for the development of whatever factors, objective or subjective, good or bad, are involved in the use it is put to. It is least true of the total ownership of money of any group to say that its unequal and changing distribution is only a matter of formal change not affecting its overall significance. It is precisely this formal change which produces the most substantial differences with regard to the economy and wealth in their entirety. Nor is it a matter only of quantitative but also rather of qualitative differences, a point of central importance for our problem, albeit one which at the same time brings us back to the question of quantity. The same commodity in different hands generally signifies, in economic terms, only a quantitative difference in the monetary return. But the same amount of money in different hands signifies chiefly a qualitative difference in its material consequences. The social purposiveness which undoubtedly comes into operation here explains why modern wealth tends to stay in the same family for much shorter periods than used to be the case when wealth was not of a capitalistic kind. Money seeks, as it were, the more fruitful owner, and this is all the more striking, and must arise from all the more profound necessity, in view of the fact that money can apparently be owned more tranquilly, securely and passively than any other possession. Since money at any given moment develops a minimum or maximum of economic productivity simply by virtue of its distribution, and since furthermore its change of ownership tends to entail less loss through friction and intermediate stages of ownership than other commodities, money provides economic purposiveness which is a particularly rich field for its task of distributing property in such a way as to maximize its total importance.

Our special concern now is to continue the interrupted investigation of the extent to which a money economy can increase the sum total of human freedom by liberating it from that primary form of social value in which anything that is given to one person must be taken away from another person. To begin with, some immediately visible manifestations of capitalism evince this bilaterial advantage. The customary exchange of goods, in which they are personally examined and handed over, obliges the buyer in his own interest to check the goods thoroughly and expertly, because the seller, once he has provided the opportunity for such a check, can reject any subsequent complaint. When commerce evolves to the point where goods are sold on the basis of samples, the onus is transferred to the seller: not only is he responsible for ensuring that the goods supplied tally exactly with the sample, but also the buyer will naturally profit without scruple from any error made by the seller to his own disadvantage with regard to the quality of the sample. Business at our present-day commodity exchanges takes a form which relieves both parties of these responsibilities by employing a permanent universal standard. The buyer no longer has to carry out a prior check, with all its attendant risk of error, either of the goods in their entirety or of a sample. The seller no longer has to supply his wares to match an individual sample which, being in some degree subject to chance, entails a variety of risks for him. Rather, both parties now know for certain that if they conclude an agreement regarding a particular specified quality of wheat or petroleum, they are committed to an objectively fixed standard independent of any personal uncertainty or inadequacy. Thus, at the zenith of capitalism, a mode of commerce has become possible which, by objectifying its subjective basis, alleviates the responsibilities of both parties and makes the advantage of one entail no disadvantage to the other. A precise parallel can be seen in credit trading. In the Middle Ages it was very difficult to determine an individual merchant's creditworthiness, which meant that both the merchant and the creditor were obstructed and restricted in their dealings. Not until the sixteenth century did the bills of exchange of certain houses (especially at the exchanges of Lyon and Antwerp), come to be regarded as 'good' as a matter of course. The idea of unqualified creditworthiness pure and simple arose. This made the promissory notes of these houses into an objective functional value independent of any personal assessment of creditworthiness; the standing of houses might vary greatly in other respects, but they could be relied on to meet their commitments. Thus these commitments, being sufficient for this particular purpose, became separated from other individual qualities. By creating the general objective concept of being 'in credit', the exchanges—which everywhere raised the money economy to its purest form—typically alleviated the burdens of some people without imposing any extra burden on others, but rather achieving equal alleviation for both debtor and creditor by transmuting uncertain individual assessments into an objectively valid quality.

The significance of a money economy for individual freedom is deepened when we investigate the actual form taken by those dependency relationships which survive in it. It makes possible not only a solution as put forward above, but a special kind of mutual dependence compatible with a maximum of freedom. To begin with, it creates, on the face of it, a number of previously unknown commitments. Once a substantial working capital (which can usually only be raised through mortgage loans) has to be put into the land for it to yield the necessary quantity of produce, once tools are no longer manufactured directly from raw materials but from a number of prefabricated components, once the worker operates essentially with means of production which are not his own property—then dependence on third parties spreads to quite new areas. The more material conditions human existence and activity become dependent on, the more people they are bound also to become dependent on. But these people acquire their significance for the individual concerned solely by virtue of those functions: as owners of capital or purveyors of work requisites. It is irrelevant in this connection what sort of people they are in other respects.

This general fact, the significance of which will be elaborated in the following pages, presupposes the process by which a person becomes a definite personality in the first place. This clearly requires the coalescence of a number of qualities, characteristics and abilities in a single person. A person is, of course, a unity, relatively speaking, but only the unity of a *variety* of attributes is real and effective. Just as a physical organism exists by forming the unity of a life process out of a multiplicity of material constituents, a man's inner personal unity is also based on the interaction and coherence of a number of elements and properties. Each individual element, considered in isolation, is objective in character, i.e. it is not really personal *per se*. Neither beauty nor ugliness, neither physical nor intellectual powers, neither vocation nor personal inclination nor any of the other innumerable human attributes can by themselves unmistakably determine a personality. For any one of them can be combined with any other elements, even mutually incompatible elements, and may occur in identical form in the make-up of an unlimited variety of personalities. Only when several such attributes meet and fuse, as it were, at a focal point do they constitute a personality, which then in its turn imparts to each individual characteristic a personal subjective quality. A person is a unique personality not by virtue of being either one thing or another, but by being both one thing *and* another. The mind cannot apprehend the mysterious unity of the soul directly, but only when it is broken down into a variety of elements which have to be re-synthesized before a particular individual personality can be identified.

The personality thus constituted disintegrates almost completely under the conditions of a money economy. The supplier, the financier, the worker, people on whom one is dependent, do not operate as personalities at all, because they are involved in the relationship only by virtue of one single activity, i.e. supplying goods, lending money or performing work. Their contribution does not involve any of those other qualities which are essential to give their activity some personal colouring. This applies, of course, only to the ultimate stage of a development which, though in progress, is as yet incomplete in many ways. At the present time, personal interdependence is not as yet wholly objectified, subjective factors are not entirely excluded. But the general tendency is undoubtedly to make the individual dependent on the contributions of more and more people, but increasingly independent of their personalities as such. Both phenomena have a common root, they are the twin aspects of one and the same process: modern division of labour both increases the number of dependencies and causes personalities to disappear behind their functions, because it permits only one aspect of a personality to come into play, while all those other aspects which together make up a personality recede into the background. If this development were fully completed, the inevitable consequence would be a form of society with a pronounced affinity to socialism, at least to an extreme state socialism. For the aim of state socialism is to transform to an extreme degree all socially relevant activity into objective functions. Just as today a civil servant occupies a 'position' which is objectively performed and absorbs only very special individual aspects or energies of his personality, so in a fully fledged state socialism the world of personalities would, as it were, be overlaid by a world of objective forms of socially effective activity which would allow and prescribe only very specific and precisely defined modes of self-expression to the personality and its powers. This world would be to the world of personalities as geometrical shapes are to actual objects. A man's whole personality and its subjective elements could then only be translated into external activity under the restrictions of one of the specialized functions into which all necessary social action would be broken down, fixed and objectified. The essence of a person's activity would thus be completely transferred from the personality, as the *terminus a quo*, to the material purpose, the *terminus ad quem*. The form of man's activity would then hover above man's full psychological reality as the realm of platonic ideas hovers over the real world. The beginnings of such a form of society already exist, as said, in many respects. Often a specialized function becomes separated from the person who performs it, it becomes a self-contained ideal construct, so that people, no longer individually distinguishable, merely pass through the function, so to speak, without being able or allowed to find in its narrowly circumscribed specialized demands scope for their whole personality. The personality which merely performs a function or occupies a position is as irrelevant as that of the occupant of a hotel room. In a society completely constituted in this way, the individual would be infinitely dependent; the one-sided nature of his allotted contribution would make him dependent on complementary contributions from the nexus of all other persons, and satisfaction of needs would come only to a very limited extent from an individual's own abilities, and much more from a work organization determined by purely impersonal considerations, and existing independently of the individual. If there were ever a state socialism which lived up to its fundamental conception, this is the form of life it would produce.

Such a differentiated form of life is adumbrated, however, in a money economy in the sphere of private interests. On the one hand, the infinite flexibility and divisibility of money makes that multiplicity of economic dependencies possible, while on the other hand its neutral, objective nature is conducive to the elimination of the personal element from human relationships. Compared with modern civilized man, the member of an ancient and primitive economy is dependent on only a minimum of persons. Not only is the range of our needs very much wider, but even the basic necessities of life which we have in common with the primitives (food, clothing and shelter) require, where we are concerned, a far more complex organization involving many more people. Not only does our specialized activity require an infinitely greater number of other producers to exchange products with, but the actual activity itself is dependent on an increasing number of prior processes, assistants and semi-prefabricated articles. But in an undeveloped, or only slightly developed, money economy the relatively narrow range of dependence of its members was of a much more specific personal nature. It was with such fixed, familiar, as it were irreplaceable people that the ancient Germanic peasant or the American Indian tribesman, the member of the Slav or Indian domestic community, indeed in many cases even medieval men had relationships of economic dependency. The fewer interdependent functions are involved, the more permanent and significant were their representatives. On how many 'suppliers' alone is modern capitalist man dependent by contrast. But he is incomparably more independent of any particular individual one of them, and can change them without difficulty and as frequently as he wishes. Even today, we need only compare life in a small town with that of a large city to see this development, on a small scale of course, but none the less unmistakably. While at the earlier stage people paid for the small number of their dependencies with the closeness of personal relationships, often personal irreplaceability, the multiplicity of our dependencies is compensated for by our indifference and freedom of substitution regarding the individuals concerned. And if, because of the complexity of our needs on the one hand and the specialization of our abilities on the other, we are much more dependent on society as a whole than primitive man, who could always get through life one way or another in his very close-knit isolated group, we are on the other hand extremely independent of any *particular* member of this society, because his significance for us now lies only in his limited and specific material contribution, of which any number of other people of different personality are equally capable, with whom we have no connection save interests which can be completely expressed in terms of money.

This is the most favourable situation for achieving inner independence, the feeling of individual self-sufficiency. Mere isolation from other people does not engender the positive state of mind which we are talking about here. In purely logical terms: independence is not just non-dependence—just as immortality is not just non-mortality, for stones and metals are non-mortal but could not be called immortal. After all, even in its other sense of loneliness, 'isolation' is not the purely negative concept it may appear to be. Loneliness as a psychological state certainly does not simply mean the absence of society in any form; on the contrary, it implies its existence as an idea followed by its negation. It is a long-distance effect of society, a positive effect on the individual of negative sociation. If mere isolation does not produce either desire for others or happiness at being away from them, in short, an emotional response of some sort, then it sets the person concerned beyond the dichotomy of dependence and freedom. He cannot become conscious of his actual freedom as a value because of the absence of its antipode: friction, temptation, proximity. If the evolution of individual personality, the conviction that in all our personal emotions and desires we are developing the nucleus of our ego, is to be regarded as freedom, then it is so not as mere absence of relationships, but on the contrary as a quite definite relationship with others. These others must exist and be perceived in the first place for them to be of no importance. Individual freedom is not a purely inner quality of an isolated individual, but a correlational phenomenon, which becomes meaningless if there is no correlative. If any human relationship consists of elements of closeness and elements of distance, then independence is a relationship in which, although the latter have been maximized, the former cannot have entirely ceased to exist, any more than the concept of 'left' can exist entirely without that of 'right'. The only question then is, what is the concrete form of the two elements most conducive to the creation of independence both as an objective fact and in subjective awareness. Such a form appears to be provided by extensive relationships with other people from which all actual individual elements have been removed; influences exerted anonymously on both sides; regulations which apply without respect of persons. Both the cause and the effect of such objective dependencies, in which the individual as such is free, lie in the replaceability of persons: the change of persons, either voluntarily or resulting from the nature of the relationship, demonstrates that irrelevance of the subjective factor of dependence on which the sense of freedom is based. May the reader recall the empirical fact with which this chapter began: that we very often perceive a change of obligation as freedom; what we have here is merely an extension of this relationship between commitment and freedom into the individual commitment itself. A rudimentary example is the characteristic difference between medieval vassals and serfs: the former could change their master, whereas the latter were ineluctably tied to the same master. Even if the degree of obligation towards the master had been *per se* identical, this would constitute an incomparably higher degree of independence for the one than for the other. The real antipode of freedom is not obligation in itself but obligation towards a particular individual master. The modern master–servant relationship is still characterized by the fact that the master selects the servant on the basis of references and personal impression, but the servant, in general, has neither the opportunity nor the criteria for making a similar choice. Only in very recent times has the shortage of servants in the bigger cities occasionally put them in a position to turn down offers for imponderable reasons. This is felt on both sides to be a major step towards the independence of servants, even if the actual demands of a position, once accepted, commit the servant no less extensively than in earlier times. Thus when an anabaptist sect justified their large number of wives and their frequent change by arguing that this destroyed an inner dependence on the feminine principle—the same phenomenon as above transferred to a completely different sphere—the sentiment is valid in principle, albeit in the nature of a caricature. Our overall situation at any particular time comprises a certain degree of obligation and a certain degree of freedom, often, within the individual sphere of life, in such a way that the one relates more to the form and the other to its content. The restriction imposed on us by a particular interest is felt to be tempered by freedom as soon as we are able, as it were, to rearrange it, i.e. to select for ourselves the concrete, abstract or personal authority on whom we are dependent, without reducing the degree of dependence. A formally similar development occurs with wage-earners under capitalism. Considering the harshness and forced nature of the work, wage-earners might seem to be only slaves in disguise. We shall see later how their slavery to the objective production process can be interpreted as a transitional stage towards their emancipation. But the subjective aspect of the matter is that in comparison with former forms of work, the relationship to the individual entrepreneur is an altogether more flexible one. Of course, the worker is tied to his work just as the peasant is tied to the land, but the frequency with which entrepreneurs change under capitalism, and the many opportunities which the worker has of choosing and changing his employer, through being paid wages in money, do give him a quite new kind of freedom for all his ties. The slave could not change his master even if he was willing to accept far worse living conditions; the wage-earner can do so at any time. When the pressure of irrevocable dependence on a particular individual master thus disappears, then whatever concrete commitment may still be involved, a step is taken on the road to personal freedom. We must not be blinded to this incipient freedom by its frequent failure to influence the worker's material situation. For here, as in other spheres, there is absolutely no necessary connection between freedom and eudemonistic enhancement such as tends to be automatically assumed in the aspirations of theorists and agitators. A prime factor here is that the worker's freedom is counterbalanced by freedom for the employer too of a kind which he did not enjoy in more restrictive forms of work. The slave-owner and the lord of the manor both had a personal interest in keeping their slaves or bondmen in good condition and fit for work; their rights over them became, in their own interest, duties. In the relationship of the capitalist to his workers, this is either not the case or, where it is, is not always realized. The emancipation of labour has to be paid for, as it were, by emancipation of the employer, i.e. by the loss of that concern for his welfare enjoyed by the bondman. Thus the harshness and insecurity of his present position is a proof of the process of emancipation which begins with the removal of dependence on specific individuals. Freedom in the social sense, just as much as unfreedom, is a relationship between people. The development from unfreedom to freedom proceeds thus: the relationship first changes from one of stability and permanence to one of instability and change of persons. If freedom is general independence from the will of other people, then it begins with independence from the will of *particular* other people. The isolated hermit in the Germanic or American forest is non-dependent; the modern city-dweller is independent in the positive sense of the word. True, he needs innumerable suppliers, workers and colleagues—without them he would be completely helpless. But his association with them is a completely impersonal one mediated solely by money, so that he is not dependent on any of them as particular individuals, but only on their objective contribution, which is evaluated in terms of money, thus making the individual contributor unimportant and replaceable. Because the purely monetary relationship ties the individual closely to the group as an abstract whole—money being, as argued earlier, the embodiment of abstract forces—the relationship of an individual to others merely duplicates his relationship to objects, as this is determined by money. The rapid increase in the supply of goods, combined with the peculiar devaluation and loss of emphasis which objects undergo in a capitalist economy, make the individual object less important, even valueless. At the same time, the overall category of these same objects not only retains its importance, but as culture increases we become more and more dependent on more and more objects. Thus an individual pin is practically valueless to us—a point of importance earlier in our investigation—but modern cultured man would be lost if he had no pins at all. And finally the importance of money itself develops along similar lines: the enormous cheapening of money makes individual sums of money more and more valueless and unimportant, but the role of money as a whole becomes more and more powerful and all-embracing. In all these manifestations of a money economy, specific individual objects become less and less important to us, more insubstantial and interchangeable, whereas the material function of the category as a whole assumes increasing importance and makes us increasingly dependent on it.

This development is one example of a more general pattern to be discerned in an extraordinary number of forms and aspects of human life. These usually originate as an integral unity of the material and the personal. Aspects of life such as property and work, duty, knowledge, social position and religion, do not—as we feel to be the case today—first have some sort of independent existence, either real or conceptual, which is then taken over by a personality in a close joint association. On the contrary, the primary state is one of completely undifferentiated unity wholly transcending as yet the antithesis of personal and impersonal aspects of life. Thus, for example, on the lower levels of mental life, no distinction is made between objective logical truth and subjective artifacts of a purely psychological nature. Children and primitives automatically accept momentary psychological phenomena, fantasies and subjectively produced impressions as reality. For them the word and the thing, the symbol and its referend, the name and the person, are identical, as is proved by innumerable findings of ethnology and child psychology. It is not that two intrinsically separate sets of phenomena erroneously coalesce or become entangled, but rather that duality does not as yet exist at all, either in the abstract or in any concrete manifestation. The contents of the mind are completely unified phenomena from the moment of their inception. Their unity consists not in the resolution of an antithesis, but in being wholly uncontaminated by it. Thus aspects of life such as those mentioned above evolve directly in a personal form; the emphasis of the ego on the one hand and its object on the other develops only as the result of a long and never wholly completed process of differentiation from the original naïve unity. This evolution of personality from life in its undifferentiated state, which also produces as its complement the objectivity of the material world, is also the genesis of freedom. What we call freedom is linked in the closest possible fashion to the idea of personality, so closely that moral philosphy has often enough declared the two concepts to be identical. For that unity of the psyche, that congruence as at a single point, that fixed, defined, unique quality of seeing what we call personality, signified the independence and self-sufficiency *vis-à-vis* all external factors, the development determined solely by the laws of one's own being, which we call freedom. Both concepts equally emphasize an ultimate, profoundest point of seeing which stands apart from all that is material, external and sensory, both within our own nature and without. Both are but two ways of stating the single fact that, at this point, a partner has come into being to our natural, continuous, materially determined being, a partner which demonstrates its separateness not only by claiming a special position *vis-à-vis* this being, but equally by striving for reconciliation with it.

If the idea of personality, being a counterpart and correlate to that of material existence, must develop at the same pace as the latter, then clearly a more rigorous evolution of the concepts of the material sphere will go hand in hand with a similar evolution of individual freedom. Thus we can see the dual development peculiar to the last three hundred years: on the one hand, the laws of nature, the material order of things, the objective necessity of events have become ever more clearly and precisely visible, while on the other hand, independent individuality, personal freedom and independence of all external factors and natural forces have received increasingly pointed and vigorous emphasis. Even the aesthetic development of recent times began with the same dual character: the naturalism of Van Eyck and the Quattrocento is also a demonstration of the most individual qualities of phenomena. The first forms of satire, biography and drama, which appear at the same time, are both naturalistic in style and centred on the individual as such. They appeared, incidentally, at the time when the social consequences of the money economy were just becoming perceptible. Even Greek antiquity at its zenith created as one aspect of its philosophy of life a very objective image of the world close to that based on the laws of nature, while its other aspect was the complete inner freedom and self-sufficiency of the personality. And to the same extent that the theoretical elaboration by the Greeks of the concepts of freedom and the self was imperfect, the stringency of their theories relating to natural laws also left something to be desired. Whatever difficulties metaphysics may encounter in the relationship between the objective determinism of material things and the subjective freedom of the individual, as aspects of culture they have evolved parallel to each other, and any extension of the one seems to demand an extension of the other in order that the balance of inner life be preserved.

And here this general reflection leads back to our more specific sphere. Economy also begins without differentiation of the personal and the impersonal aspects of work. Only gradually does a split occur: the personal element recedes by degrees from production, from the product and from its turnover. But it is this process which creates individual freedom. As we have seen above, freedom develops to the same extent that nature becomes for us more objective, material and subject to its own laws. Similarly, it increases with the objectification and depersonalization of the economic cosmos. A positive sense of individual independence is no more possible in the economic isolation of an unsocial existence than in a philosophy of life still innocent of the causality and strict objectivity of nature. Only these twin antitheses produce the feeling of a peculiar power and a peculiar value of self-sufficiency. Indeed, even in man's relationship to nature it appears that in the isolation of a primitive economy—i.e. in the period of ignorance concerning the laws of nature as understood today—there prevailed a corresponding degree of unfreedom arising out of the superstitious conception of nature. Only the development of the economy to its full extent, complexity and internal reciprocity creates that interdependence which, by eliminating the personal element, makes the individual more self-reliant and conscious of freedom in a more positive way than would be possible in the total absence of relationships. Money is ideally suited to provide the basis for such a state of affairs. It creates relationships between people, but does not include them in those relationships. It provides an exact measure of material contributions, but a very inadequate one of their individual personal element. The restrictions of the material dependence which it creates is, for the discriminating consciousness, the necessary background against which the personalityand its freedom, differentiated out of these dependencies, stand out clearly.

[New translation. From Georg Simmel; *Philosophie des Geldes*, Chapter 4, part 1, Duncker & Humblot, Leipzig, 1900]

# The Style of Life (1)

The mental energy underlying the specific phenomena of a money economy is intellect, in contrast to those energies generally denoted as emotions or sentiments which predominate in periods and spheres of interest that are not determined by a money economy. This is, in the first place, because money is a means to an end. All means as such are an indication that the various interconnected aspects of reality are taken into account in our volitional process. They are only possible because we have an objective image of actual causal connections. Clearly, a mind which could encompass all such connections without error would, intellectually, have at its command the most appropriate means to any end in any initial situation. But even such an intellect, containing within itself all possible means, would not thereby produce the slightest means in reality, because means require the choice of an *end*. Only in relation to an end do those concrete energies and connections acquire the status of means, and an end can, it its turn, be created only by an act of will. Without the operations of the will there are no ends in the intellect any more than there are in the objective world, for the intellect is only a more (or less) perfect representation of the world. It has been correctly said, but generally misunderstood, that the will is blind. It is not blind in the sense of acting violently and at random, after the fashion of the blinded Cyclops. It does not produce irrational effects, if we understand rationality as a value-concept; but rather it cannot produce any effect at all unless it is given some object, which is never inherent in the will itself. For the will is merely one of the psychological modes (like being, obligation, hope, etc.) in which things exist in us, one of the categories (which are probably the mental concomitants of muscular or other sensations) which we attach to the things of the world—which are *per se* of a purely ideal nature—in order to give them some practical significance for us. Thus mere consciousness of reality, i.e. intellectuality, does not create ends any more than the will *per se*, which is merely the above mode given a name and elevated to a degree of independence, chooses any definite object. Rather, intellect, being completely neutral, must at some point be joined by the will, which attaches itself to reality in ways which cannot be predicted from that reality. Of course, once this has occurred, the will is transferred in a purely logical objective manner to other ideas causally connected with the first, which thus acquire the status of 'means' to that 'end'. Wherever the intellect leads us, we are wholly dependent, for it leads us only through the objective nexus of reality; it is the agency by which volition accommodates itself to independent being. If we consider exactly what is meant by working out means to an end, we see that we are acting in a purely theoretical, absolutely non-practical way when we are thus engaged. Volition accompanies our various deliberations only in the manner of an organ-point: it is the general precondition of a sphere in whose specific details it does not intervene, though it alone imbues that sphere with life and reality.

The extent and complexity of the means which make up our activity thus evolve in proportion to intellectuality, the subjective spokesman of the objective order of things. But since all means are in themselves completely neutral, all emotional values are in practice attached to ends, those points where action halts and the fact that we have reached them casts a glow not over activity but only over the responsive mind. The more such terminal points practical life contains, the more active will the emotional function become in comparison with the intellectual function. The impulsiveness and emotional intensity which are so frequently reported in primitive peoples must surely be connected with the shortness of their teleological series. The work which makes up their lives does not have the continuity provided in more advanced cultures by the occupation which runs consistently through life. It consists rather of simple series of aspirations which, if they are fulfilled at all, require relatively few means. An important factor here is the directness of their methods of obtaining food, which in more advanced societies is almost entirely replaced by complex series of ends. Under such circumstances, ends are relatively frequently imagined and achieved, and awareness of objective reality, i.e. intellectuality, comes into operation less frequently than the emotions which are the characteristic concomitants of both the direct image and the concrete achievement of ends. Even in the Middle Ages, widespread gearing of production to personal needs, the pursuit of crafts, the great variety of close-knit social groups and above all the Church provided a much greater number of fixed points of gratification in the course of purposive activity than does the present age. In our age, the elaborate preparations for such moments of gratification become endless, the purpose of the present moment so much more frequently lies beyond the moment, indeed outside the individual's range of awareness. This extension of series is the result of money, which in the first instance creates a central interest common to otherwise unrelated series, thus linking them in such a way that one can become a preparation for another, even if objectively wholly remote from it, as, for example, when an enterprise in one series is financed by money earned from another series—and thus served by that series *in toto*. The crux of the matter, however, is the general fact (which was discussed earlier in terms of its origins) that money is ubiquitously felt to be an end, thereby reducing to mere means an extraordinary number of things which are really ends in themselves. Because, however, money itself is an omnipresent means to all ends, life becomes one vast teleological system in which nothing is either the first or the last element. And since money evaluates all things with merciless objectivity, and since their value, thus measured, determines their interconnections, the result is a nexus of material and personal aspects of life whose complete cohesion and strict causality approach those of the cosmos of natural laws. It is held together by the all-pervading value of money as nature is held together by universal vital energy. Both take on a thousand forms, but by virtue of their unvarying real nature and the reversability of all their conversions, they make all things interconnected and interdependent. Just as all emotional elements have vanished from our conception of natural processes and been replaced by a uniform objective intelligence, so also the interconnected things of the practical world, by forming increasingly close-knit series, leave no room for emotional responses, which occur only in relation to teleological end-points. These things become mere objects of intelligence, to be used under its guidance. The increasing transformation of everything that constitutes life into means, the interlinking of series which at one time ended with self-sufficient ends, in a complex of relative factors is the practical counterpart of increasing insight into natural causality and the transformation of the absolutes of nature into relative factors. But it also means that because all structures of means (in the context of our present reflections) are causal connections viewed from in front, the practical world increasingly becomes a challenge to the intelligence. To put it more precisely, the mental elements of action fuse objectively and subjectively into calculable, rational connections, thereby progressively eliminating emotional reactions and decisions, which only arise at the points of life where its course is interrupted, i.e. at its ends.

Because of this relationship between the significance in life of the intellect and that of money, the quality which we initially attribute to those eras or spheres of interest which are dominated by both is a negative one: a certain lack of character. Character always means that people or things have a decided and permanent individual mode of being, which differs from and excludes all others. This is alien to intellect as such, for intellect is but the neutral mirror of reality in which all elements are equally valid, their validity consisting simply in the fact of their existence. Of course, there are characteristic differences in people's intellectuality, but strictly speaking they are either differences of degree (depth or superficiality, breadth or narrowness), or differences produced by the admixture of other mental energies, viz. emotion or volition. Intellect, in its pure form, is absolutely lacking in character, not in the sense of being deficient in some necessary quality, but because it completely transcends the selective limitation in which character consists. This is evidently also the sense in which money has no character. It is *per se* a mechanical reflection of the relative value of things, equally available to everyone, and in money matters everyone is equal, not because they are all of value, but because none of them is of any value, only money. But the lack of character of money and intellect tends to go beyond this pure, negative sense. We expect everything (perhaps not always with objective justification) to have a definite character, and we take it ill if the purely theoretical thinker forgives everything because he understands everything: an objectivity which would befit a deity, but never man, who, we feel, thereby does open violence both to the promptings of his nature and to his role in society. Likewise we take it ill that money economy makes its central value the utterly compliant tool of the most squalid machinations. The fact that it is equally willing to serve the most high-minded enterprise is no compensation, but simply the most glaring illustration of the wholly fortuitous relationship between the series of monetary operations and the series of our higher values, indeed the meaninglessness of the one when measured against the other. The peculiar loss of depth in emotional life which is said to be typical of the present time by comparison with the rugged energy and forthrightness of earlier ages; the ease of intellectual communication even between people of the most disparate natures and attitudes (whereas even Dante, with his towering intellect and deep interest in philosophy, said that there were certain philosophical opponents who should be answered not with reasons but only with the knife); the trend towards conciliatoriness which arises from indifference to the basic issues of inner life, which are ultimately the questions of the soul's salvation and which cannot be decided by intellect—including the idea of world peace which is particularly cultivated in liberal circles, the historical representatives of intellectualism and money dealings: these are all positive consequences of the negative attribute of lack of character. Where monetary dealings reach their culminating point, colourlessness becomes, as it were, the colour of men's working lives. In the modern cities, there are a great number of occupations without any clear-cut objective form: certain types of agent, middle-men, all the indeterminate people to be found in cities who earn their living by the most diverse fortuitous opportunities of making money. For them, economic life, the web of its teleological series, consists of nothing that can be defined with certainty except earning money, which is absolutely indeterminate, but which for them is the one fixed point around which their activities revolve with unlimited scope. We have here a particular kind of 'unqualified work' compared with which the work that we usually thus describe is seen to be 'qualified'. Its essence lies in simple muscular labour where the amount of energy employed completely outweighs the form of its application, so that this work of the humblest labourer does have a specific colouring, without which even such attempts as have recently been made in England to organize them in trade unions would not be possible. The lives of those individuals who pursue the most disparate opportunities for earning money are much more lacking in any predetermined character—unlike the bankers, for whom money is not only the end but also the raw material of activity, a capacity in which it can very well have the features of a definite profession with its own special fixed laws and its own particular kinds of interest. Only in the case of the above-mentioned problematic individuals have the routes to the final goal of money forfeited any objective unity or affinity. Only here does the levelling of individual activities and interests resulting from the pursuit of money encounter a minimum of resistance. The character and quality that the personality could derive from its economic activities are lost. Such a life is clearly only at all successful, indeed only possible, where there is an unusually high degree of intellectuality—of the kind, moreover, that is commonly known as 'cunning', i.e. intelligence not restricted by any concrete or ideal standards, unreservedly at the service of any particular personal interest. Rootless individuals are, understandably, particularly suited to such 'callings', where the element of 'being called', i.e. a firm ideal connection between a person and his life, is precisely what is absent. Equally understandably, they tend to be suspected of unreliability. Even in India the word for 'agent' has also come to be used occasionally as the word for 'someone who lives by cheating his fellow-creatures'. Such products of the city, whose only ambition is to earn money in one way or another, quite regardless of how, are therefore all the more in need of intellect as a general function because there can be no question for them of any special expertise. They constitute a major proportion of the class of indeterminate personalities who are difficult to pin down because their flexibility and versatility save them from the necessity of pinning themselves down in any particular situation. These phenomena are possible only because money and intellect share the quality of neutrality, or lack of character. They could not arise anywhere else than where these two forces meet.

The apparent contradiction between these features of a money economy and the relentless violence of modern economic struggle is not a real one, for that struggle is itself unleashed by direct interest in money. Not only does it take place in an objective realm where people matter not as individual personalities but as embodiments of a particular impersonal economic potential, where today's mortal enemy is tomorrow's cartel ally. Also, and especially, the internal qualities fostered by a particular sphere may be entirely different from those which it displays towards outside spheres which come under its influence. Thus a religion may, within the sphere of its followers and doctrines, be peacableness itself, and yet be extremely militant and cruel towards both heretics and neighbouring spheres of life. Similarly, a person may awaken in others thoughts and feelings which are quite unlike anyting anything in his own life, so that he gives what he does not possess. Again, a movement in the arts may, in terms of its own convictions and artistic intentions, be wholly naturalistic, aiming merely at the direct reproduction of nature; but the very existence of such faithful devotion to reality and the struggle to reproduce it is an absolutely idealistic element in the system of life and, by comparison with its other constituents, far transcends any naturalistic reality.

Struggles between vested interests in a money economy are not incompatible with that economy's principle of neutrality (which raises the struggle above the personal level to a sphere where communication is always basically possible), any more than the acrimony of logical or philosophical controversy is incompatible with the fact that intellectuality is a principle of reconciliation: once a dispute moves from the realm of opposing emotions and desires or unprovable emotive axioms into the sphere of theoretical discussion, it must be fundamentally possible to reach agreement. Certainly, there is something callous in a purely intellectual approach to people and things; but this callousness is not a positive impulse, it is simply that pure logic is unaffected by considerateness, good nature or sensitivity. That is why the man who is interested only in money tends to be baffled if he is accused of callousness and brutality, for all he is aware of is the pure objective logic of his behaviour, not of any evil intentions. One must remember withal that we are speaking only of money as the *form* of economic dealings; these may, for all that, have quite different features arising from other sources. One can describe as objectivity in the style of life this indefinite character which life takes on as a result of intellectuality and money economy, notwithstanding all other intensification of conflict which arises from them. Objectivity is not a quality added to intelligence, it is its very nature. It is the only way open to man of achieving a relationship with things that is not determined by fortuitous subjective factors. Even supposing that objective reality is totally determined by the functions of the human mind, we still describe as intelligent those functions by virtue of which it appears to us as objective in the specific sense of the word, no matter to what degree intelligence itself may be animated and directed by other forces. The most outstanding example is Spinoza, in whose philosophy we see the most objective attitude towards the world: every individual spiritual act is required to be a harmonious echo of the universal exigencies of existence; nowhere is individual unpredictability allowed to violate the logical-mathematical structure of the universal unity; the image of the world and its norms is based on the function of pure intellect. This philosophy is itself subjectively constructed to the end of merely understanding things, and understanding is adequate to fulfil its demands. But this intellectuality is itself founded on a profound religiosity, a wholly meta-theoretical relationship to the ultimate ground of things—which, however, never intervenes in the particulars of the self-contained intellectual process. On a larger scale, the Indian race demonstrates the same combination. It is reported that in both the most ancient and the most modern times the peasant is left to till his fields in peace between the warring armies of Indian states, without being molested by any hostile party, for he is regarded as the 'common benefactor of friend and foe'. This is clearly an extreme degree of objectivity in practical matters. What appear to be natural subjective impulses are completely pushed aside by a practical approach which is concerned only with the objective import of things. Differentiation of behaviour is governed only by objective expediency, not personal passions. This race was, at the same time, of a completely intellectual cast. In logical precision, in the meditative profundity of its conception of the world, indeed in the austere intellectuality of even its most gigantic artifacts of fantasy and its loftiest ethical ideals, it was, in ancient times, as superior to all other races as it was inferior to very many of them in warmth of emotional life and strength of will. They had become mere spectators and logical designers of the universe. But the *fact* that they had become these things had, for all that, had its roots in ultimate emotional decisions, in immeasurable suffering which had acquired the dimensions of a metaphysical, religious sense of the cosmic necessity of that suffering, because the individual could not come to terms with it, either within the emotional sphere itself or by channelling his energies into a vigorous practical life.

This same objective stance towards life also arises from the role of money in it. I have pointed out in an earlier context how great an advance even trade constitutes beyond man's original undifferentiated subjectivity. There are still today tribes in Africa and Micronesia who know no other form of change of ownership than robbery and gift. But, at a more advanced stage of human evolution, the subjective motives of egoism and altruism (alternatives to which ethics, alas, still tends to restrict human motivation) are joined and transcended by objective interests which have nothing to do with subjective factors but with dedication or commitment to concrete expediency and ideals. Similarly, the egoistical impulsiveness of robbery and the equally altruistic impulsiveness of giving gifts are transcended by transfer of ownership according to the criteria of objective correctness and fairness: exchange. Money, however, is the pure, self-sufficient embodiment, so to speak, of the objective factor in exchange. For it has none of the specific properties of individual exchangeable commodities, and thus has *per se* no closer relationship to any particular subjective economic element than to any other. Similarly, theoretical laws constitute the independent objectivity of natural events, set against which any individual case determined by them appears as fortuitous—the counterpart of the subjective element in human nature. The fact that nevertheless different people have very different inner relationships to money proves precisely that it transcends all subjective particularity, a quality which it shares with other great historical forces, which are like vast lakes where men can take from any side whatever is permitted by the size and shape of their vessels. The objectivity of human interaction (which is, of course, only the form given to raw material originally supplied by subjective energies, but one which eventually takes on its own independent existence and norms), finds its most thoroughgoing form in purely money-economic interests. What is sold for money goes to the person who gives most for it, regardless of who or what he is in other respects. Where other rewards are involved, where property changes hands for the sake of honour, service or gratitude, one scrutinizes the character of the recipient. Conversely, when I myself spend money it does not matter to me from whom I buy what I want, as long as it is worth the price. But wherever one pays for something with service or personal commitment of either an internal or external kind, one looks very carefully to see whom one is dealing with, because money is the only thing of ours which we are willing to give to anybody. The promise printed on bank notes to pay the bearer 'on demand', i.e. without checking his credentials, is typical of the absolute objectivity of monetary transactions. In this sphere, we find even in a much more passionate race than the Indians a counterpart to the Indian peasant's exemption from acts of war: in some American Indian tribes, traders are allowed free passage to trade with tribes which are at war with their own! Money sets human actions and relationships as far beyond human subjectivity as the purely intellectual component of inner life goes beyond the sphere of personal subjectivity into the objective sphere, of which it then becomes the mirror. This clearly creates a position of superiority. Just as the man who has money is in a superior position to the man who has the commodity, the intellectual as such has a certain power with regard to the more emotional, impulsive man. For however much greater the value of the latter's overall personality may be, however superior his powers may ultimately be to those of the former, he is for all that more restricted, more involved, more biased than the man of pure intellect; he does not have his sovereign understanding and free, unlimited command of practical resources. This element of superiority common to both money and intellect by virtue of their objectivity towards any individual aspect of life, led Comte to give bankers leadership of secular government in his Utopian state, because they were the class with the most abstract and universal functions. We hear a pre-echo of the same combination in the associations of medieval journeymen in which the treasurer was usually also the head of the brotherhood.

There is, however, a weighty counter-argument to this explanation of the correlation between intellectuality and money-economy in terms of their shared objectivity and indeterminacy of character. Alongside the impersonal objectivity peculiar to intelligence, it also has an extremely close relationship with individuality and the whole principle of individualism. Money for its part, much as it transmutes subjective impulsive behaviour into supra-personal behaviour with objective norms, is for all that a breeding-ground for economic individualism and egoism. There are evidently conceptual ambiguities and intricacies here which require precise analysis if we are to understand the life style to which they can be applied. This dual role of both intellect and money is explicable once one distinguishes between their actual concrete content and their underlying function, or the use to which they are put. In the former sense, intellect has a standardizing, indeed one might say communistic quality: in the first place, because the essence of its content is that it is universally communicable and that, provided it is correct, any adequately trained mind must be open to persuasion by it. There is no parallel at all to this in the spheres of will or emotion. There, to communicate any internal configuration depends on the character of the individual concerned, who will only yield to any such pressure under particular conditions. Here there are no *proofs* such as intellect, in principle at least, has at its command for the universal propagation of convictions. The ability to learn, which is unique to the intellect, means that one is on the same plane as everybody else. In addition, the jealous exclusivity so often encountered in the practical aspects of life is alien to the contents of intelligence, apart from chance complications. Certain emotions, e.g. those involved in intimate personal relationships, would utterly forfeit their essence and their value if they could be shared in the same form by a number of people. It is essential to certain goals of the will that others be precluded from even pursuing them, let alone achieving them. Theoretical ideas, as has been well said, are, by contrast, like a torch whose light does not become dimmer if any number of others are lighted from it. Their infinite potential propagation, because it does not affect their significance, makes it more impossible for them than for any other elements of life to be privately owned. Finally, the precision of which they are capable makes it possible, in principle at least, for them to be absorbed unadulterated by any chance individual elements. There is no way of fixing emotions and energies of the will so completely and unequivocally that anyone can at any moment refer back to them and use the objective structure to reproduce the same inner event at will. Only with regard to intellectual matters do we possess, in the language of concepts and their logical connections, adequate resources for such repeated reproduction which are relatively independent of individual make-up.

The significance of the intellect develops in a quite different direction, however, the moment concrete historical forces begin to channel its abstract, objective potential. To begin with, the very universality of knowledge and its consequent irresistible pervasiveness make it a fearsome weapon in the hands of anyone of superior intelligence. Against a superior will there are defences, at least for those who are not too easily influenced, but the only defence against superior logic is wilful stubbornness, which is itself an admission of defeat. Furthermore, although major decisions in human affairs are the result of supra-intellectual energies, the daily struggle for existence and possessions tends to be decided by the available resources of practical intelligence. The power of superior intelligence lies precisely in its communal quality: because it is universally valid, and ubiquitously effective and acknowledged, possession of a greater quantity by virtue of individual make-up is enough to give a more unconditional advantage than could arise from any possession of a more individual nature, which would not be so universally useful and able to find some domain for itself anywhere in the practical world. Here as elsewhere it is precisely the basis of equal rights for all which gives full scope for the development and exploitation of individual differences. Precisely because a purely intellectual conception and arrangement of human affairs which eschews any arbitrary volitional or emotional discrimination recognizes no *a priori* differences between individuals, it has just as little reason to curtail in any way the intrinsic potential for development of differences which emerge *a posteriori*—as is so often done out of a sense of social obligation or sentiments such as charity and compassion. That is why rationalist philosophy (although, being as impartial as money, it has also nourished the socialist view of life) has become the nursery of modern egoism and ruthless individualism. In the usual, not particularly profound way of looking at things, the ego is, in practice no less than theory, a man's obvious natural basis and inevitable prime interest. Any selfless motives appear not as equally natural and autochthonous, but as artificially cultivated afterthoughts. The result of this is that to act in one's own selfish interest is considered to be genuinely and simply 'logical'. Any selflessness or self-sacrifice is seen as emanating from irrational emotions or desires, so that men of pure intellect tend to regard them ironically as revealing a lack of practical intelligence, or to expose them as stratagems of disguised egoism. This is certainly erroneous, if for no other reason than that an egoistic will is also will, just as much as an altruistic will, and cannot any more than the latter be derived from intellectual thought alone. On the contrary, such thought, as we have seen, can only ever provide the means for either one kind of will or the other; it is completely neutral as regards the practical purpose which selects and actualizes these means. But since the combination of pure intellectuality and practical egoism is undeniably a widespread notion, it must presumably have some reality, if not in the direct logical sense claimed for it, then in some indirect psychological form. Not only ethical egoism proper, however, but also social individualism appears to be a necessary correlate of intellectuality. Any collectivism which creates a new vital unity transcending its individual constituents seems to the sober intellect, wherever it cannot break the unity down into the mere sum of its individual members, to contain some impenetrable mystical element, similar to the vital unity of an organism, in so far as the intellect cannot comprehend it as the mechanism of its parts. That is why we associate eighteenth-century rationalism, which culminated in revolution, with radical individualism; it was only opposition to rationalism, leading from Herder via Romanticism, which by acknowledging the supra-individual emotional forces of life also recognized supra-individual collective forms as unities and as historical realities. The universality of intellectual ideas, which are valid for every individual intelligence, is conducive to the atomization of society. Both as a result of the intellect, and seen in terms of it, everyone appears as a separate, self-sufficient element: abstract universality never takes on any concrete form in which only the combination of individuals could constitute a unity. Finally, the practical implications of the inner accessibility and reproducibility of theoretical insights (which can never be fundamentally beyond some people's capacities in the way certain emotions and desires are) are offset by a consequence which produces exactly the opposite effect. To begin with, because of this general accessibility, factors quite independent of personal capacities decide how the latter are actually put to use: hence the enormous advantage of the most unintelligent 'educated' man over the most intelligent proletarian. Reality makes a cruel mockery of the appearance of equal access to the materials of education for anyone who desires to make them his own. The same applies exactly to the other freedoms of liberal orthodoxy, which does indeed permit the individual to gain possessions of all kinds but overlooks the fact that only people who are privileged in one way or another have any real chance of acquiring them. Despite, or because of, its universal availability, education can, in fact, only be acquired by individual activity. It thus creates the most unassailable, because most intangible, aristocracy, a distinction between superiors and inferiors which, unlike social, economic distinctions, cannot be eliminated by decree or revolution, not even by the good will of the people concerned. It was possible for Jesus to say to the rich young man: 'give all your goods to the poor', but not: 'give your education to the humble'. There is no advantage which makes the person of inferior status feel so despised, defenceless and out of his depth as the advantage of education; which is why endeavours to create practical equality have so often and in so many various ways entailed condemnation of intellectual education: from Buddha, the ancient cynics and certain manifestations of Christianity down to Robespierre's *Nous n'avons pas besoin des savants.*' Added to this, there is the vital fact that because knowledge can be permanently enshrined in language and writing (which, viewed in the abstract, are a basis of its communal character), it can be accumulated and, especially, concentrated, thus steadily widening the gulf between superiors and inferiors in this respect. The more extensive and concentrated the available material of education, the more opportunity will the person of intellectual disposition, or even one who is relatively free from material needs, have to stand out above the mass of men. The working man of today has access to many amenities and cultural pleasures which used to be denied him, but at the same time (especially if we look back several centuries and millennia) the great gulf between his standard of living and that of the upper classes has become very much greater. Similarly, the general raising of the level of knowledge has not by any means brought a general levelling, but rather quite the opposite.

I have discussed this point at such length because these two contrary implications of the concept of intellectuality are exactly paralleled with regard to money. Understanding of money is thus facilitated not only by its interaction with intellectuality, which gives them a formal similarity, but perhaps also by the suggestion thus given of a deeper common principle underlying the similarity of their evolution—perhaps the fundamental nature or ambiance of the historical factors which gave them their form, and thus also their style. Money, though fundamentally universally accessible and objective, nonetheless promotes the growth of individualism and subjectivity; . . . its constant ubiquitous identity and communal quality mean that any quantitative difference immediately produces qualitative distinctions. But here also, in the scope of its power (with which no other cultural factor can compare), which procures equal validity for the most contrary vital impulses, one can see that money is the concentration of cultural energy as pure form, which can be combined at will with any content in order to intensify its own specific character and make possible its increasingly pure expression. I propose therefore to highlight only some specific parallels with intellectuality to show how the impersonality and universality of its abstract objectivity put money, wherever it is a matter of its function and use, at the service of egoism and differentiation. The rational, logical nature of egoism that we have seen is also characteristic of the full ruthless exploitation of the possession of money. We have established earlier that the characteristic feature of money, in contrast to other kinds of property, is that it gives no intrinsic indication of any specific use to which it might be put. For the same reason, it contains no impediment which might make any one use more unlikely or difficult than any other. It can adapt completely to whatever use happens to be involved: no relationship between it and any concrete object is specifically conducive or obstructive. In this, it is comparable to the forms of logic themselves, which lend themselves equally to the elaboration or permutations of any content, and hence, of course, make it equally possible for both what is of supreme value, and what is, in concrete terms, utterly meaningless or pernicious, to be presented in a formally correct manner. There is a similar parallel with the forms of the law, which often enough lack any precautions to prevent grave material injustice from being presented under the guise of unimpeachable formal justice. This unrestricted possibility of exploiting the power of money to the very last degree is felt to constitute not only a justification but, so to speak, a logical conceptual necessity for actually doing so. Lacking any intrinsic impulses or counter-impulses, it follows the strongest subjective urge, which in all money matters tends to be egoistic. Inhibitions such as the notion that certain money is 'blood money', or under a curse, are mere sentimentality, they lose all significance as money grows increasingly neutral, i.e. as it becomes more and more simply money. The purely negative fact that no material or ethical considerations such as arise with regard to other kinds of property, determine the use of money, leads directly to ruthlessness as a positive mode of behaviour. Its flexibility, arising from its complete independence of any specific interests, origins or relationships, appears logically to imply an invitation to cast off all self-restraint in the areas of life which it governs. Its absolute objectivity, the result of excluding any relative objectivity, gives *carte blanche* to egoism, just as does pure intellectuality, for no other reason than that egoism is logically the simplest and most obvious impulse and thus offers the purely formal and neutral forces of life their primary, as it were natural, congenial fulfilment.

It is not only, as touched on above, the forms of law in general which are of a piece with both pure intellectuality and monetary dealings in that none of them eschews even the most materially and morally perverse content: it is above all the principle of equality before the law in which this discrepancy between form and real content is greatest. All three: law, intellectuality and money are characterized by indifference towards specific individual attributes. All three extract from the dynamic concrete totality of life an abstract general factor; this factor develops in obedience to its own independent norms, which then cause it to intervene in and determine the totality of vital interests in its own way. Thus, because all three have the power to prescribe the form and direction of content towards which they are essentially indifferent, they inevitably introduce those paradoxes with which we are concerned here into life in its entirety. Where equality takes hold of the formal foundations of human relationships, it becomes a means of giving the most radical and far-reaching scope to individual inequality. By respecting the restrictions imposed by formal equality, egoism need pay no further heed to internal or external obstacles. It then possesses, in the universality of that equality, a weapon which, since anybody can use it, can also be used against anybody. The forms of equality before the law are the typical forms which also characterize both intellectuality, in the sense described above, and money. Their general accessibility and validity and their potential communal character remove, for superiors, inferiors and equals alike, certain barriers which were entailed by *a priori* class boundaries with regard to kinds of property. As long as the ownership of land and the professions were monopolized by particular classes, they entailed obligations towards social inferiors, solidarity with others of the same class, and automatic limits to the ambitions of outsiders. But in 'enlightened' rationalism, there are no longer any grounds for such behaviour once all property can be converted to a value which nobody in principle can be precluded from acquiring in unlimited quantity. (This, of course, gives no answer to the question of whether *on the whole* egoism has increased or declined in the course of history.)

I would like finally to mention the extremely characteristic fact that the accumulation of intellectual attainments which gives a disproportionate and rapidly increasing advantage to anyone who is privileged in any way, also has a parallel in the accumulation of monetary capital. The structure of capitalism, the way money produces profit and regular income, means that after a certain point it multiplies automatically without needing to be fertilized by any proportionate effort on the part of its owner. In the world of culture, this is paralleled by the structure of knowledge. After a certain point, less and less effort is needed on the part of the individual to acquire it, because knowledge takes on a more concentrated form the higher one progresses. At the highest level of education, each further step often demands far less effort compared with the pace at which lower stages were mastered, while also yielding a greater increase of knowledge. At a certain stage, the objectivity of money allows it to 'work' in relative independence of personal energies, and the accumulated fruits of this work lead on, as if automatically, to further accumulation in increasing proportions. Likewise, the objectivization of knowledge, the separation of the achievements of intelligence from its actual processes, means that these achievements accumulate in the form of concentrated abstractions, so that a man of sufficient stature can pluck them like fruit that has ripened without any effort on his part.

As a result of all this, money, which intrinsically and conceptually is an absolutely democratic, classless entity devoid of any specific individual relationships, is repudiated most unequivocally by those whose aim is general equality: the same result, for the same reason, as was observed in the case of intellectuality. In both spheres, universality in the logical, objective sense and universality in the practical social sense do not coincide. In other spheres, they often enough do coincide: the essence of art, for instance, has been defined (no matter whether this is a complete definition or not) as the presentation of typical universal features of phenomena so as to evoke typical human responses in us, thus basing the fundamental claim of art to general subjective acknowledgement of its validity on the exclusion of all fortuitous individual elements from its presentation. Likewise, religions are conceived as rising above all the particularities of earthly forms to the universal Absolute, thus taking on a relationship to the secular absolute that unites all individual men. By their universality, they redeem us from our merely individual attributes, by relating them to those fundamental common features which are felt to be the roots of all humanity. Kantian morality is a similar case: an action which can be logically universalized without self-contradiction is a moral imperative valid for all men without regard to persons. The criterion that one must be able to imagine practical maxims as natural laws, i.e. the criterion of conceptual, objective universality, decides their general validity as moral claims for all individuals. By contrast with these spheres, modern life seems in other areas to create a tension precisely between objective universality of content and practical, personal universality. Certain elements acquire increasing universality of content, their power expands to cover more and more details and aspects of life, their definition encompasses, directly or indirectly, a growing proportion of reality. This is the case with the law, the processes and results of intellectuality, and money. But along with this goes the intensification of these entities in subjectively differentiated forms of life, the exploitation of their significance, as they engulf all spheres of interest in the service of egoism. Because money is standardized and universally accessible and valid, it offers no impediment to any particular desire and can thus be used to maximize personal differences. The confusion and sense of internal self-contradiction which in so many ways are characteristic of the style of present-day life, are surely to some extent the result of this imbalance and tension between the objective content and significance of these spheres, and their personal use and development with regard to universality and equality.

I come now to a final feature in this stylistic portrait of the present day in whose rationalistic character the influence of money can be seen. The intellectual functions which assist modern man to come to terms with the world and order his relationships (both individual and social), can for the most part be described as *calculative* functions. His epistemological ideal is to grasp the universe as one vast arithmetical calculation, to capture all events and qualities of things in a mathematical system. Kant believed that natural philosophy contained only as much actual science as it offered scope for applied mathematics.

But the ambition is not only to master the physical world intellectually by quantifying it. Both pessimists and optimists aspire to determine the value of life itself by calculating its balance of pleasure and suffering. Their ideal, at least, would be to find mathematical formulae for both factors. The same tendency can be seen in public life, where so much is decided by majority decisions. It is by no means as self-evident as it appears today that it is right for an individual to be outvoted because the majority, who *a priori* have no greater rights than he, are of a different opinion. Ancient Germanic law did not have this feature: anyone who dissented from a communal decision was not bound by it. In the tribal council of the Iroquois, the 'cortes' of Aragon until the sixteenth century, the Polish Parliament, and other communities, majority decisions were unknown; no resolution was valid unless unanimous. The principle that a minority must bow to the wishes of the majority means that the absolute, qualitative value of an individual vote is reduced to a unit of purely quantitative importance. Democratic levelling, which makes everybody a single person and nobody more than a single person, is the correlative, or precondition, of this arithmetical procedure, in which a numerical majority or minority of unspecified units expresses a group's inner reality and controls its outer reality. This measuring, weighing, calculating precision of the modern age is the purest development of its intellectualism, which, of course, here also promotes the growth, on the basis of abstract equality, of the most selfish individualism. There is a subtle instinctive insight in the way language always means by a 'calculating' person someone who is calculating in an egoistic way. Just as in the way we use 'sensible' or 'unreasonable', here, too, an apparently neutral formal concept is revealed in its true nature by its tendency to acquire a particular specific content.

It seems to me that there is a close causal connection between money economy and this psychological feature of the present age, which contrasts so strongly with the more impulsive, emotional, integrated character of earlier ages. Money economy makes continual mathematical operations a daily necessity. Many people's lives are filled with such calculation, weighing, adding up—i.e. with the reduction of qualitative to quantitative values. The encroachment of monetary evaluation was bound to bring much greater precision and discrimination into life, for it taught people how to isolate and determine any value right down to the last farthing. Where things are directly related to one another, rather than reduced to their common denominator of money, there will be much more rounding off and acceptance of one unit as the equivalent of another. Precision and rigour in the economic aspects of life keep pace with the growing influence of money (though this is not conducive to living in a grand style), and, of course, rub off on other aspects of life also. It was money that first introduced the ideal of numerical calculability into practical life—and perhaps, who knows, into theoretical thinking also? This effect also shows money to be merely an intensified, sublimated form of the essence of economic life. A historian, writing of the commercial dealings whereby, especially in the thirteenth and fourteenth centuries, the English people purchased a variety of rights and liberties from their monarchs, comments: 'This provided a practical way of deciding difficult questions which were in theory insoluble. The monarch has rights as sovereign of his people, the people have rights as free men and as the estates of the realm which is personified in the monarch. To determine the rights of each was extremely difficult in theory, but became easy in practice once the question was reduced to one of buying and selling.' That is to say, once a qualitative practical relationship is restricted to that aspect which permits it to be treated as a commercial transaction, it can be precisely determined, although this is impossible as long as it is conceived directly and in terms of all its qualities. Money is not essential for this; such transactions often involved natural commodities, such as wool. But clearly the more precise determination of values and demands entailed in any kind of commercial transaction can be achieved by money with much more rigorous accuracy. In this sense also one can perhaps say that money transactions are to commercial transactions in general what commercial transactions are to other modes which existed prior to exchange. Money embodies, as it were, the purely commercial element in the commercial treatment of things, just as logic embodies the comprehensibility of comprehensible things. And because the abstract system which determines the value to be attached to things is one of arithmetical precision and hence absolute rationality, these qualities are bound to reflect back on things themselves. If it is true that artistic fashion gradually determines how we see nature, if the artist's spontaneous subjective abstraction shapes our conscious image of reality, which we appear to perceive directly with the senses—if this is so, then the superstructure of monetary relationships erected over qualitative reality must even more drastically impose its forms on our inner image of that reality. The mathematical nature of money has brought into various areas of life an exactitude, a certainty in weighing things up against one another and a precision in agreements and arrangements, similar to those created in the external sphere by the general spread of pocket watches. Both the calculation of abstract time by watches and that of abstract value by money, produce a system of the subtlest, most accurate measurement and organization, which absorbs the contents of life and gives them, at least as regards practical management, an otherwise unattainable transparency and calculability. The calculating intellectuality embodied in these forms may, in its turn, derive from them some of the energy which enables it to dominate modern life. All these aspects can be, as it were, negatively focused in the fact that the type of mind which would be most aloof and hostile towards the economic vision and basis of human affairs, men such as Goethe, Carlyle or Nietzsche, were on the one hand fundamentally anti-intellectual in their thinking, and at the same time utterly rejected that mathematically exact interpretation of nature which, as we have seen, is the theoretical counterpart of money.

[New translation. From Georg Simmel, *Philosophie des Geldes*, Chapter 6, part 1, Dunker & Humblot, Leipzig, 1900]

# The Style of Life (2)

By giving the name of culture to those refined and spiritualized forms of life which are the products of our internal and external endeavours, we set these values in a perspective which does not automatically ensue from their actual objective import. They are products of culture for us inasmuch as we regard them as the intensified realization of natural impulses and potential, intensified beyond the degree of naturally attainable development, abundance and differentiation. The concept of culture presupposes a natural energy or tendency (which is necessary only so that it may be surpassed by actual development). Seen in relation to culture, the values of life are cultivated *nature*; they do not have here the autonomous significance which is measured from above, as it were, against the ideals of happiness, intelligence or beauty. They appear, rather, as developments of a basic raw material which we call nature, whose degree of energy and ideas they surpass to the degree that they become culture. Thus, although an improved garden fruit and a statue are both equally products of culture, language subtly indicates the difference by calling the fruit tree itself cultivated, whereas the block of rough marble has certainly not been 'cultivated' to produce a statue. In the former case, the assumption is that the tree has a natural potential and impetus towards the fruit which has been pushed beyond its natural limit by means of intelligent manipulation, whereas no such impetus towards a statue is assumed in the block of marble. The culture embodied in the statue constitutes the enhancement and refinement of certain human energies whose original manifestations we describe as 'natural'.

It appears, at first sight, to go without saying that impersonal things can only symbolically be described as cultivated. After all, such application of will and intelligence to the development of reality beyond the limit of its purely natural vital powers is something which we bestow only on ourselves or on things whose development accords with our own impulses and, in its turn, stimulates our own emotions.

Material culture—furniture and cultivated plants, works of art and machinery, appliances and books—in which natural materials are developed into forms which, though possible for them, are never created by their own energies, is the actualization, by means of ideas, of our own desires and emotions, which absorb the evolutionary potential of nature where this lies in their path. The same applies to the culture which gives shape to people's relationships with others and with themselves: language, morals, religion, law. Inasmuch as these values are considered aspects of culture, we distinguish them from such stages of development of their inherent energies as they can reach unaided. These are merely raw material for the process of cultivation, like wood and metal, plants and electricity. By cultivating things, i.e. increasing their value beyond the degree achieved by their natural constitution, we cultivate ourselves. Both external nature and nature within us are submitted to the same process of enhancement of value, which begins with us and ends with us. This idea of culture is illustrated in its most clear-cut form by the visual arts, which show the greatest tension between these poles. Here it seems at first sight quite impossible to integrate the shaping of the object into our subjective processes. What the work of art interprets for us is the meaning of the phenomenon itself, whether this lies in the shaping of spatial factors, or the relationships of colours, or the spirituality which exists both in and behind what is visible. It is always a question of eliciting the mystery and significance of things in order to represent them in a purer or more lucid form than that attained by their natural evolution—but *not* in the manner of chemical or physical technology, which discovers natural laws in order to integrate them into human aims extrinsic to them. Rather, the process of artistic creation is finished once the subject has attained its own essential significance. This is indeed sufficient to fulfil the purely artistic ideal, for which perfection of the work of art is an objective value, wholly independent of its effect on our subjective feelings. The catchword of *l'art pour l'art* aptly denotes this self-sufficiency of the pure artistic impulse. Things are different, however, when seen in terms of the cultural ideal. The essence of *this* ideal is to subsume the autonomous values of aesthetic, scientific, moral, eudemonistic and even religious achievements as elements, or components, in the evolution of the human being beyond his natural state. To put it more precisely, they are sections of the path taken by this development, which must at any moment occupy one such section. Development can never proceed purely formally, independently of any content; but this does not mean that it is identical with such content. The contents provided by culture consist of such entities as the above. Each of them has its own autonomous dominant ideal, but here they are considered in relation to the development of our energies, or our being, beyond the degree considered to be purely natural. They underlie this development and provide various stages in it. By cultivating objects, man creates them in his own image. Regarded as a cultural process, the supra-natural actualization of their energies is merely the visible form of embodiment of the identical actualization of *our* energies. Of course, in the development of individual aspects of life, the boundary at which their natural form becomes a cultural form is blurred; it is impossible to agree as to exactly where it lies. But this is merely an example of one of the most universal difficulties of thought. The categories to which we allocate individual phenomena in order to integrate them into an organized, coherent body of knowledge are clearly demarcated. They often owe their very meaning to the existence of their opposites. They form discontinuous series. Individual phenomena, however, which have to be grouped under these concepts, do not by any means tend to fit in so neatly. On the contrary, it is often quantitative features which determine their allocation to one of two categories. Since all quantitative series are continuous, it is always possible for an item to be at the centre between two measurements, each of which indicates a definite category. In such cases, an individual phenomenon can belong to either one category or the other, and thus appear to be located indeterminately between them, or even to be compounded of concepts which *per se* are mutually exclusive. The fundamental certainty that one can draw a boundary between nature and culture, that one ends exactly where the other begins, is not, therefore, impaired by any uncertainty regarding the categorization of individual phenomena, any more than the concepts of day and night are difficult to separate because the hour of twilight can be seen as belonging to either of them.

From this discussion of the general notion of culture, I wish now to move to a particular aspect of contemporary culture. If one compares the latter with, for example, the period a hundred years ago, one can surely say that (many individual exceptions notwithstanding) the material things which fill and surround our lives are cultivated to an indescribable degree: the gadgets, means of transport, the products of science, technology and art. But individual culture, at least in the privileged classes, has by no means advanced proportionally; indeed, it has in many respects declined. This scarcely requires detailed proof. I propose therefore to point out only a few phenomena. During the last hundred years the expressive resources of language, in both German and French, have been enriched and refined to an extraordinary degree. Not only have we been given the language of Goethe, but many subtleties, shades of meaning and individual modes of expression have also been added. Yet if one looks at the speech and writing of individuals, they are, on the whole, becoming increasingly incorrect, undignified and trivial. As for content, during the same period the range of subjects for conversation has objectively increased considerably as a result of advances in theory and practice, yet it seems as if conversation, both social and intimate, and letter-writing are much more superficial, boring and frivolous now than at the end of the eighteenth century. The fact that machines are now much more 'intelligent' than workers is in the same category. How many workers today, even in smaller-scale industries, understand the machine with which they work, that is to say, the intelligence embodied in the machine? It is the same in military culture. The demands made on the individual soldier have remained essentially unchanged for a long time; indeed, in some respects they have been lessened by the techniques of modern warfare. The material instruments of war, on the other hand, and especially the impersonal organization of the army, have been refined to an extraordinary degree to become a veritable triumph of objective culture. As regards the purely intellectual sphere, even the most knowledgeable and thoughtful men operate with an ever-increasing number of ideas, concepts and statements with whose precise meaning and content they are only very imperfectly familiar. The vast expansion of objective, existing knowledge allows, indeed compels, people to use phrases which are, in effect, passed on from one person to the next like sealed containers; the actual ideas concentrated in them do not reveal themselves to the individual user. Just as our external lives are surrounded by more and more objects without our remotely encompassing in our minds the objective intellect employed to produce them, so our intellectual lives, personal and social, are also filled (as was pointed out above in a different context) with complexes which have acquired symbolic status, in which a wide-ranging spirituality is garnered, but of which the individual mind generally makes only minimal use.

The preponderance of objective over subjective culture which came about during the nineteenth century is more or less summed up by the fact that the educational ideal of the eighteenth century was the cultivation of man as a personal inner value, whereas in the nineteenth century this was supplanted by the concept of cultivation in the sense of a sum total of objective knowledge and modes of behaviour. The gulf between the two conceptions appears to be steadily widening. Daily and from all sides the quantity of material culture is increased, but the individual can only follow at a great distance and can only slightly increase the speed at which he expands the form and content of his culture.

How is this phenomenon to be explained? If all culture of things is, as we have seen, only a culture of people, if by cultivating things we only cultivate ourselves—what then is the import of this evolution, elaboration and spiritualization of objects which happens as if by their own energies and norms, without any corresponding individual human evolution being involved either in it or by means of it? We are faced here with an intensified form of the enigmatic general relationship between social life and its products on the one hand, and fragmentary individual lives on the other. Language and morals, political constitutions and religious doctrines, literature and technology, all embody the labours of countless generations as objectified spirit from which each man takes as much as he desires or is able, but which no one man could possibly absorb entirely. The relative amount which is taken from this stock is extremely varied and haphazard. But the low degree or irrational quality of individual use does not impair the substance and dignity of mankind's heritage, any more than the existence of any physical object is dependent on its being individually perceived. The content and significance of a book are *per se* quite unaffected by its readers, be they few or many, perceptive or otherwise. Similarly, any other product of culture is independent of the circle of cultured people, ready to be taken up by anyone, but never encountering more than a sporadic response to this readiness. Thus the relationship between this concentrated spiritual achievement of a cultural community, and the degree to which it comes to life in individual minds, is the same as that between the vast plenitude of the possible and the limitations of the real. In order to understand the mode of existence of such objective intellectual structures, they must be located in a special system of the categories by which we apprehend reality. Within this system there will then also be a place for the discrepancy between objective and subjective culture.

In the Platonic myth, the soul during its pre-existence sees the pure essence of things, their absolute significance, so that its later knowledge is but a memory, occasioned by sensory stimuli, of that truth. The most obvious impulse underlying this conception is our perplexity regarding the origins of knowledge, if we reject, as Plato did, empirical origins. But over and above the question of its genesis, this metaphysical speculation gives a profound indication of the epistemological activity of the human soul. For whether we regard the acquisition of knowledge as the direct effect of external objects or as a purely internal process in which all external things are immanent forms or conditions of spiritual factors, we always feel that our thinking (to the extent that we regard it as truthful) is the response to an objective demand, the reproduction of something that is ideally prefigured. Even if our ideas were an exact mirror-image of things as they are in themselves, the unity, correctness and completeness to which knowledge approaches, mastering one item after another in an infinite series, would not lie in things themselves. On the contrary, our epistemological ideal would never be anything but the content of things in the form of ideas. The ambition of even the most extreme realism is not things themselves, but knowledge of things. Thus, if we describe the sum total of fragments which constitute our knowledge at any given moment in terms of the development to which that knowledge aspires and which determines the significance of any particular stage in it, we can only do this by presupposing the basis of the Platonic doctrine: that there is an ideal realm of theoretical values, of perfect intellectual meaning and coherence, which neither coincides with the world of objects (which are, after all, only its *objects*) nor with the degree of psychologically real knowledge possessed at any particular time. On the contrary, such knowledge only gradually, and always imperfectly, achieves congruence with the ideal realm which includes all possible truth. Knowledge is true to the extent that it succeeds in doing this. Plato appears to have shared this basic feeling that our knowledge at any moment is part of a complex of knowledge which exists only in ideal form, but which invites and demands mental actualization by us. He merely expressed this as a decline of real knowledge from the former possession of its totality, in terms of 'no longer', whereas we today are compelled to think of it in terms of 'not yet'. But both interpretations are obviously consistent with the identical basic feeling (just as the same number can be obtained by subtraction from a higher number or addition of lower numbers). The mode of being peculiar to this epistemological ideal, as a norm or totality contrasted with our actual knowledge, is the same as that of the totality of moral values and prescriptions in relation to actual individual behaviour. Here, in the ethical sphere, we are more immediately aware that our activity actualizes, in varying degrees of perfection or deficiency, a norm that has its own intrinsic validity. This norm (which, be it said, may vary in content from person to person and from one period of life to the other) exists neither in space nor time, nor does it coincide with ethical awareness, which rather perceives itself as dependent on that norm. This is, in the last analysis, the general formula of our lives, from mundane practicalities to the supreme pinnacles of intellectuality: over every activity is set a norm, a criterion, an ideal prefigured totality which is given reality through that very activity. This does not merely mean the simple general fact that all volition is guided by some ideal. It is rather a question of a definite, more or less distinct characteristic of our actions, which can only be expressed by saying that in action, no matter if in terms of value it may run quite counter to any ideal, we actualize some prefigured possibility, an ideal programme, as it were. Our practical existence, inadequate and fragmentary as it is, is given a certain significance and coherence by being, so to speak, the partial actualization of a totality. Our actions, indeed our entire being, whether beautiful or ugly, righteous or wicked, great or petty, appear to be taken from a stock of possibilities. At any moment they stand in relationship to their ideally determined content as does a concrete individual object to the concept which expresses its inner law and logical essence; the significance of this ideal content does not depend on whether, how or how often it is actualized. We cannot conceive of knowledge other than as an actualization within consciousness of those ideas which have, so to speak, been awaiting actualization at the point in question. To describe, as we do, our knowledge as necessary, in the sense that as regards its content it can exist only in one single form, is merely another way of expressing our awareness that we feel knowledge to be a mental actualization of a pre-established ideal content. This one single form does not by any means imply, however, that there is only one single truth for the entire multitude of diverse minds. It is rather that, given an intellect of particular constitution on the one hand and a particular objective reality on the other, the 'truth' for that particular mind is objectively pre-formed, as is the result of a calculation with given factors. Any change in the given intellectual structure changes this truth, but this does not make it any less objective and independent of that mind's consciousness. The very fact that certain things, once known, irrevocably demand that we also accept certain other things, reveals this essential nature of knowledge: all knowledge is consciousness of something which is fixed and valid in advance within the objectively determined context of facts. From the psychological point of view, finally, this is an aspect of the theory that to consider something true is always a *feeling* which accompanies a mental image; what we call proof is merely the creation of a psychological configuration in which this feeling occurs. It is never sense perception or logical deduction which actually constitute the conviction of truth; they are only conditions which evoke the trans-theoretical feeling of assent, affirmation or whatever one cares to call this indefinable sense of reality. This constitutes the psychological mediator between the two epistemological categories: the valid, objective meaning of things, based on internal cohesion and organization of elements; and our idea of them, which constitutes their subjective reality.

This fundamental general relationship is paralleled on a smaller scale in the relationship between objectified mind and culture, and the individual. Just as, epistemologically speaking, we derive the content of our lives from the realm of what is objectively valid, so, historically speaking, we derive the greater part of it from the storehouse of mankind's accumulated intellectual labours. Here, too, there are pre-formed contents, available for actualization in individual minds; but they retain their character quite independently of such actualization, a character which is also by no means that of a material object. Even where the mind is tied to matter, as in tools, works of art or books, it never coincides with the part of them that is perceived with the senses. It inhabits them in a potential form, that cannot be more precisely defined, which can be actualized by individual consciousness. Objective culture is the historical manifestation or concentration (in varying degrees) of the objectively valid truth which our knowledge reproduces. If it can be said that the law of gravity was valid before Newton formulated it, the law as such is not inherent in physical matter, since it only signifies the form taken by the condition of matter in a mind organized in a particular way, and since its validity does not depend at all on the real existence of matter. To this extent, then, it exists neither in objective things themselves, nor in subjective minds, but in the sphere of objective mind, which our consciousness of truth concentrates and actualizes section by section. Once this has been alchieved by Newton in respect of the law in question, that law has become part of objective historical mind, and its ideal significance therein is now, in its turn, fundamentally independent of its reproduction by particular individuals.

By establishing this category of objective mind as the historical manifestation of the valid intellectual content of things in general, we can see how the cultural process, which we have seen to be one of subjective evolution (the culture of things as the culture of people), can become separated from its content. On entering this category, the content assumes, as it were, a different overall condition. This, fundamentally, provides the basis for the phenomenon which we have encountered as the separate development of material and personal culture. The objectification of mind produces the form which enables the work of consciousness to be preserved and accumulated. It is the most significant and far-reaching of the historical categories of mankind. For it makes into a historical fact what is so dubious as a biological fact: the hereditary transmission of acquired characteristics. The superiority of man over the animals has been defined as the fact that he is not merely a descendant, he is also an heir. The objectification of mind in words and works, organizations and traditions, is the precondition of this distinction, without which man would not possess his world, or indeed any world at all.

Although this objective mind of a society and its history is its culture in the widest sense, the practical cultural significance of its individual constituents is to be measured by the extent to which they become elements of individual development. For, supposing that Newton's discovery were only to be found in a book which nobody knew of, it would still be objectified mind and a potential possession of society, but it would not then be a cultural value. Since such cases, of which this is an extreme example, can occur in innumerable varying degrees, it follows directly that, in any fairly large society, only a certain proportion of objective cultural values will ever become subjective values. If one imagines society as a whole and arranges all its objectified intellectuality in a temporal-causal system, then its overall cultural development, thus hypothetically unified, is richer than the development of any of its members. For each individual achievement belongs to the total complex, but the total complex does not belong to each individual. A community's entire style of life depends on the relationship between objectified culture and subjective culture. I have already indicated the importance of numerical considerations. In a small community at a less advanced stage of culture, the relationship will be almost one of equality: the objective cultural potential will not far outstrip actual subjective culture. A raising of the level of culture (especially if accompanied by growth of the community) will be conducive to the divergence of the two. The incomparable situation of Athens at its peak was that, despite the very high level of its culture, it managed to avoid this (except perhaps as regards its loftiest philosophical currents of thought). But the size of a community does not, in itself, explain the divergence of subjective and objective culture. On the contrary, what we must now do is seek the concrete effective causes of this phenomenon.

If one wishes to summarize this phenomenon and its contemporary magnitude in a single concept, then that concept is *division of labour*, in its significance for both production and consumption. With regard to production, it has often enough been pointed out that improvement of the product is achieved at the expense of the development of the producer. The increased psycho-physical energies and skills resulting from specialized activity tend to be of little benefit to the personality as a whole. This, indeed, is often left to atrophy by being robbed of energy essential for the harmonious development of the self. In other cases, these energies and skills develop as if cut off from the nucleus of personality, as a wholly autonomous sphere whose fruits do not accrue to the centre. Experience seems to show that inner wholeness is created essentially in interaction with a complete, rounded task in life.

Objects only acquire unity at all for us by our projecting on to them our awareness of the ego. We shape them in our own image, in which a wide variety of characteristics fuse in the unity of the ego. Similarly, on the psychological, practical level, the unity of an object which we create, or the lack of such unity, have the same effect on the parallel shaping of our personality. Where our energies do not produce something whole which gives them an outlet appropriate to their own peculiar unity, there is no real relationship between the two. The intrinsic character of the product relates it to other products produced by other people, with which it needs to be combined to constitute a totality; but it does not relate back to the person who produced it. This lack of vital congruence between the worker and his product, resulting from a high degree of specialization, makes it particularly easy for the product to become completely divorced from the worker. It acquires significance, not from the spirituality of the worker, but from its association with other products of different origin. Because of its fragmentary character, it lacks the spiritual quality which is so easily detectable in any product that is entirely the work of a single person. Thus its significance can lie neither in the reflection of a subjective impulse nor in the illumination of a creative spirit of which it is an expression. Its significance is solely that of an objective achievement detached from the individual.

This relationship can be seen equally clearly, at the other far end of the spectrum, in works of art. The essence of a work of art runs utterly counter to such distribution of labour between a number of workers, none of whom create anything whole. Of all the works of man, the work of art is the most self-contained unity, the most self-sufficient totality, not even with the exception of the State. For much as the State may, in special circumstances, be sufficient unto itself, it never absorbs its elements so completely that none of them have separate lives and interests of their own. We only ever identify a part of our personality with the State; other parts revolve around other centres. Art, by contrast, leaves none of the elements which it absorbs any significance outside their allotted context. The individual work of art nullifies the multiplicity of meaning of words and sounds, colours and shapes. We are allowed to be conscious only of such aspects as are relevant to the work. This closed nature of the work of art signifies, however, that it is the expression of a unified subjective spirituality. A work of art requires only one single person, but it requires the whole of that person, his innermost essence. His reward is that the form of the work of art allows it to be his purest mirror and self-expression. The complete repudiation of division of labour is thus both a cause and a symptom of the connection between the self-sufficient totality of the work and the unity of the spirit. Conversely, where division of labour prevails, it creates an incommensurability of the person and his achievement. The person can no longer see himself in his activity, whose form is so unlike anything personal and spiritual; it appears only as a wholly specialized part of our being, indifferent to the unified whole man. Thus, where work is highly labour-divided and the worker is aware of this characteristic, it has an inherent impulse towards the category of objectivity. For ther worker himself it appears increasingly appropriate to regard it and treat it as purely impersonal and autonomous, for he no longer feels that it has any contact with the roots of his life as a whole.

The more completely a whole entity absorbs its partial subjective components, the more the status and function of each part is exclusively that of a part of that whole, then the more objective that whole is, the more its existence transcends all the individuals involved in its production. Generally speaking, this specialized production goes hand in hand with increased consumption. Today even the most intellectually and professionally specialized man reads a newspaper, thereby indulging in a more extensive intellectual consumption than was possible a hundred years ago even for a man of the most versatile and wide-ranging intellectual activity. Increased consumption comes from the growth of *objective* culture, for the more objective and impersonal a product is, the more people it is suitable for. Such extensive individual consumption requires that goods be made available and attractive to very many individuals; they cannot appeal to subjectively differentiated desires. At the same time, only the utmost differentiation of production is capable of mass-producing goods as cheaply as such extensive consumption necessitates. Thus extensive consumption is, in its turn, a link connecting the objectivity of culture with the division of labour.

Finally, the process described as the separation of the worker from the means of work, which is itself a division of labour, clearly has the same effect. Because it is now the capitalist's function to acquire, organize and distribute the means of production, they are bound to be objectively quite different for the worker than if he works with his own tools and materials. This capitalistic differentiation drastically separates the subjective and objective elements of work, a separation for which there was no psychological cause when the two were unified in one person. Because work itself and its immediate materials belong to different people, the objective character of these materials must loom very large in the worker's mind, the more so since work and its materials do of themselves form a unity, so that their very proximity is bound to make their polarity very obvious. An extension and counterpart of this separation is that, in addition to the means of work, actual work itself becomes separated from the worker. This is what is meant by saying that labour has become a commodity. Where the worker works with his own material, his work remains within the sphere of his personality, and only the completed work leaves this sphere when it is sold. But lacking the opportunity to deploy his labour in this way he offers it to another person at the current market price, thus separating himself from his labour from the moment it leaves its source. The fact that henceforward it shares a common character, mode of evaluation and destiny with all other commodities, signifies that it has become something objective in relation to the worker himself, something which not only *is* no longer him, but which he no longer even *has*. For once his potential working capacity has been converted into actual work, he no longer owns it, but only its monetary equivalent. The work itself belongs to somebody else, or rather to an objective organization of labour. The transformation of labour into a commodity is thus only one aspect of the far-reaching process of differentiation which detaches the individual elements of personality and establishes them as separate objects with independent character and dynamics. Finally, the effect of this fate which has befallen both the means of work and work itself can be seen in the product. We become most forcefully aware that the products of capitalist labour are objects with a definite independent existence, possessing their own dynamic laws and alien to the very individuals who produce them, where the worker is compelled to *buy* the product of his own labour if he wishes to possess it. There is a general pattern of development here which applies far beyond the sphere of the wage-earner. The extreme division of labour in, for example, scientific work, means that only a very small number of scientists indeed can themselves supply the prerequisites of their work. Innumerable facts and methods have to be simply taken over from outside as objective materials. Other people's intellectual property becomes material for one's own work. As regards technology, the reader may recall that even at the beginning of the nineteenth century, when, especially in the iron and textile industries, the most impressive inventions were appearing in rapid succession, the inventors had still not only to manufacture themselves, unaided, the machines which they had devised, but in most cases had also to devise and manufacture the necessary tools first. The present state of affairs in science can be described as a separation of the worker from the means of work in a broader sense, and certainly in the sense at issue here. For, in the actual process of scientific production, an objective material becomes separated from the subjective work processes of the producer. The more undifferentiated the pursuit of science used to be, the more the scientist had to master personally all the prerequisites and materials of his work, the less of a dichotomy existed for him between his subjective achievement and a world of objectively established scientific facts. Here, too, the dichotomy extends to the product of work also: the scientific finding itself, however much it is *per se* the fruit of subjective endeavours, is all the more bound to be elevated to the category of an objective fact, independent of the person who discovered it, the more results of other people's labours are from the outset combined in it and contribute to it. Hence we also see that in the branch of inquiry with the least division of labour, viz. philosophy (especially metaphysics), on the one hand the objective material involved plays a very subordinate role, and on the other the product is least detached from its subjective origin. On the contrary, it is seen wholly as the achievement of a specific individual.

Thus division of labour in its broadest sense, including division of production, breakdown of work processes and specialization, detaches the working personality from the end product, and bestows an objective independence on the latter. A related phenomenon occurs in the relationship of labour-divided production to the consumer. Here it is a matter of demonstrating the psychological consequences of universally familiar concrete facts. The work to order prevalent in the medieval crafts, which only in the last century dwindled considerably, gave the consumer a personal connection with the commodity. Being made specifically for him, embodying as it were an interaction between him and the maker, it belonged inwardly to him in somewhat the same way as it belonged to the maker. The radical polarity of subject and object, which has been tempered in theory by allowing the object to exist in the subject in the form of an idea, is likewise not fully felt in practice as long as the object is made either by or for one specific person. Since division of labour is the death of production to order (because, if for no other reason, the customer can make contact with one manufacturer but not with a dozen part-manufacturers), the subjective aura of the product vanishes for the consumer also now that it is manufactured independently of him. The commodity is now an objective external entity with its own autonomous existence and quality. The difference, for example, between a modern ready-made clothes store designed for the utmost specialization, and the tailor who used to make fittings in the home, most clearly highlights the increased objectivity of the economic cosmos, its supra-personal independence in relation to the individual consumer with whom it was originally so closely identified. It has been pointed out that the breakdown of work into increasingly specialized partial operations makes exchange relationships increasingly complex and indirect, with the result that economic life necessarily entails more and more relationships and commitments *which are not directly reciprocal*. It is obvious how much the general character of commerce thereby becomes objectified. Subjectivity is bound to retreat into cool reserve and anonymity once a number of intermediate agencies spring up between the manufacturer and the customer, removing any personal contact between them.

This autonomy of production *vis-à-vis* the customer is connected with one effect of the division of labour which is now very commonplace, though its importance has for the most part gone unnoticed. There is a widespread simple notion, derived from former modes of production, that the lower classes of society work for the higher. The plants live from the soil, animals from plants, men from animals, and this order of things is thought to continue (whether rightly or wrongly, in moral terms) in the structure of society: the higher the social or intellectual status of individuals, the more their lives are supported by the labour of those lower down the scale, whom they reward not by working for them in return but only by means of money. This notion is quite wrong nowadays, for the needs of the masses are met by large-scale industries which draw on immeasurable scientific, technical and organizational energies from the highest social strata. The eminent chemist in his laboratory pondering over the description of aniline colours is working for the farmer's wife who selects the brightest-coloured scarf at her local shop. The international wholesale merchant speculator who imports American grain into Germany is the servant of the poorest proletarian. A cotton mill which employs people of the highest intelligence is dependent on customers in the lowest social class. There are, today, innumerable examples of this feed-back of services whereby the lower classes purchase the work of the higher classes; they affect our entire culture. This phenomenon is possible only because the objectification of production as regards both manufacturer and consumer sets it above any social or other distinctions between the two. The fact that producers of culture of the highest status work in the service of consumers of the lowest status simply indicates that there is no relationship between them at all. The object stands between them, with producers on one side and consumers on the other, separated by the very thing which holds them together. The basis of this is clearly a division of labour: production techniques are so specialized that its various operations are allotted not only to an increasing number, but also an increasing variety of people. Eventually a point is reached where some of the work involved in the humblest necessities is performed by persons of the highest intelligence. Conversely, in an exactly parallel objectification, the breakdown of mechanical work means that the coarsest hands contribute to the most sophisticated products of the highest culture. (Let the reader think, for example, of a present-day printing works in contrast to the production of books before the invention of printing.) This inversion of what is regarded as the typical relationship between the upper and lower strata of society demonstrates, in the clearest possible fashion, how division of labour makes the former work for the latter. But the only form in which this is possible is the complete objectification of production itself in relation to both groups. The inversion is merely an extreme logical consequence of the connection between division of labour and the objectification of culture.

Division of labour has been considered hitherto as a specialization of personal activity. Specialization of products themselves, however, contributes equally to their alienation from the individual, which is perceived as the independence of the product and the individual's inability to assimilate it, to impose his own rhythms on it. This applies, to begin with, to the means of work. The more these are differentiated, i.e. constructed from a number of specialized parts, the less possible it is for the worker's personality to express itself through them, and the less visible is his personal contribution to the product. The tools of art are, relatively speaking, quite undifferentiated and hence provide the widest scope for the expression of personality. They do not confront the personality like an industrial machine whose specialized complexity gives it a clearly defined, quasi-personal character, which cannot be imbued with the worker's own personality as can the more indeterminate tools of art. During thousands of years of the sculptor's tools have not evolved beyond their wholly unspecialized form. Where an artistic instrument has evolved to such a decisive extent, as, for example, the piano, it has also taken on a highly objective character. Its excessive autonomy creates a far more formidable barrier to subjective personal expression than is the case with, for example, the violin, which is technically much less differentiated. The automatic character of modern machinery is the result of a drastic breakdown and specialization of materials and energies. Likewise, the identical character of a highly developed state administration necessitates sophisticated division of labour between its officials. By becoming a complete entity and taking over an increasing proportion of work, the machine becomes an autonomous power in relation to the worker, while in relation to the machine he is not an individual personality, but merely carries out an objective prescribed task. Let the reader compare, for example, a worker in a shoe factory with a maker of bespoke shoes in order to see how much the specialization of tools eliminates the importance of personal qualities, whether superior or inferior, and makes subject and object develop as essentially independent elements. An undifferentiated tool is really a mere extension of the human arm; only more specialized tools are elevated to the pure category of objects. This process also occurs in an obvious and very characteristic way in the instruments of war, culminating in the battleship, the most specialized and perfect of machines. Here objectification has progressed to the point that in modern sea warfare there is scarcely any decisive factor other than simple numerical superiority in terms of ships of equal quality.

Finally, the process of objectification of culture, based on specialization, which increasingly alienates the individual from what he creates, is spreading to the sphere of personal daily life. Even in the early nineteenth century, domestic furniture, the useful or ornamental articles of the immediate environment, were, relatively speaking, extremely simple and durable, from the needs of the lower classes to those of the most cultivated. This produced that close personal bond between people and the objects of their environment which today appears even to the middle generation as old-fashioned eccentricity. The differentiation of objects has removed this bond in three ways, with the same result in each case. To begin with, the mere number of specifically formed objects makes a close, as it were, personal relationship to individual objects difficult. A small number of simple articles can be more easily assimilated by the personality, whereas an abundance of various articles becomes, so to speak, an adversary. This is the source of the housewife's complaint that looking after the home requires a positively fetishistic devotion, as also of the occasional outbursts of hatred by people of earnest and meditative temperament against the innumerable articles with which we encumber our lives. The former case is so typical for our culture because the housewife's task of maintenance and preservation used in former times to be more extensive and demanding than it is now. But this did not make them feel that their freedom was restricted by objects, because the objects were more closely linked with the personality. The individual personality could more easily impart its aura to a few, undifferentiated articles; they did not confront one as independent entities as does a multitude of specialized objects. Only these latter are felt by us as hostile when we are at their service. Freedom is not something negative, it is our positive control of unresisting objects, and conversely the only things which have objective status for us are those which paralyse our freedom, that is to say, things with which we are associated but cannot assimilate to our ego. The feeling of being stifled by the external objects surrounding us in modern life is not only the consequence but also the cause of their existence as autonomous objects. The irksome thing is that we are, at bottom, indifferent to all these objects that crowd in on us, for reasons specific to a money economy: their impersonal origin and easy replaceability. The fact that large-scale industry fosters the idea of socialism is a consequence not only of working men's conditions but also of the objective nature of its products. Modern man is so completely surrounded by such impersonal things that he is bound to feel an increasing affinity with (though also, admittedly, increasing hostility to) the idea of a fundamentally anti-individualistic social order. The objects of culture increasingly evolve into a world with its own coherence which touches the subjective soul, with its desires and emotions, at fewer and fewer points. This coherence is supported by a certain independent mobility of objects. It has been pointed out that the merchant, the artisan or the scholar are much less mobile today than they were, for example, during the period of the Reformation. Both material and intellectual objects now move independently, however, without personal representation or transportation. Things and people have parted company. Ideas, labour and skills, through being increasingly embodied in objective artefacts, books and commodities, have acquired a mobility of their own, of which modern advances in transportation are merely the actualization or expression. Only by virtue of this independent, impersonal mobility does the differentiation of objects away from people reach its final stage. The ultimate example of this mechanical quality of modern economy is the self-service machine, which completely eliminates the human agency even from retail selling, where transactions remained the longest on an inter-personal basis. The monetary equivalent is now converted automatically into the commodity. The same principle operates, on a different level, in the '50 pfennig market' and similar establishments, where the psychological process involved in economic decisions does not begin with the commodity and move thence to the price, but vice versa. Here, the fixed price for all articles obviates the necessity for a variety of reflections and deliberations on the part of the buyer and efforts and elucidations on the part of the seller. This minimizes the extent and importance of the personal element in the economic transaction.

This concurrent differentiation has the same effect as consecutive differentiation. Changes of fashion interrupt the inner process of acquisition and assimilation between subject and object which prevents any discrepancy between the two. Fashion is one of those social phenomena which combine, in a particular proportion, the appeal of variety and change with that of similarity and solidarity. All fashion is essentially class fashion, that is to say, it always indicates a social class which uses similarity of appearance to assert both its own inner unity and its outward difference from other classes. Once the lower classes, aspiring to emulate the upper classes, adopt a fashion, the upper classes abandon it and create a new fashion. That is why there have always been fashions wherever social distinctions have sought visible expression. But the social dynamism of the last hundred years has greatly increased their speed of change. This, on the one hand, because of the increasing flexibility of class boundaries and the widespread upward social mobility of individuals, and sometimes of whole social groups; on the other hand, because of the predominance of the third estate. Because of the first factor, the fashions of the leading classes have to change extremely quickly, for the lower classes are hot on their heels, which rapidly deprives existing fashions of their point and appeal. The second factor owes its effect to the fact that the middle class and the urban population, unlike the conservative upper class and peasantry, are the real class of social change. Restless individuals and classes clamouring for variety discover, in fashion, the vehicle of change and contrast, a pace to match their own mental dynamism. Present-day fashions, it is true, are not nearly as extravagant and expensive as those of earlier centuries, but on the other hand they change much more rapidly. This is partly because they influence much larger circles, partly because it has to be made much easier for those lower down the scale to adopt them, and partly because their real centre is now the affluent middle class. The result of this growing influence and speed of change of fashion is that it appears to have its own independent impetus as an objective force evolving by its own energies, running its course independently of any individual. As long as fashion (and this by no means applies only to fashions in dress) lasted for comparatively longer periods and gave uniformity to comparatively restricted social circles, it was possible for individuals to feel a kind of personal relationship with the various aspects of fashion. Their speed of change (i.e. their consecutive differentiation) and their wide-ranging influence destroy any such relationship, and fashion suffers the fate of not a few similar modern shibboleths: fashion comes to depend less on the individual, the individual less on fashion, they develop like separate evolutionary universes.

Thus differentiation, both concurrent and consecutive, of omnipresent aspects of culture helps to give them an independent objectivity. I would like now, thirdly, to mention just one of the factors which have this effect, viz. the multiplicity of styles encountered in the visible objects of daily life, from architecture to the design of books, from sculpture to horticulture and furnishings, with their juxtaposition of Renaissance and Orientalism, Baroque and Empire, Pre-Raphaelitism and utilitarian realism. This arises from the interaction of the spread of historical knowledge and that predilection of modern man for change which has already been noted. All historical understanding demands mental flexibility, the ability to empathize with and re-create casts of mind very remote from one's own. All history, however much it may deal with visible things, is meaningful and intelligible only as the history of basic interests, emotions and aspirations. Even historical materialism is merely a psychological hypothesis. To make history one's own therefore requires mental receptivity and impressionability, a sublimated form of liking for change. The historicizing tendencies of our century, its incomparable ability to reproduce and revitalize the most remote things (historically and geographically) is simply the internal equivalent of its generally increased adaptability and wide-ranging mobility. Hence the bewildering variety of styles which are adopted, presented and appreciated in our culture. Any style is a language in itself, with its own special sounds, inflections and syntax for expressing life, and it is evident that, as long as we have only one style to shape ourselves and our environment, we are not conscious of it as an autonomous force with a life of its own. Nobody, as long as he speaks his native language spontaneously, sees in it any objective laws transcending his subjective individuality which he has to consult in order to borrow from them the resources for expressing his inner life—resources obedient to independent norms. On the contrary, for such a person, the means of expression and the thing expressed are identical. It is only when we become acquainted with foreign languages that we come to see not only our native language but language in general as something independent, existing separately from us. Similarly, people whose entire life is encompassed by a wholly unified style will unquestioningly identify that life-style with its contents. Since everything that they either create or contemplate is automatically expressed in that style, they have no psychological reason at all to dissociate it in their minds from the matter of what they see, or create and establish it as a separate entity with its own provenance. Only where there is a plurality of available styles will any particular style be dissociated from its content. Its autonomy and independent significance will then be balanced by our freedom to choose that style or another.

Differentiation of styles makes each individual style, and thus style in general, something objective, whose validity is independent of the individual with his subjective interests, influences, likes and dislikes. The breakdown of all the visual elements of our cultural life into a multiplicity of styles destroys the original relationship to them, in which subject and object were still as one. It leaves us facing a world of expressive possibilities that have evolved in accordance with their own norms, as forms for giving utterance to life. Thus these forms and our subjectivity are like two separate factions with a purely fortuitous relationship of contact, harmony or dissonance.

This, then, is more or less the area within which division of labour and specialization, personal as well as material, underlie the great process of objectivization of our most recent culture. All these phenomena make up the overall picture, in which culture increasingly, and with our increasing awareness, becomes *objective mind*, in relation to recipients and producers alike. As this objectivization proceeds, the strange phenomenon which provided our starting-point becomes more comprehensible: the fact that the cultural improvement of individuals can lag perceptibly behind that of things, be they tangible, functional or spiritual.

The fact that the opposite occasionally occurs demonstrates the same mutual independence of the two forms of mind. This can be seen in a somewhat disguised and modified form in the following phenomenon. It would appear that the long-term preservation of the peasant economy in North Germany is possible only on the basis of one kind of hereditary entitlement, viz. where one of the heirs takes over the farm and compensates the others with a lower payment than they would receive if it were based on the selling price of the farm. If the payment is based on the latter (which far exceeds present revenue) the farm is thereby over-mortgaged to the extent that only very poor management is possible. Nevertheless, the modern individualistic sense of justice demands this mechanical equality of monetary entitlement for all heirs and refuses to allow any one child an advantage, even though this is the prerequisite of objectively proper farm management. Undoubtedly cultural improvement of particular individuals is often achieved by this means at the cost of letting objective culture lag behind by comparison. Such discrepancies occur to a very pronounced degree in actual social institutions, whose evolution proceeds at a more sluggish, conservative pace than that of individuals. To this category belong those cases whose common element is that methods of production which have existed for a certain time are outstripped by the productive energies which they themselves called into being but for which they no longer provide commensurate scope for expression and employment. These energies are largely of a personal nature: there is no longer any place in the objective forms of work for what people are capable of achieving or entitled to desire. The requisite modification of these forms never comes about until the pressures have built up to massive proportions. Until then, the objective organization of production lags behind the evolution of individual economic energies. Many of the motives of the feminist movement are of this kind. The advances of modern industrial technology have removed from the home an extremely large number of domestic activities which used to be woman's responsibility; the articles concerned can be manufactured more cheaply and expediently elsewhere. This has meant that very many middle-class women have been deprived of the activities that made up their lives, without easily finding alternative activities and goals to fill the vacuum. The widespread 'dissatisfaction' of modern women, their unused energies, whose backlash brings about all manner of disturbance and destruction, their search—partly healthy, partly pathological—for opportunities to prove themselves outside the home, all these come about because technology, with its objectivity, has advanced at its own pace, which outstrips human capacity for development. The same state of affairs is said to lie at the root of the widespread dissatisfaction in modern marriages. It is said that the fixed forms and habits of marriage, with the compulsion that they exert over individuals, are incompatible with the personal development of the partners, especially the wife, who has far outgrown these forms. Individuals, it is felt, now aspire to freedom, understanding, equal rights and educational opportunities for which married life, in its traditional, objectively fixed form, does not give proper scope. The objective spirit of marriage, so one might put it, has lagged behind subjective spiritual development. The same applies to jurisprudence: logically derived from certain basic facts, laid down in a fixed code of laws, represend by a particular social class, it takes on that inflexibility towards people's feelings regarding the needs and conditions of life, which leads eventually to its being transmitted from one generation to the next like a hereditary disease which turns reason into absurdity and a blessing into a curse. Religion fares no better once religious impulses have crystallized into a body of specific dogmas, administered on a basis of division of labour by a specific body separate from the remainder of the faithful.

If one bears in mind this relative independence of the objectified contents of culture, the precipitate of elemental historical dynamics, in relation to individuals, then the question of historical progress should become much less vexing. The reason why any answer we give to this question can be proved or disproved with equal plausibility, may often be that it is not, in fact, the same thing which is being proved or disproved. It can, for example, be asserted with equal justification that there has, or has not, been progress in ethical standards, depending on whether one is referring to the established principles and organizations and the moral imperatives that have become part of general awareness, or to the relationship of individuals to these objective ideals, the ethical adequacy or inadequacy of their behaviour. Progress and stagnation can thus coexist in immediate proximity, not only in different historical spheres but in one and the same sphere, depending on whether one looks at the evolution of subjective individuals or of the structures which, though originating in individual contributions, have acquired an objective spiritual life of their own.

Having established that not only can the development of objective mind outstrip that of subjective mind, but that the reverse is also possible, let us now take a further look at the part played by the division of labour in actualizing the former possibility. This dual possibility arises, to put it briefly, as follows. Mind, as objectified in production of any kind, is superior to any individual because of complex manufacturing techniques which presuppose a vast number of historical and material factors, forerunners and contributors. This makes the product a repository of energies, qualities and intensified potential wholly external to the individual who produces it. This is especially the case in specifically modern technology as a result of division of labour. As long as a product was manufactured basically by a single person or a co-operative group of relatively unspecialized workers, its objectified substance could not very far exceed the intellect and energies of the individuals involved. Only a sophisticated division of labour makes the individual product the focal point of energies derived from a great number of individuals. Considered as a unity and compared with any particular individual, the product is therefore bound to be superior in a whole variety of ways. This accumulation of quality and excellence in the object which is their synthesis knows no bounds, whereas the development of individual personalities in any given period of time encounters immutable natural limits. By absorbing individual aspects of very many personalities, the objective product acquires an objectively outstanding development potential, but also forfeits certain kinds of excellence which are only possible where energies are synthesized in a *single* person. The most comprehensive example of this is the State, especially in its modern form. Rationalists have denounced as a logical paradox the fact that a monarch, who is after all only an individual person, rules over a vast number of other persons. But they overlook the fact that these latter, inasmuch as they constitute the State ruled by the monarch, are not 'persons' in the same sense that he is. On the contrary, only a certain fraction of their lives and energies go to make up the State; the remainder goes into other spheres, none of which encompass their entire personality. The monarch's role, on the other hand, absorbs his entire personality, i.e. more than that of any individual subject. Admittedly, there may be an imbalance where the ruler's power is unrestricted in the sense that he can dispose of his subjects' entire lives. But a modern constitutional state precisely defines the limits of its own purview. It constitutes itself from certain elements detached from people by differentiation. The more pronounced this differentiation, the more objective is the State in relation to the individual, an artefact detached from the forms of individual spirituality. By being a synthesis of differentiated individual elements, it is clearly as much an infra-personal as a supra-personal entity. All structures of objective mind created by combining differentiated individual contributions are similar in the State. However much they may surpass any individual intellect in objective intellectual content and evolutionary potential, we nevertheless feel them to be soulless and mechanical, the more so as their degree of differentiation and number of labour-divided elements increase.

Here we see most clearly what we might call the difference between mind and soul. Mind is the objective content of what the soul is conscious of as a vital function. The soul is, as it were, the form which the mind, i.e. the logical-conceptual content of thought, assumes for our subjectivity; it is our subjectivity. Mind, thus understood, does not therefore need the unity without which there is no soul. It is as if the contents of the mind somehow lay strewn about and were only assembled and unified by the soul, somewhat as inanimate matter is integrated in an organism and its vital unity. Therein lies the greatness and the limitation of the soul in relation to the individual contents of consciousness, considered in their autonomous validity and objective significance. No matter in what radiant perfection and total self-sufficiency Plato depicted the realm of ideas, which are merely the objective contents of thought detached from all the hazards of thinking—and no matter how imperfect, restricted and crepuscular the human soul appeared to him, with its pallid, blurred, scarcely grasped reflection of those pure ideas—for us such pellucid clarity and logical fixity of form is not the only evaluative criterion for either the ideal or the real. For us the personal unity in which consciousness assembles the objective intellectual meanings of things is of incomparable value. Only there is that mutual friction created which constitutes life and energy, only there does that mysterious, radiant warmth of feeling arise, for which there is no place, no sympathy, in the lucid perfection of pure objective ideas. The same applies to the mind which, through the autonomy of intelligence, treats the soul as its object. The gulf between the two evidently widens as the number of people involved in the labour-divided production of the object concerned increases. For it becomes thereby increasingly impossible to embody in one's work, by the way one works and the way one lives, that unity of personality with which we associate the value, warmth and uniqueness of the soul. The fact that objective mind lacks this form of spirituality as a result of the modern differentiation involved in its genesis (closely connected with the mechanical quality of our cultural products) may be the ultimate reason for the frequent contemporary hostility of highly individualistic and meditative people towards the 'progress of culture'. This is particularly so since this shaping of objective culture by division of labour is one aspect or consequence of the general phenomenon which is usually described by saying that what is significant in the present age is achieved not by individuals but by the masses. Division of labour does, indeed, mean that any individual article is a product of the mass. The breakdown of individuals into their separate energies, on which the organization of present-day labour is based, and the synthesis of these differentiated elements in the objective cultural product means that the more people are involved in the manufacture of a particular product, the less humanity there is in it. There is thus a parallel between the splendour and magnitude of modern culture and the radiant Platonic realm of ideas where the objective mind of things exists in reality and immaculate perfection, but where the values of actual personality, which cannot be broken down into objective components, are not to be found. This deficiency cannot be outweighed by the awareness, however acute, that personality is fragmentary, irrational and ephemeral. Indeed, the mere form of personal spirituality asserts its value however inferior or contrary to any ideal its particular content may be. It retains its peculiar existential significance independently of all the objective aspects of life, even in those cases which provided our starting point, where individual subjective culture regresses while objective culture advances.

The relationship between objective mind and its development, and subjective minds, is clearly of the utmost importance for any cultural community, particularly as regards its style of life. For if the significance of style is that it can give the same formal expression to any number and variety of contents, then it is certainly possible for the relationship between objective and subjective mind in terms of quantity, level and pace of development to be the same even where the *contents* of the cultural mind are very different. It is precisely the general pattern of life, the context provided by social culture for individual impulses, that is defined by the answers to questions such as the following: does the individual know that his inner life is lived in affinity with or alienation from the objective cultural trends of his age? Does he feel these trends to be something superior, something almost entirely beyond his reach; or does he feel his value as a person to be superior to all objectified mind? Are, within his own intellectual life, the objective, historically given elements a power with its own laws, developing independently of the real nucleus of his personality, or is the soul master in its own house, or does it at least create a harmony of level, meaning and rhythm between its own inmost life and what it has to absorb into that life as impersonal content? These questions, abstract as they are, provide the paradigm for innumerable concrete interests and moods, both temporary and permanent, and thus indicate the extent to which the relationships between objective and subjective culture determine the style of life.

If the present form of this relationship arose from division of labour, then it is also an offshoot of money economy. On the one hand, this is because the breakdown of production into a large number of partial operations requires an organization that functions with absolute precision and reliability, which is only possible, now that slavery no longer exists, if workers are paid in money. Any other basis of the relationship between an entrepreneur and his employees would entail some less predictable elements, partly because payment in kind cannot be so readily provided and precisely quantified, partly because only a purely monetary relationship has the exclusively objective, automatic character which is indispensable to highly differentiated, complex organizations. It is also because, as production becomes more specialized, the fundamental reason for the existence of money becomes more urgent. For economics is a matter of one person giving up what another desires, on condition that the other person does likewise. In economics, the moral rule that one should do unto others as one would be done by is obeyed in the most comprehensive fashion. When a producer finds someone willing to take object A, which he wishes to exchange, then object B, which the latter is able to offer in exchange, will often not be what the producer desires. The fact that two people's different desires do not always accord with the different products they each have to offer necessitates, as we know, the introduction of a medium of exchange. Then, if the owners of A and B cannot agree to a direct exchange, the former will give A in return for money with which to obtain C, which he wants, while the owner of B obtains the money to buy A by means of a similar transaction involving B and a third party. Since money thus comes into being as a result of *differences* in products, or in the desires relating to them, its role will clearly become more extensive and indispensable as the variety of articles involved in commerce increases. Conversely, any substantial specialization of operations is only possible if direct exchange is no longer necessary. The likelihood that the person taking a product will happen to be able to offer in return an object which the producer is willing to accept dwindles as the specialization of products and human desires increases. Seen in this light, the connection between modern differentiation and the exclusive dominance of money is not by any means the result of any new emergent factor. On the contrary, these two cultural values are linked at their deepest roots. The fact that the specialization which I have described has interacted with money economy to form a total historical unity, is merely an intensification in degree of a synthesis inherent in the nature of both.

Thus, by virtue of this connection, the style of life, in so far as it depends on the relationship between objective and subjective culture, is linked with the use of money. Furthermore, the nature of money is fully revealed by the fact that it underlies both the preponderance of objective over subjective mind, and also the reserve, independent enhancement and autonomous development of the latter. What makes the culture of things so superior to that of individuals is the unity and autonomous self-sufficiency which it has acquired in modern times. Production, with its technology and its achievements, is like a cosmos with, so to speak, fixed logical characteristics and its own development, confronting the individual as fate confronts the inconstancy and irregularity of the human will. This formal self-sufficiency, this inner force which unifies the contents of culture into a mirror-image of the coherence of nature, only becomes reality through money. On the one hand, money acts as the articular system of this organism, making its various elements interdependent and enabling them to move in relation to one another and transmit any impulses throughout the system. At the same time, it is comparable to the bloodstream, which, by continually circulating through all the intricacies of the body's limbs and nourishing them all equally, unifies their functions. As regards the second point: money enables people, by separating them from things, to lead an abstract life, as it were, free of the need to take objects into direct consideration, free of any direct relationship to them. Without this freedom, certain potential spiritual developments could not be realized. Modern man's ability to stake out, under favourable conditions, an area of subjective privacy, a secret sealed-off sphere of intimate personal being (not in a social but in a profoundly metaphysical sense) which to some extent compensates for the loss of the religious style of life of earlier ages, is dependent on the fact that money exempts us to an ever-increasing degree from direct contact with objects, while at the same time making it infinitely easier for us to control them and select from them what meets our needs.

Hence this opposing tendency, which does exist, may develop towards an ideal of absolute, clear-cut separation, where all the material aspects of life become more and more objective and impersonal, but thereby also make its residue, which defies objectivization, all the more personal, all the more the indisputable property of the self. A typical specific example of this tendency is the typewriter. Writing, an external concrete activity but one which always has a characteristic individual form, can now cast off this form and replace it with mechanical uniformity. But, at the same time, it achieves the dual effect that, first, what is written now functions purely as content, without being either reinforced or obscured by its visual form, and, secondly, intimate personal characteristics are no longer betrayed, as is so often the case with handwriting (quite regardless of whether the actual communication is wholly superficial and unimportant, or highly personal). Thus, for all the socializing effect of such mechanical inventions, they do at the same time intensify what remains of the privacy of the spiritual self, making it guard that privacy all the more jealously. Such banishment of subjective spirituality from all external things is, of course, as hostile to the aesthetic ideal of life as it can be conducive to that of pure inwardness.

This explains both the despair of people of purely aesthetic temperament with regard to the present age, and the slight tension between such people and others who are concerned only with spiritual salvation, which is beginning to appear in, as it were, subterranean forms (quite unlike those of the age of Savonarola). Money, both the symbol and the cause of the process whereby everything that can be rendered superficial and neutral is so rendered, becomes at the same time the gatekeeper of the most intimate sphere, which can then develop within its own limits.

The extent to which this produces personal refinement, individuality and spirituality, or conversely, as a result of the ease with which they can be acquired, makes men the slaves of the objects thus brought under control, depends not on money but on people themselves. Here, too, one can see the formal affinity of money economy to socialism: what people expect from socialism, release from the individual struggle for existence, secure access to the lower economic values and easy access to the higher ones, could be expected to have the same differentiating effect, viz. that a certain section of society would rise to unprecedented heights of spirituality utterly remote from all mundane considerations, while another section would sink into an equally unprecedented practical materialism.

By and large, money is probably most influential in those aspects of our lives whose style is determined by the preponderance of objective over subjective culture. But the fact that it is equally capable of reinforcing the converse situation illuminates most clearly the nature and extent of its historical power. The only other thing to which it could, in some respects, be compared is language, which also reinforces, clarifies and elaborates the most disparate tendencies of thought and feeling. Money is one of those forces whose particular quality lies precisely in the lack of any particular quality, but which can none the less influence life in very different ways, because the purely formal, functional and quantitative character which is their mode of existence combines with qualitative aspects and tendencies of life to engender further qualitative innovations. Its significance for the style of life is not nullified but increased, not refuted but proved by the fact that it helps to intensify and bring to fruition *both* possible relationships between the objective and the subjective mind.

[New translation. From Georg Simmel, *Philosophie des Geldes*, Chapter 6, part 2, Dunker & Humbolt, Leipzig, 1900]

# The Conflict of Modern Culture

As soon as life progresses beyond the purely biological level to the level of mind, and mind in its turn progresses to the level of culture, an inner conflict appears. The entire evolution of culture consists in the growth, resolution and re-emergence of this conflict. For clearly we speak of culture when the creative dynamism of life produces certain artefacts which provide it with forms of expression and actualization, and which in their turn absorb the constant flow of life, giving it form and content, scope and order: e.g. civil laws and constitutions, works of art, religion, science, technology and innumerable others. But a peculiar quality of these products of the life-process is that from the first moment of their existence they have fixed forms of their own, set apart from the febrile rhythm of life itself, its waxing and waning, its constant renewal, its continual divisions and reunifications. They are vessels both for the creative life, which however immediately departs from them, and for the life which subsequently enters them, but which after a while they can no longer encompass. They have their own logic and laws, their own significance and resilience arising from a certain degree of detachment and independence *vis-a-vis* the spiritual dynamism which gave them life. At the moment of their establishment they are, perhaps, well-matched to life, but as life continues its evolution, they tend to become inflexible and remote from life, indeed hostile to it.

This is ultimately the reason why culture has a history. Life, as it becomes mind, continuously creates such artefacts: self-sufficient and with an inherent claim to permanence, indeed to timelessness. They may be described as the *forms* which life adopts, the indispensible mode of its manifestation as spiritual life. But life itself flows on without pause. With each and every new form of existence which it creates for itself, its perpetual dynamism comes into conflict with the permanence or timeless validity of that form. Sooner or later the forces of life erode every cultural form which they have produced. By the time one form has fully developed, the next is already beginning to take shape beneath it, and is destined to supplant it after a brief or protracted struggle.

The transformation of cultural forms is the subject of history in the widest sense. As an empirical discipline, it is content to identify in each individual case the concrete basis and causes of these external manifestations of change. But the deeper underlying process is surely a perpetual struggle between life, with its fundamental restlessness, evolution and mobility, and its own creations, which become inflexible and lag behind its development. Since, however, life can take on external existence only in one form or another, this process can be clearly identified and described in terms of the displacement of one form by another. The never-ending change in the content of culture, and in the long run of whole cultural styles, is the sign, or rather the result, both of the infinite fertility of life and of the profound opposition between its eternal evolution and transformation and the objective validity and self-assertion of those manifestations and forms in which, or by means of which, it exists. It moves between the poles of death and rebirth, rebirth and death.

This nature of the process of cultural history was first observed in respect of economic developments. The economic forces of any age give rise to an appropriate form of production: slavery, the guilds, peasant statute labour, free wage-labour, and all the other forms of the organization of labour. When they arose, they were all the adequate expression of the capacities and aspirations of the age. But always within their norms and restrictions there arose economic energies whose nature and proportions could not find adequate scope in these forms. They therefore broke free of them, either gradually or in violent upheavals, and the former mode of production was replaced by one more suited to the current energies. But a mode of production has, as a form, no inherent energy to oust a different mode. It is life itself (in this case in its economic aspect) with its impetus and dynamism, its transformation and differentiation, which provides the driving force behind the entire process, but which, being itself formless, can only manifest itself as a phenomenon by being given form. However, it is the essence of form to lay claim, the moment it is established, to a more than momentary validity not governed by the pulse of life. This can be seen even more clearly in intellectual than in economic spheres. That is why there is from the very outset a latent tension between these forms and life, which subsequently erupts in various areas of our lives and activity. This can, in the long run, accumulate as a pervasive cultural malaise in which all form comes to be felt as something forcibly imposed on life, which then tries to break out of any form, not just one specific form or other, and to absorb it into its own spontaneity, to put itself in the place of form, to allow its force and plenitude to gush forth in their primal untrammelled spontaneity, and in no other way, until all cognition, values and structures can only be seen as the direct revelation of life. We are at present experiencing this new phase of the age-old struggle, which is no longer the struggle of a new, life-imbued form against an old, lifeless one, but the struggle against form itself, against the very principle of form. The moralists, the eulogists of the good old days, the stylistic purists have the facts on their side when they complain of the ubiquitous and growing formlessness of modern life. But they tend to overlook the fact that what is happening is not merely something negative, the death of traditional forms, but that an altogether positive vital impulse is sloughing off these forms. But because the magnitude of this process does not as yet permit this impulse to focus on the creation of new forms, it makes, as it were, a virtue of necessity and feels obliged to struggle against form simply because it *is* form. This is perhaps only possible in an age which feels that all cultural forms are like exhausted soil, which has yielded all it can but which is still entirely covered with the products of its earlier fertility. In the eighteenth century, of course, something similar occurred, but first it happened over a much longer period of time, from the English Enlightenment of the seventeenth century to the French Revolution; and secondly, each upheaval was inspired by a very definite new ideal: the emancipation of the individual, the rational conduct of life, the reliable progress of humanity towards happiness and perfection. And from each upheaval there arose, giving men a sense of inner security, the image of new cultural forms which in a way were already prefigured. Hence they did not produce the cultural malaise as we know it, which we of the older generation have seen grow gradually to the point where it is no longer a question of a new cultural form struggling against an old, but of life, in every imaginable sphere, rebelling against the need to contain itself within any fixed form at all.

This situation, which is now clear for all to see, was anticipated in a way some decades ago when the concept of life began to assume a dominant role in philosophy. In order to relate this phenomenon correctly to the general history of ideas, it is necessary to digress a little. In any great cultural era with a definite character of its own, one particular idea can always be discerned which both underlies all intellectual movements and at the same time appears to be their ultimate goal. Whether the age itself is aware of this idea as an abstraction, or whether it is merely the ideal focal-point of such movements, whose import and significance for the age become apparent only to later observers, makes no difference. Every such central idea occurs, of course, in innumerable variants and disguises, and against innumerable opposing factors, but it remains withal the hidden governing principle of the intellectual era. In every such era it is to be found (and can hence be identified), where the highest life, the absolute, the metaphysical dimension of reality coincides with the supreme value, the absolute demand made of ourselves and of the world. A logical paradox is involved here, of course: what is absolute reality does not need anything to make it real; it cannot, clearly, be said that what most indubitably exists has yet to come into being. But at its highest peaks, philosophy is not inhibited by this conceptual difficulty; indeed, the point where this paradox appears, where the series of that which is and that which ought to be, otherwise alien to each other, meet, is, one may be sure, an authentic central aspect of that particular philosophy of life.

I will only indicate with the utmost brevity the ideas which seem to me to be central in this way to certain broad eras. In the era of Greek classicism, it was the idea of *being*—being which was unified, substantive and divine, but not of a pantheistic formlessness, yet which rather existed, and could be shaped, in meaningful concrete forms. The Christian Middle Ages replaced this idea with that of God, at once the source and goal of all reality, the unconditional lord of our lives, yet one who demanded free obedience and devotion from those lives. From the Renaissance onwards, this supremacy was gradually accorded to the idea of Nature: it appeared to be the absolute, the sole embodiment of existence and truth, but at the same time also the ideal, that had yet to be endowed with presence and authority—initially in artistic activity, for which, of course, the vital prerequisite is *a priori* the unity of the ultimate essence of reality and the highest value. Then the seventeenth century focused its philosophy on the idea of natural laws, which alone it regarded as fundamentally valid, and the century of Rousseau erected upon this foundation an ideal of 'nature' as the absolute value, aspiration and challenge. In addition, at the end of the era, the ego, the spiritual personality, emerges as a central idea: on the one hand, existence in its entirety appears as the creative idea of a conscious ego, while on the other hand personality becomes a goal. The assertion of the pure individual ego comes to be seen as the absolute moral imperative, indeed the universal metaphysical goal of life. The nineteenth century, with its motley variety of intellectual currents, did not produce any comparable all-embracing guiding concept. If we restrict ourselves to the human sphere, we might here speak of the idea of society, which in the nineteenth century is proclaimed for the first time to be the true reality of our lives, reducing the individual to a point of intersection of various social series, or even a hypothetical entity such as the atom. But on the other hand, man is *required* to relate his entire life to society; complete social integration is regarded as an absolute obligation subsuming all other obligations, moral or otherwise. Only at the turn of the twentieth century did large groups of European intellectuals appear, as it were, to be reaching out for a new basic idea on which to construct a philosophy of life. The idea of *life* emerged at the centre where reality and values—metaphysical or psychological, moral or artistic—both originate and intersect.

As for which individual phenomena, among those which make up the general tendency of our most recent culture as described above, find in the multi-facetted 'metaphysics of life' the soil to nourish their growth, the vindication of their proclivity, their conflicts and their trage- dies—this will be investigated later. But it must be mentioned here how remarkably the emergent philosophical significance of the concept of life is anticipated and confirmed by the fact that the two great adversaries in the modern articulation of values, Schopenhauer and Nietzsche, have precisely this idea in common. Schopenhauer is the fist modern philosopher to inquire at the most profound, crucial level, not into any specific contents of life, any conceptions or aspects of existence, but to ask exclusively: what is life, what is its pure significance *qua* life? The fact that he does not use the term, but speaks only of the will to life, or just of the will, must not be allowed to obscure this fundamental stance. Notwithstanding all his speculative exploration of areas beyond life, the 'will' provides his answer to the question of the meaning of life as such. This answer is that life cannot attain to any meaning and goal beyond itself, because it always follows its own will, albeit in innumerable shapes and forms. Precisely because its metaphysical reality condemns it to remain within its own bounds, any apparent goal can only bring disappointment and an endless series of further illusions to pursue. Nietzsche, on the other hand, started in exactly the same way from the idea that life is entirely self-determining and constitutes the sole substance of all its contents. But he found in life itself the purpose that gives it the meaning which it cannot find outside itself. For the essence of life is intensification, increase, growth of plenitude and power, strength and beauty from within itself—in relation not to any definable goal but purely to its own development. By its increase, life itself takes on potentially infinite value. However profoundly and vitally these two opposing responses to life, despair and jubilation, differ—beggaring any attempt to make a rational choice or compromise between them—they have in common the basic question which sets them apart from all earlier philosophers: what does life mean, what is its intrinsic value? For them, questions of knowledge and morality, of the self and reason, art and God, happiness and suffering, can only be asked after they have solved that prime mystery; and the answer to them depends on the solution given. Only the fundamental fact of life itself gives to all other things positive or negative value, meaning and proportion. The idea of life is the point of intersection of the two diametrically opposed ways of thinking, which between them have mapped out the crucial decisions to be taken in modern life.

I shall now attempt to illustrate in relation to some of the manifestations of our most recent culture, i.e. that which had evolved up to 1914, how it has diverged from all former cultural evolution. In the past, old forms have always been destroyed by a desire for new forms. But today the ultimate impulse underlying developments in this sphere can be identified as opposition to the principle of form as such, even where consciousness is actually or apparently advancing towards new forms. The fact that for at least several decades we have no longer been living by any sort of shared idea, nor indeed, to a large extent, by any idea at all, is perhaps—to anticipate a later point—only another manifestation of the negative aspect (as regards its identifiable phenomena) of this intellectual current. The Middle Ages, by contrast, had the idea of the Christian Church; the Renaissance had the restoration of secular nature as a value which did not need to be legitimized by transcendental forces; the eighteenth-century Enlightenment lived by the idea of universal human happiness through the rule of reason, and the great age of German idealism suffused science with artistic imagination, and aspired to give art a foundation of cosmic breadth by means of scientific knowledge. But today, if one were to ask educated people what idea actually governs their lives, most of them would give a specialized answer relating to their occupation. One would not hear much of any cultural idea governing them as whole men and guiding all their specialized activities. If even within the individual cultural sphere the present peculiar stage of historical evolution is a stage where life aspires to manifest itself in pure immediacy; and, this being possible only in some form or other, if the inadequacy of any such form reveals that this is indeed the truly decisive impulse, then not only is there no raw material, as it were, for an all-embracing cultural idea, but also the spheres whose new forms it would encompass are far too diverse, indeed disparate, to permit any such ideal unification.

Turning now to specific phenomena, I propose first to discuss art. Of all the hotch-potch of aspirations covered by the general name of futurism, only the movement described as Expressionism seems to stand out with a certain identifiable degree of unity and clarity. If I am not mistaken, the point of Expressionism is that the artist's inner impulse is perpetuated in the work, or to be more precise, *as* the work, exactly as it is experienced. The intention is not to express or contain the impulse in a form imposed upon it by something external, either real or ideal. Thus the impulse is not concerned with the imitation of any entity or event, either in its objective natural form or, as was the ambition of the Impressionists, as registered by our momentary sense impressions. For, after all, even this impression is not the artist's purely personal creation, coming exclusively from within. It is, rather, something passive and secondary, and the work which reflects it is a kind of blend of artistic individuality and a given alien entity. And just as this non-subjective element is rejected, so likewise is the formal procedure, in the narrower sense, which is only available to the artist from some external source: tradition, technique, a model or an established principle. All these are obstructions to life, whose urge is to pour out spontaneously and creatively. If it were to accommodate itself to such forms it would survive in the work only in a distorted, ossified and spurious guise. I imagine the creative process, in its purest form, of an Expressionist painter (and similarly, though less simple to formulate, in all the other arts) as a process whereby the emotional impulse is spontaneously transferred into the hand holding the brush, just as a gesture expresses an inner feeling or a scream expresses pain. The movements of the hand obediently follow the inner impulse, so that what eventually takes shape on the canvas is the direct precipitate of inner life, unmodified by any external, alien elements. The fact that even Expressionist paintings have names denoting objects, although they bear no 'resemblance' to them, is, of course, rather puzzling, and perhaps superfluous, but it is not as pointless as it is bound to appear in the light of traditional expectations regarding art. The artist's inner impulse, which simply gushes forth as an Expressionistic work, can, of course, originate in nameless or unidentifiable spiritual sources. But it can clearly also originate in the stimulus of an external object. It used to be thought that the artistically productive result of such stimulus must show a morphological similarity to the object that provided it (the entire Impressionist movement was based on this assumption).

But Expressionism rejects this assumption. It takes seriously the insight that a cause and its effect can have wholly dissimilar external manifestations, that the dynamic relationship between them is purely internal and need not produce any visual affinity. The sight of a violin or a human face, for example, may trigger off emotions in the painter which, transmuted by his artistic energies, eventually produce an artefact with a completely different appearance. One might say that the Expressionist artist replaces the 'model' by the 'occasion' which awakens an impulse in that life in him which is obedient only unto itself. In abstract terms (but describing a very real act of will), it is the struggle of life to be itself. Its ambition is to express itself purely as itself, and hence it refuses to be contained in any form which is thrust upon it by some other reality which is valid because it is real, or by a law which is valid because it is a law. Conceptually speaking, the artefact eventually produced in this way does, of course, have a form. But as far as the artistic intention is concerned, this is merely an unavoidable extraneous appendage, as it were. It does not, as in all other conceptions of art, have any significance in itself, requiring creative life merely as the basis of its actualization. That is why this art is also indifferent to beauty or ugliness. These are qualities associated with such forms, whereas the significance of life lies beyond beauty and ugliness, for its flux is governed not by any goal but merely by its own driving force. If the works thus created do not satisfy us, this merely confirms that a new form has not been discovered, and is thus not at issue. Once the product is completed, and the life process which engendered it has departed from it, we see that it lacks that meaning and value of its own which we expect from any objective created thing existing independently of its creator. Life, anxious only to express itself, has, as it were, jealously withheld such meaning from its own product.

Perhaps this is the basic explanation of the peculiar preference for the late works of the great masters observable in recent times. Here creative life has become so sovereignly itself, so rich in itself, that it sloughs off any form which is at all traditional or common to other works also. Its expression in the work of art is purely and simply its own inmost essence and destiny at that particular time. However coherent and meaningful the work may be in relation to this essence, it often appears, when measured against traditional forms, uneven, fragmentary and disjointed. This is not a senile waning of formal artistry; it reveals not the infirmity but the strength of old age. Having perfected his creative powers, the great artist is so purely himself that his work shows only the form spontaneously generated by the flow of his life: form has lost its autonomy *vis-a-vis* this life.

It would, in theory, be perfectly possible, of course, for a form with its own intrinsic perfection and significance to be the wholly appropriate expression for such spontaneous life, to fit it like a living skin. This is doubtless the case with the truly great classic works. But, disregarding these works, one can observe here a peculiar structural feature of the spiritual world which far transcends its consequences for art. It is true to say that, in art, whose forms are available in their perfection, something which exists beyond those forms is articulated. In all great artists and all great works of art there is something more profound, more expansive, of more mysterious origin than is offered as art considered purely as artistry, something which is, however, accommodated, presented and made visible by art. In the case of the classics, this something fuses entirely with art. But where it actually conflicts with, or indeed destroys, the forms of art, we feel it, we are conscious of it rather as something separate, something with a voice of its own. An example of this is the inner fate which Beethoven attempts to articulate in his last works. Here it is not a matter of a particular art form being shattered, but rather of the form of art itself being overwhelmed by something different, vaster, something from another dimension. The same applies to metaphysics. Its aim, after all, is knowledge of truth. But in it something which lies beyond knowledge struggles to be heard, something greater, or more profound, or merely different, which reveals itself unmistakably by doing violence to truth as such, making paradoxical, easily refutable claims. It is a typical intellectual paradox (which, of course, a superficial and complacent optimism tends to deny) that some metaphysical beliefs would not have the truth they do as symbols of life or the expression of a particular typical human stance towards life as a whole if they were true as 'knowledge'. Perhaps there is in religion also something that is not religion, something profounder lying beyond it which transcends all its concrete forms, however genuinely religious these are, and reveals itself as heresy and dissent. Some, perhaps all, human creations which spring entirely from the creative power of the soul, contain more than can be accommodated in their form. This property, which distinguishes them from anything produced in a purely mechanical fashion, can only be seen unmistakably when there is a tension between the work and its form.

This is the reason, in a general if not so extreme a way, for the interest currently enjoyed by the art of Van Gogh. For here, more than with any other painter, one surely feels that a passionate vitality far transcending the limits of painting, erupting from an altogether unique breadth and profundity, has merely found, in the gift for painting, a way of channelling its surging flux—by chance, so to speak, as if it could equally well have found fulfilment in religious, literary or musical activity. It seems to me that it is more than anything else this incandescent, palpable spontaneous vitality—which, it is true, only occasionally conflicts with its pictorial form to the extent of destroying the latter—which attracts large numbers of people to Van Gogh in line with the general intellectual tendency under discussion. The existence, on the other hand, in some young people of today of a desire for a wholly abstract art probably arises from the feeling that an insurmountable paradox is created when life acquires—no matter how blithely—a passion for direct, unveiled self-expression. It is precisely the tremendous dynamism of these young people which pushes this tendency to an absolute extreme. It is, incidentally, perfectly understandable that the movement we are describing is, above all, a movement of the young. Revolutionary historical change, external or internal, is generally brought about by the young, and this is particularly true of the current change with its special nature. Age, with flagging vitality, concentrates more and more on the objective *content* of life (which in the present context can equally appropriately be described as its form). But youth is primarily concerned with the *process* of life, it is anxious only to develop to the utmost its powers and its surplus vitality; it is relatively indifferent, and quite often unfaithful, to the particular objects involved. In a cultural climate which enthrones life itself, with its utterances that are well-nigh contemptuous of all form, the significance of youthful life as such is, as it were, objectified.

Finally, we encounter within our sphere of discourse a further fundamental confirmation both in the pursuit of art and also, to a large extent, in other areas. The *mania for originality* in so many young people of today is often, but by no means invariably, vanity and sensationalism, both private and public. In the better cases, the passionate desire to articulate an authentic personal sense of life plays an important part, and the conviction that it really is authentic appears to require the exclusion of anything pre-established or traditional—any permanent forms objectified independently of spontaneous creativity. For when personal life is channelled into such forms, it not only forfeits its uniqueness, it also runs the risk of squandering its vitality on something that is no longer alive. The intention in these cases is to preserve not so much the individuality of life as the life of individuality. Originality is only the *ratio cognoscendi*, so to speak, which guarantees that life is purely itself and that no external, objectified, rigid forms have been absorbed in its flux, or its flux in them. We may have here a more general underlying motive for modern individualism (a point which I can only suggest in passing here).

I shall now try to demonstrate the same basic impulse in one of the most recent movements in philosophy, one which departs most radically from the historically established modes of philosophy. I will refer to it as pragmatism, because the best-known offshoot of the theory, the American version, has acquired this name—a version, incidentally, which I consider to be the most narrow and superficial one. Independently of this or any other specific version that has become current hitherto, the following seems to me to be the crucial motivation in the context of our present interests. Of all the individual spheres of culture, none is as independent *vis-à-vis* life, none as autonomous, as remote from the stress and turbulence, the individual patterns and destinies of life, as knowledge. Not only are the statements that twice two is four, or that matter attracts matter in inverse proportion to the square of distance *true*, regardless of whether they are known to any living minds or not, or of what changes the human race may undergo during the period in which they are known. It is also true to say that knowledge which is directly interwoven with life owes its importance precisely to its complete independence of the fluctuating fortunes of life. Even so-called practical knowledge is, of course, simply theoretical knowledge that is put to practical use at some later stage, but which, *qua* knowledge, remains part of an order of things obedient to its own laws, an ideal realm of truth.

This independence of truth which has always been accepted in the past is denied by the pragmatists. Both inner and outer life are based at every step—so their argument runs—on particular imagined ideas. These ideas sustain and foster our lives if they are true, or they bring us to ruin if they are false. But our ideas are dependent on our mental make-up, they are by no means a mechanical reflection of the reality with which our practical life is interwoven. It would therefore be the most remarkable coincidence if ideas shaped exclusively by the logic of subjective thinking were to produce desirable and predictable results within that reality. On the contrary, it is more likely that of the innumerable ideas which determine our practical life some are regarded as true because they affect that life in a dynamic, positive way, while others which have the opposite effect are dismissed as false. There is therefore no independent, pre-existent truth which is merely later incorporated, as it were, into the stream of life in order to guide its course. On the contrary, the opposite is the case: among the vast mass of theoretical elements which are engendered by the stream of life and are subsequently fed back and affect its course, there are some whose effects match our vital desires (by chance, one might say, but without this chance we could not exist). These we call true, epistemologically correct. The truthfulness of our ideas is not a matter of objects *per se*, nor of any sovereign intellect in us. Life itself, rather, creates, sometimes on the basis of crude expediency, sometimes of the most profound spiritual needs, the scale of values within our ideas, the one pole of which we call the complete truth, the other complete error. I can neither elaborate nor criticize this doctrine here. I am, indeed, not concerned with whether it is correct or not, merely with the fact that it has evolved at the present time, and that it denies the time-honoured claim of knowledge to be an autonomous realm governed by independent, ideal laws. It now becomes one element interwoven with and sustained by life, guided by the totality and unity of vital impulses and goals, and legitimized by the fundamental values of life. Life has thus reasserted its sovereignty over a sphere which hitherto appeared to be separate and independent of it. In more profound philosophical terms: the forms of knowledge whose internal consistency and self-sufficient meaning constitute a firm framework or an indestructive backcloth for our entire mental world, are dissolved by and in the ebb and flow of life. They are seen to be moulded by its evolving and changing energies and ambitions, not standing firm in their own rightness and timeless validity. Life as the central concept of philosophy finds its purest form where, far transcending the reformulation of the problem of epistemology, it becomes the prime metaphysical fact, the essence of all being, making every existing phenomenon a heart-beat, or a mode of representation, or a stage of development of absolute life. Life ascends as spirit, in the course of the overall evolution of the world towards spirit; it descends as matter. This theory answers the question of knowledge in terms of an 'intuition' which transcends all logic and all the operations of the intellect and directly apprehends the essential inner truth of things—which means that only life is capable of understanding life. That is why, in this way of thinking, all objective reality (the *object* of knowledge) had to be transformed into life, so that the epistemological process, conceived entirely as a function of life itself, could be sure of encountering an object essentially similar to itself, which it can thus wholly penetrate. Thus, whereas the original pragmatism dissolved our conception of the world into life only from the point of view of the subject, this has now been performed from the point of view of the object also. Nothing remains of form as a universal principle external to life, as a governing factor of existence with its own import and its own power. Any surviving remnant of form in this conception would exist only by the grace of life itself.

The repudiation of the principle of form culminates not only in pragmatism, but also in all those thinkers imbued with a modern sense of life who reject the coherent systems in which an earlier age, dominated by the classical notion of form, saw its entire philosophical salvation. Such systems attempt to unify all knowledge (at least with regard to its most general concepts) symmetrically, as it were, in a regular, harmonious edifice with dominant and subordinated elements, all based on one fundamental principle. In such a system, the architectural, aesthetic perfection, the achieved harmony and complete-ness of the edifice is regarded as proof (and this is the crucial point) of its objective correctness, the proof that existence has been truly grasped and comprehended in its entirety. This is the final culmination of the principle of form, for it makes intrinsic formal perfection and completeness the ultimate touchstone of truth.

It is against this that life is now on the defensive, for although it is forever creating forms, it is also forever bursting their bounds. These theories specify in two ways the philosophical significance which they claim for life. On the one hand, mechanism is rejected as a fundamental principle of the universe; it is, perhaps, a technique employed by life, perhaps a symptom of its decadence. On the other hand, the belief in ideas as metaphysically autonomous, as the supreme and absolute guiding principle or substance of all existence, is also rejected. Life refuses to be governed by anything subordinate to itself, but it also refuses to be governed at all, even by any ideal realm with a claim to superior authority. If, for all that, no higher life can escape the awareness of some guiding idea, be it a transcendental power, or some ethical or other value-based obligation, if this is so, it now seems to be possible, or to have any prospect of success, only by virtue of the fact that the ideas themselves come from life. It is the nature of life to produce within itself that which guides and redeems it, and that which opposes, conquers and is conquered by it. It sustains and enhances itself by way of its own products. The fact that these products confront it as independent judges is the very foundation of their existence, their *modus vivendi*. The opposition in which they thus find themselves to the life which is superior to them is the tragic conflict of life as mind. This conflict is now, of course, becoming more perceptible with the growing awareness that it is in fact created by life itself, and is therefore organically and ineluctably bound up with life.

In the most general cultural terms, this entire movement constitutes the repudiation of classicism as the absolute ideal of humanity and its evolution. For classicism is altogether dominated by form: harmonious, fulfilled, serene and self-contained, the confident norm of life and creativity. Here, too, it is certain that nothing positive, clear and satisfactory has, as yet, been found to put in place of the former ideal. This is why one can see that the battle against classicism is not, for the moment, concerned with creating a new cultural form at all. What is happening is simply that life, with its own self-assurance, is endeavouring to emancipate itself altogether from the formal restraint historically embodied in classicism.

A very brief look may be taken at the same basic trend underlying a specific phenomenon from the sphere of ethics. The term 'the new ethics' has been adopted for a critique of existing sexual relationships being propagated by a small number of people, but whose aspirations are widely shared. The critique is directed chiefly against two elements of the existing order of things: marriage and prostitution. The theme of the critique is, fundamentally, that erotic life is striving to assert its own authentic, inmost energy and natural proclivity against the forms in which our culture has in general imprisoned it, robbed it of its vitality and caused it to violate its own nature. Marriage is contracted in innumerable cases for other than actual erotic reasons, and thus, in innumerable cases, the vital erotic impulse either stagnates or perishes when its individuality comes up against inflexible traditions and legal cruelty. Prostitution, which has almost become a legalized institution, forces young people's love life to take on a debased form, a caricature which trangresses against its inmost nature. These are the forms against which authentic spontaneous life is in revolt. Under different cultural conditions, they would perhaps not be quite so inadequate, but at the present time they are being challenged by forces which spring from the deepest source of life. One can see here very much more clearly than in the other areas of our culture the almost complete lack hitherto of any positive new forms as a concomitant of the basic (and entirely positive) desire to destroy existing forms. No proposal put forward by these reformers is regarded at all generally as an adequate substitute for the forms which they condemn. The typical process of cultural change —struggle against an old form by a new form in a successful bid to replace it—has conspicuously failed to occur. The energy which should by rights occupy the new form is, for the time being, aimed directly, as it were naked, against those forms from which authentic erotic life has departed. Thus, in perpetrating the paradox which has by now been repeatedly stressed, it finds itself in a vacuum, for the moment erotic life enters any sort of cultural context, it simply must adopt a form of some kind. For all that, as in the areas discussed earlier, it is only the superficial observer who sees here merely licentiousness and anarchic lust. In this sphere, formlessness in itself does indeed appear in such a light; but at a deeper level (wherever this exists) matters are different. Authentic erotic life flows along wholly individual channels, and the above forms arouse hostility because they trap this life in institutionalized patterns and thus do violence to its special individuality. Here, as in many of the other cases, it is the struggle between life and form which, in a less abstract, metaphysical way, is being fought out as a struggle between individuality and standardization.

A tendency in current religious life must, it seems to me, be interpreted similarly. I refer here to the fact, which has been observable for the past ten or twenty years, that quite a number of intellectually progressive people find satisfaction for their religious needs in mysticism. It can be reasonably assumed, by and large, that they all grew up within the intellectual orbit of one of the existing churches. Their turn to mysticism very clearly reveals two motives. First, the forms which channel religious life by means of a series of specific, objective images no longer do justice to that life. Secondly, religious longings are not thereby killed, they merely seek other paths and goals. The decisive factor in the turn towards mysticism seems to be more than anything else its freedom from the clear contours and boundaries of religious forms. Here there is a divinity which transcends any personal (and hence, in people's minds, ultimately specific) form. Here there is an indefinite expansiveness of religious emotion, free from all dogmatic restrictions, given profundity in a formless infinity, and evolving solely from the yearning of the soul, transmuted into energy. Mysticism appears to be the last resort of religious individuals who cannot as yet dissociate themselves from all transcendental forms, but only (for the time being, as it were) from any fixed, specific form.

But the most profound impulse (no matter if it be self-contradictory and its goal eternally remote) is to my mind the impulse to replace the structures of faith by a religious life that is purely a functional quality of inner life: the spiritual state which once gave rise, and still does give rise, to such structures of faith. In the past, the evolution of religious culture has followed the course demonstrated throughout these pages: a particular form of religious life, initially wholly appropriate to the nature and energies of that life, gradually becomes externalized, constricted and inflexible. It is then ousted by a new form, which once again accommodates the spontaneous dynamism of the religious impulse in its current manifestation. What takes the place of the obsolete form is thus still a religious form, with various articles of faith. Today, however, the other-worldly objects of religious faith are being radically rejected, at least by very many people. But this does not mean that these people no longer have any religious needs. In the past, these basic needs revealed themselves in the creation of appropriate new dogmas. But today the whole situation of a believing subject confronted by something that is believed in is no longer felt to be a proper expression of the religious life. Taken to its ultimate conclusion, this whole spiritual evolution would make religion into a kind of direct mode of living, not a single melody, so to speak, within the symphony of life, but the key of the entire symphony. Life, in all its secular aspects, action and fate, thought and feeling, would be permeated in its entirety by that unique inner blend of humility and exaltation, tension and peace, vulnerability and consecration, which we can describe in no other way than as religious. Life thus lived would itself produce the sense of absolute value which, in the past, appeared to be derived from the specific forms of religious life, the particular articles of faith in which it had crystallized. A pre-echo of this, albeit transposed into the last surviving form of mysticism, can be heard in the writings of Angelus Silesius, where he rejects any restriction of religious values to specific forms and locates them in life itself as it is lived: 'The saint, when he drinks, pleases God as much as when he prays and sings.' It is not a question of so-called secular religion.

This, too, is still associated with a specific content, which is simply empirical rather than transcendental. It, too, channels religious life into certain forms of beauty and grandeur, sublimity and lyric emotion. It is, in essence, an obscure hybrid form, animated by the disguised surviving remnants of transcendental religiosity. What we are speaking of is religiosity as an all-embracing, spontaneous process of life. It is a state of being, not of having, a piety which is called faith when it has an object, but which now lies in the way life itself is lived. Needs are no longer satisfied by anything external. (The Expressionist painter likewise does not satisfy his artistic needs by faithful adherence to an external object.) What is sought is a continuity at that profound level where life has not yet split into needs and satisfactions and thus requires no object which would impose a specific form upon it. Life seeks religious expression of a direct kind, not using a language with a given vocabulary and fixed syntax. One might say (and it only appears to be a paradox) that the soul desires to preserve the quality of faith even though it no longer accepts any specific predetermined articles of faith.

This desire of religious souls is often perceptible in tentative beginnings, bizarre confusion, and critique that is wholly negative because its proponents do not understand their own sentiments. It faces, of course, the most intractable difficulty in the fact that spiritual life can, from the outset, only become articulate in *forms*. Its *freedom* likewise can only be actualized in forms, even though they also immediately restrict that freedom. Certainly piety or faith is a spiritual state entailed by the very existence of the soul; it would give life a particular colouring even if it never had any religious object—just as people of an erotic temperament would perforce retain and fulfil that temperament even if they never met anybody worthy of their love. Nevertheless, I doubt whether a fundamental religious need does not inevitably require an object. A purely functional quality, a formless dynamism which does no more than give a colour, a spiritual quality to the universal ebb and flow of life, appears to be the essence of much contemporary religious feeling. But I doubt whether this is not merely an interlude of an ideal nature which can never become reality, the symptom of a situation where existing religious forms are being repudiated by the inner religious life, which is, however, unable to replace them with new ones; and where, as elsewhere, the notion then arises that this life can entirely dispense with forms that have their own objective significance and legitimate claims, and be content to give free rein to its eruptive inner force. One of the most profound spiritual dilemmas of innumerable modern men is that although it is impossible to preserve the traditional church religions any longer, the religious impulse still exists. No amount of 'enlightenment' can destroy it, for it can only rob religion of its outer garment, not of its life. The intensification of religious life to the point of complete self-sufficiency, the transformation, as it were, of 'faith' from a transitive into an intransitive concept, is a tempting way out of the dilemma, but one which in the long run perhaps involves no small degree of self-contradiction.

Thus all these phenomena (and a number of others besides) reveal the conflict which arises from the inescapable essence of all cultural life in the widest sense of the word, whether creative or responsive to what has already been created. Such life must either produce forms, or proceed within given forms. What we *are* is, it is true, spontaneous life, with its equally spontaneous, unanalysable sense of being, vitality and purposiveness, but what we *have* is only its particular form at any one time, which, as I have stressed above, proves from the moment of its creation to be part of a quite different order of things. Endowed with the legitimacy and stature of its own provenance, it asserts and demands an existence beyond spontaneous life. This, however, goes against the essence of life itself, its surging dynamism, its temporal fortunes, the inexorable differentiation of all its elements. Life is ineluctably condemned to become reality only in the guise of its opposite, i.e. as *form*. This paradox becomes more acute, more apparently insoluble, to the degree that the inner being which we can only call life *tout court*[1] asserts its formless vitality, while at the same time inflexible, independent forms claim timeless legitimacy and invite us to accept them as the true meaning and value of our lives—i.e. the paradox is intensified, perhaps, to the degree to which culture progresses.

Thus life here aspires to the unattainable: to determine and manifest itself beyond all forms, in its naked immediacy. But knowledge, volition and creation, though wholly governed by life, can only replace one form by another; they can never replace form itself by the life that lies beyond form. All the onslaughts on the forms of our culture, passionate and iconoclastic or slow and cumulative, which either overtly or covertly oppose them with the power of life purely *qua* life because it is life, are revelations of the most profound internal paradox of the spirit wherever it evolves as culture, that is to say, takes on forms. Indeed it seems to me that of all the periods of history in which this chronic conflict has become acute and affected the entirety of life, no period has revealed as clearly as our own that this is its fundamental dilemma.

It is, however, pure philistinism to assume that all conflicts and problems are meant to be solved. Both have other functions in the history and make-up of life which they fulfil independently of any solution. Hence they are by no means pointless, even if the future resolves them not by solving them but merely by replacing their forms and contents with others. For, of course, all these problematic phenomena which we have discussed make us aware that the present state of affairs is far too paradoxical to be permanent. The dimensions of the problem clearly indicate some more fundamental change than the mere reshaping of an existing form into a new one. For, in such cases, the link between the past and the future hardly ever seems so completely shattered as at present, apparently leaving only intrinsically formless life to bridge the gap. But it is equally certain that the movement is towards the typical evolution of culture, the creation of new forms appropriate to present energies. This will only replace one problem, one conflict by another; though it may perhaps take longer to become conscious of it, open battle may be postponed for a longer period. But this is the true destiny of life, for life is struggle in the absolute sense that overrides the relative distinction between struggle and peace, while absolute peace, which perhaps also overrides this distinction, remains a divine mystery.

[New translation of *Der Konflict der modernen Kultur*, 2nd edition, Duncker & Humblot, Leipzig, 1921]

## NOTES AND REFERENCES

1. Life is the opposite of form, but obviously an entity can be conceptually described only if it has a form of some sort. Hence the term 'life', in the very fundamental sense meant here, is inevitably somewhat vague and logically imprecise. Life precedes or transcends all forms, and to succeed in giving a conceptual definition of it would be to deny its essence. Life can become conscious of itself only directly, by virtue of its own dynamism, not via the stratum of mediating concepts, which coincides with the realm of forms.

Thus the nature of the case restricts our ability to describe it, but this does not make the fundamental philosophical antagonism any less evident.

# The Meaning of Culture

All series of events arising from human activity can be regarded as nature, that is to say, as a causally determined development in which each stage must be explicable in terms of the configuration and dynamic forces of the preceding situation. Nor need any distinction be made between nature and history, thus understood. What we call history takes its place, when considered purely as a sequence of events, within the natural pattern of events in the material world, which can be causally apprehended. But as soon as any of the elements of these series are grouped under the concept of culture, the concept of nature thereby takes on a more restricted specific meaning. The 'natural' development of the series then only leads to a certain point, at which it is replaced by cultural development.

The wild pear tree produces hard, sour fruit. That is as far as it can develop under the conditions of wild growth. At this point, human will and intelligence have intervened and, by a variety of means, have managed to make the tree produce the edible pear; that is to say, the tree has been 'cultivated'. In just the same way we think of the human race first developing, by virtue of psycho-physical constitution, heredity and adaptation, to certain forms and modes of existence. Only then can teleological processes take over and develop these existing energies to a pitch that was quite impossible, in the nature of things, within the limits of their foregoing development. The point at which this change to a new evolutionary energy occurs marks the boundary between nature and culture.

Since, however, culture can also be causally derived from its 'natural' origins, we see, first, that nature and culture are only two different ways of looking at one and the same thing, and secondly, that 'nature', for its part, is being used in two different senses. It means both the all-embracing nexus of causally and temporally connected phenomena, and also a phase of development, viz. that phase in which only inherent energies are developed. This phase ends as soon as an intelligent will with *means* at its disposal takes up these energies and, with them, creates states which could not be attained by those energies unaided. If this seems to mean that the concept of culture is identical with that of purposive human activity in general, the concept needs to be qualified in order to pin down its special meaning. If one schoolboy trips another up so as to make him fall and make his friends laugh, this is without doubt an eminently teleological action, in which will and intelligence make use of natural circumstances. But it will not be regarded as an element of culture. The use of that concept depends, rather, on a number of conditions—operating unconsciously, if one wishes to put it thus—which can be determined only by a process of analysis which is not immediately obvious.

Cultivation presupposes the prior existence of an entity in an uncultivated, i.e. natural state. It also presupposes that the ensuing change of this entity is somehow latent in its *natural structure or energies*, even if it cannot be achieved by the entity itself but only through the process of culture. That is to say, cultivation develops its object to that perfection which is predetermined as a potential of its essential underlying tendency.

Hence we regard the pear tree as cultivated because the work of the gardener only develops the potential dormant in the organic constitution of its natural form, thus affecting the most complete evolution of its own nature. If, on the other hand, a tree trunk is made into a ship's mast, this, too, is undoubtedly the work of culture, but not a 'cultivation' of the tree trunk, because the form given it by the shipbuilder is not inherent in its nature. It is, on the contrary, a purely external addition imposed by a system of purposes alien to its own character.

Thus all cultivation, as the word is generally understood, is not only the development of some entity beyond the form attainable by natural processes alone. It is development in accordance with an original inner essence, the perfection of an entity in terms of its own significance, its most profound impulse. But his perfection is unattainable at the stage which we call natural, which consists in the purely causal development of initial inherent energies. It comes into being, rather, by the combination of those energies and the new teleological intervention, an intervention in the potential direction of the entity itself, which may thus be called the culture of that entity.

Strictly speaking, this means that only man himself is the real object of culture. For he is the only being known to us with an inherent *a priori* demand for perfection. His 'potential' is not simply the fact of latent energies, not the considerations and speculations aroused in the mind of an onlooker (as is the 'potential' garden pear seen in the wild pear tree), but rather it already has, so to speak, its own language. Whatever can be attained by the development of the soul is already present in its state at any time, as a feeling of urgency, as some invisible inner pattern. Even if its content is actualized only in a vague, fragmentary way, it is, for all that, a positive feeling of direction. Full development, as destiny and as capacity, is inseparably bound up with the existence of the human soul. It alone possesses the potential for development towards goals that are exclusively inherent in the teleology of its own being. However, it too cannot attain these goals purely through that growth from within which we call natural growth, but beyond a certain point it requires a 'technique', a procedure directed by the will.

Thus when we speak of the 'cultivation' of lower organisms, plants and animals (usage does not permit the term to be applied to inorganic entities), this is clearly only a transference based on the loose analogy between man and other organisms. For even if the state to which culture develops such entities is a potential of their organization and is in due course reached with the aid of their own energies, it is never inherent in the same way in the intrinsic meaning of their existence, it is never predetermined in their natural state as a kind of activity, in the way that the perfection attainable by the human soul is inherent therein.

This consideration, however, necessitates a further qualification of our concept. Even if culture is a perfection of man, it is by no means the case that any perfection of man constitutes culture. There are, on the contrary, developments which the soul achieves purely from within, or in the form of a relationship to transcendental powers, or in a direct ethical, erotic or emotional relationship with other people, and which cannot be included in the concept of culture. Religious exaltation, ethical dedication, strict preservation of the personality for its own unique task and mode of existence—all these are values which the soul achieves instinctively by its own nature or by self-improvement. They may entirely accord with our concept of culture: the maximum development of a person's potential from its natural stage, following the authentic intrinsic direction of the particular personality while necessitating the intervention of the highest spiritual powers to guide his energies. But for all that, it is not a matter of culture as we conceive it.

For culture implies also that such human development involves *something external to man.* Certainly, cultivatedness is a spiritual state, but of such a kind as is attained by the use of purposively formed *objects.*

This external, objective aspect is not to be understood only in a spatial sense. For example, forms of etiquette; refinement of taste revealed in critical judgement; the acquisition of tact, making the individual an agreeable member of society—all these are forms of culture which take the process of perfection into real and ideal spheres beyond the individual. Perfection here does not remain a purely immanent process, but takes the form of a unique adaptation and teleological interweaving of subject and object. If the development of the subjective soul does not involve any objective artefact as a means and stage of its progress back to itself, then even if values of the highest order are created, within the soul or in the outside world, it is not by way of culture in our specific sense. This also explains why certain highly introverted individuals, to whom it is abhorrent that the soul should seek self-perfection indirectly via anything external to itself, can feel hatred for culture.

This necessary duality in the concept of culture can be seen equally with regard to its objective element. We are accustomed automatically to label as cultural values the great series of artistic and moral, scientific and economic achievements. Perhaps they all are; but they are certainly not so by virtue of their purely objective, as it were autochthonous significance. The cultural significance of any particular achievement is by no means equivalent to its significance within its own series as determined by its specific nature and purpose. For example, a work of art is subject to quite different criteria and norms when considered within the sphere of art history or aesthetics, than when its cultural value is involved.

Each of these great series can be regarded on the one hand as an end in itself, so that each individual member of them constitutes a value which is proven directly by being enjoyed and giving satisfaction. On the other hand, they can all also be included in the cultural series, i.e. considered in respect of their significance for the overall development of individuals and society at large. Standing on their own ground, all these values resist inclusion in the cultural series. A work of art aspires only to perfection as measured by purely artistic criteria. In scientific research, all that matters are correct results; for the economic product, only the most efficacious manufacture and profitable utilization are of importance. All these spheres of the inner and outer world are developed teleologically beyond their 'natural' limitations; they thus, of course, become capable of functioning as cultural values. But, as autonomous objective spheres, they are *not* such values *per se*, but are subject to criteria and norms derived only from their objective content, not from the requirements of the unified centre of human personality. Their contribution to the development of human personality, i.e. their cultural value, is a different matter. Their status in this regard is by no means the same as in relation to the requirements of those specific interests pertaining only to one objective aspect of our lives. However excellently they may serve our specific ends, their value for our lives as a whole, for the wellspring of our being in its struggle for development, may be very slight. Conversely, they may be imperfect and insignificant in the objective, technical perspective of their specific province, but may, for all that, offer precisely what our life needs for the harmony of its parts, for its mysterious unity over and above all specific needs and energies.

We only ever perceive 'unity' as the interaction and dynamic interweaving, coherence and balancing of multiplicity; and so it is with that point of unity within us, whose inner significance and energy reach perfection in the cultural process by way of enhanced and perfected objects. To be more explicit: the various aspects of our lives exist in close interation, each supporting and supported by the others, harmoniously balancing and exchanging their vitality. That is why we are not cultured simply by virtue of particular knowledge or abilities. That is why specialist expertise, of no matter what objective degree, is not of itself culture, which is only created when such onesided attainments are integrated into the soul in its entirety, when they help to resolve discords between its elements by raising them all to a higher level, in short, when they help to perfect the whole as a unity. The criterion for assessing whatever we contribute or are able to appreciate within the categories of their specific objective series, must not be confused with the other criterion for evaluating these same things in the category of culture, i.e. the development of our inner *totality*.

This distinction illuminates the paradox that it is precisely the supreme achievements in various fields, especially those of a personal kind such as art, religion or speculative philosophy, whose *cultural* value is relatively secondary. The most impressive works and ideas impose their own intrinsic content and criteria on us so powerfully that their cultural significance is overshadowed. They refuse, as it were, to collaborate with other elements in the evolution of our whole being. They are too supreme within their own sphere for the subordinate role entailed in treating them as cultural factors, as means to the creation of a spiritual unity.

This will clearly apply with most force to those products of culture from which a personal life speaks most directly to the recipient. The more distinct a product is from the subjective spirituality of its creator, the more it belongs to an objective order with its own validity, then the more specific is its *cultural* significance, the more suitable it is to play a general part in the spiritual development of a large number of people.

The same is true of the 'style' of a work of art. We tend scarcely to consider the style of a really great work of art in which a sovereign spirit has found its unique mode of expression. For style is a *general* manner of expression common to many works, a form which can be abstracted from any particular content. But in the supreme work of art, the general foundation and the particular details of form are one unified revelation, in which any elements it may share with other works are wholly irrelevant. Such a work compels us to appreciate it in its uniqueness, not as an example of some general stylistic principle.

Likewise, anything very great or very personal may, in fact, have a very considerable cultural effect, but this category cannot provide the most significant locus to give the greatest prominence to its value. It can only do this with achievements which are essentially of a more general, impersonal kind, which are objectified at a greater distance from the subject, and can therefore more 'selflessly', as it were, provide stages in spiritual development.

Because culture, in a unique way, sets the contents of life at a point of intersection of subject and object, we may legitimately interpret the concept in two ways. The name of objective culture can be given to things, extended, enhanced and perfected as described above so as to lead the soul to its own perfection, or to constitute a part of the road to higher life of the individual or the community. By subjective culture, on the other hand, I understand the degree of personal development thus attained. Thus objective and subjective culture are co-ordinated concepts only if the former is understood in a figurative sense, viz. if one ascribes to things an independent impulse towards perfection, a consciousness that they ought to develop beyond their natural limits. The human energy which brings this about is then imagined to be only the means used by things, as it were, to this end. To describe things, the material contents of life, as 'cultivated' is to invert the order of the real process of cultivation which takes place within man. It is to create a symbolic parallel to this process by treating the development of things as if it were *per se* a teleological process, and then dividing it into a natural and a cultivated stage; the latter, as a self-sufficient and definitive stage proceeding in its ascent, or a part thereof, by means of the intervention of human activity.

But when understood more precisely, the two senses in which the concept of culture is used are not at all analogous. On the contrary, subjective culture is the overriding final goal, and its measure is the measure of how far the spiritual process of life has any part in those objective entities and their perfection. Clearly there can be no subjective culture without an objective culture, because a subjective development or state constitutes culture only by virtue of its inclusion of such objects. Objective culture, on the other hand, can, relatively speaking, become substantially (though not completely) independent of subjective culture, by the creation of 'cultivated' objects—i.e. 'cultivating' objects, as they should properly be understood, whose value as such is subjectively utilized only to an incomplete degree. Especially in highly developed epochs based on division of labour, the achievements of culture acquire the extent and coherence of a realm with its own kind of independent existence. Objects become more perfect, more intellectual, they follow more and more obediently their own inner logic of material expediency. But real culture, that is, subjective culture, does not progress equally; indeed, it *cannot* in view of the vast expansion of the objective realm of things, divided up as it is between innumerable contributors. To put it at its lowest, historical development tends increasingly to widen the gap between concrete creative cultural achievements and the level of individual culture. The disharmony of modern life, in particular the intensification of technology in every sphere combined with deep dissatisfaction with it, arises largely from the fact that things become more and more cultivated but people are capable only to a lesser degree of deriving from the improvement of objects an improvement of their subjective lives.

[New translation of Georg Simmel, 'Von Wesen der Kultur', *Osterreichische Rundschau*, 1908]

# The Future of Our Culture

As far as I can see, the reason for the apparent pessimism of the majority of philosophical minds regarding the present state of culture is the widening gulf between the culture of things and personal culture. As a result of the division of labour during the last few centuries, the technology at our service and the knowledge, arts, life-styles and interests at our disposal have expanded to an unprecedented variety. But the individual's capacity to use this increased raw material as means of personal culture increases only very slowly and lags further and further behind. We can no longer absorb into our lives all those things, which multiply as if in obedience to an inexorable fate indifferent to us. They develop their own purely objective life, which we are almost entirely unable even to understand.

What the Ancient Greeks created in politics and science, strategy and scope for pleasure, had a sufficiently consistent style and simple structure to be grasped to some extent by any educated man. He could, without difficulty, make use of the sum total of objective culture to build up his own subjective culture. Thus they could both evolve in a harmony which, in the modern age, has been destroyed as they have become independent of each other. In our indescribably complex culture, individual ideas and achievements leave behind permanent forms in which the fruits of individual lives become independent of those lives. There are too many of them for the individual to absorb them all: their inevitable lack of a common style is enough to make this profoundly impossible. The subjectivism of modern personal life, its rootless, arbitrary character, is merely the expression of this fact: the vast, intricate, sophisticated culture of things, of institutions, of objectified ideas robs the individual of any consistent inner relationship to culture as a whole, and casts him back again on his *own* resources.

The real cultural malaise of modern man is the result of this discrepancy between the objective substance of culture, both concrete and abstract, on the one hand, and, on the other hand, the subjective culture of individuals who feel this objective culture to be something alien, which does violence to them and with which they cannot keep pace. In many quarters today there is a feeling that we are deficient in culture by comparison with the Athens of Pericles, or with Italy in the fifteenth and sixteenth centuries, or, indeed, with many less outstanding eras. But we are not lacking in any particular elements of culture. No increase in knowledge, literature, political achievements, works of art, means of communication or social manners can make good our deficiency. The possession of all these things does not, in itself, make a man cultured, any more than it makes him happy. Culture appears to me rather to lie in the relationship of the subjective spiritual energies concentrated and unified in the self to the realm of objective, historical or abstract values. A man is cultured when these objective values, of a spiritual or even of an external nature, become part of his personality in such a way that it advances beyond the 'natural' degree of perfection, i.e. that which it can attain entirely by its own resources. Neither what we are purely in ourselves (be it the greatest ethical, intellectual, religious or other potential), nor the fruits of the labours of humanity by which we are surrounded (be they of overwhelming scope and perfection) can constitute the pinnacle of culture, but only the harmonious improvement of the former by the fruitful inward assimilation of the latter.

Throughout history, some eras have given greater emphasis to the task of increasing the elements of objective culture, others to that of enabling the individual to derive from that objective culture the subjective state of mind which is the ultimate purpose of culture. But the former has never been brought about by any explicit cultural policy as such, but always by the particular interests and energies of individual sections of society. On the contrary, the great eras that did have a cultural policy (even if not conceived or described as such) always concentrated on the subjective factor: the *education* of the *individual*. No cultural policy can eliminate the tragic discrepancy between objective culture, with its unlimited capacity for growth, and subjective culture, which can grow only slowly. But it can work towards reducing that discrepancy by enabling the individual to make better and more rapid use of the elements of objective culture in our lives as the raw material of subjective culture, which, when all is said and done, is the only thing that gives the former any real value.

[New translation of Georg Simmel, 'Die Zukunft unserer Kultur', *Frankfurter Zeitung*, 1909]

# The Crisis of Culture

Anyone who discusses culture must define this ambiguous concept in accordance with his particular purpose. I understand it to be that improvement of the soul which the latter attains not directly from within, as with the profundity that is the fruit of religion or with moral purity and primary creativity, but indirectly, by way of the intellectual achievements of the species, the products of its history: knowledge, life-styles, art, the state, a man's profession and experience of life—these constitute the path of culture by which the subjective spirit returns to itself in a higher, improved state. Therefore all behaviour intended to increase our culture is bound up with the form of means and ends. This behaviour is, however, fragmented into countless separate activities. Life is made up of modes of action which, only to a very limited extent, have, or can be seen to have, any common direction. The resulting tendency towards fragmentariness and uncertainty of purpose is maximized by the fact that the various means which serve our ends, our 'technology' in the widest sense of the word, are constantly becoming both more extensive and more intensive. The resulting immensity of the series of ends and means gives rise to a phenomenon of incalculably far-reaching consequences: certain members of these series become, in our consciousness, ends in themselves. Innumerable things which, objectively speaking, are no more than a transitional stage, a means to our real ends, appear to us while we are striving for them, and often even after we have achieved them, as the fulfilment of an ultimate ambition. We need this relative emphasis within our aspirations because they are so extensive and complex that our energy and courage would flag if we had only our real ultimate goal (which is Heaven knows how remote) as an incentive. The vast intensive and extensive growth of our technology—which is much more than just material technology—entangles us in a web of means, and means towards means, more and more intermediate stages, causing us to lose sight of our real ultimate ends. This is the extreme inner danger which threatens all highly developed cultures, that is to say, all eras in which the whole of life is overlaid with a maximum of multi-stratified means. To treat some means as ends may make this situation psychologically tolerable, but it actually makes life increasingly futile.

A second internal contradiction of culture arises from the same source. Those objective artefacts which are the precipitate of a creative life and which are, in due course, absorbed by other people as a means of acquiring culture, immediately begin to develop independently in accordance with the particular *objective* factors involved in their creation. Industries and sciences, arts and organizations impose their content and pace of development on individuals, regardless of or even contrary to the demands that these individuals ought to make for the sake of their own improvement, i.e. the acquisition of culture. The more finely wrought and perfect in their own way are those things which both have their basis in culture and are themselves the basis of culture, the more they follow an immanent logic which is by no means always appropriate to the process of individual development and self-realization, which is the whole point of all the products of culture as such. We are confronted by countless objectifications of the mind: works of art, social forms, institutions, knowledge. They are like kingdoms administered according to their own laws, but they demand that we should make them the content and norm of our own individual lives, even though we do not really know what to do with them, indeed often feel them to be a burden and an impediment. But it is not only this qualitative dissociation that sets a barrier between the objective and the subjective aspects of higher cultures. It is also, in a crucial way, a matter of quantitative vastness. One book after another, one invention after another, one work of art after another all add up to an endless, formless mass confronting the individual with the demand that he absorb it all. But the individual, with his predetermined nature and limited capacity for absorption, can only meet this demand to a visibly diminishing degree. This creates the typical problematic situation of modern man: the feeling of being overwhelmed by this immense quantity of culture, which he can neither inwardly assimilate nor simply reject, since it all belongs potentially to his cultural sphere. Left to evolve in its own way, what one might call the culture of *things* has unlimited scope for development, and the result of this is that people's interests and hopes increasingly turn towards *this* culture, at the expense of the apparently much more restricted finite task of individual personal culture.

These, then, are the two most profound dangers for ripe and over-ripe cultures: first, that the ends of life become subordinate to its means, with the inevitable result that many things which are only means acquire the psychological status of ends; and secondly, that the objective products of culture develop independently in obedience to purely objective norms, and thus both become profoundly estranged from subjective culture and advance far too rapidly for the latter to keep pace with them.

As I see the matter, all the phenomena which have, for some time now, given us the sense of an impending cultural crisis can be attributed to these two basic factors and their ramifications. All the restlessness, the overt covetousness and craving for pleasure of our age are merely a consequence of, and a reaction to, this situation: that people seek personal values on a plane where they are simply not to be found. The fact that technological progress is unquestioningly equated with cultural progress; the fact that, in intellectual fields, methods are often considered sacred and more important than results; the fact that the desire for money far exceeds the desire for the things it can buy; all these facts prove that ends and goals are gradually being usurped by means and methods. If these are the symptoms of an ailing culture, does then the war mark the outbreak of the crisis, which can become the first step towards recovery?

I do not venture to assert without reservation that the first group of phenomena in this pathology of culture—the disparity between personal culture and the culture of things—offers any prospect of a cure. We probably have here an internal paradox inseparable from the very nature of culture. For culture, after all, means the cultivation of the individual by means of the cultivation of the world of things, and the latter is capable of unlimited refinement, acceleration and expansion, whereas the capacity of the individual is ineluctably one-sided and limited. Therefore I do not see any way in theory of preventing fragmentation and the state of simultaneous dissatisfaction and over-satiation. Even so, the war does seem to be helping to narrow the rift in two ways. For the soldier, the whole system of culture pales into insignificance, not only because he is, in fact, compelled to do without it, but because in wartime the meaning and demands of life are focused on activity of whose value one is conscious without the mediation of any external things. Strength and courage, skill and stamina, prove themselves in direct activity as the values of life, and the 'war machine' visibly has a quite different, infinitely more vital relationship than a factory machine to the men involved in its operation. This is the only sphere where personal life is not usurped by objective activity, however much the vast expansion of events and the negligible quality of the individual contribution provide the conditions for this usurpation, conditions which under normal circumstances would certainly have that effect. Of course, the war situation has no actual bearing on the general cultural tension between the subjectivity of life and its material content. Of course, this tension is in the nature of things insurmountable. But even so, people who have seen it surmounted on the battlefield may perhaps also perceive the significance of their other anonymous, partial contributions to society more clearly and in a more personal way. They may more resolutely seek the connection between the work they do for the means of life and the ultimate values of personal life. And whether they find it or not, the search itself is of immeasurable value. If there is a general hope that this war may create closer bonds between the individual and the community, and may somehow temper the dichotomy of the individual as an end in himself and as a member of the community, then the problem touched on here is one context in which this dichotomy operates. By seeing how the tiny scope of his individual activity can completely absorb all his energy and willpower, the soldier—and to a certain extent also the wartime civilian—will have been given a sense at least of the *form* such a reconciliation might take, a sense of some meaningful relationship between the part and the whole, the *thing* and the *person*—even if this is no more than a pause for breath before fresh strife and alienation.

This theme can be elaborated in a particular direction in the light of our present situation. It seems to me that a number of particular contemporary cultural phenomena demonstrate in the clearest possible fashion a process which can be observed throughout the entire history of culture. It is, on the one hand, the process of interaction between life, which is in a constant state of flux and expansion of its energies, and on the other hand its historical forms of expression on forms which remain, or at least attempt to remain, fixed and permanent. The growth of Naturalism in the arts towards the end of the last century was an indication that the dominant art forms inherited from the classical era were no longer capable of accommodating a life which was clamouring for expression. It was hoped that it would be possible to capture this life in direct images of reality which, as far as possible, were not filtered through any personal artistic conception. But naturalism failed to satisfy this crucial need, just as contemporary Expressionism, which replaced concrete images by the direct expression of psychological processes, surely also fails. Here the idea is that by externalizing inner dynamics in a work of art without regard to either the form appropriate to that work or to objectively valid norms, life could at last be given the form of expression genuinely appropriate to it without any falsification by external forms. But it seems to be in the nature of inner life that it can only ever be expressed in forms which have their own laws, purpose and stability arising from a degree of autonomy independent of the spiritual dynamics which created them. Creative life is constantly producing something that is not life, that somehow destroys life, that opposes life with its own valid claims. Life cannot express itself except in forms which have their own independent existence and significance. This paradox is the real, ubiquitous tragedy of culture. What individual genius, and eras of special creativity, achieve is to give to the creative life that wells up from the inner fountainhead a felicitous and harmonious form which, for a time at least, preserves that life without hardening into an independent existence hostile to it. But, in the great majority of cases, the paradox is unavoidable. Where the expression of life attempts to avoid it by presenting itself, as it were, formless and naked, what actually results is unintelligible, inarticulate, not an expression of anything at all, but merely a chaos of fragmentary vestiges of form as a substitute for a form which is unified, even if it is also inflexible, alien and at odds with its content.

Futurism has advanced to this extreme consequence of our situation in the arts: a passionate desire for the expression of life, for which traditional forms are inadequate, but for which no new forms have been devised, and which therefore seeks pure expression in a negation of form, or in forms that are almost provocatively abstruse—a violation of the very nature of creativity in order to escape its other inherent paradox. Nowhere, perhaps, do we see more forcefully than in some of the manifestations of futurism that once again the forms that life created as dwelling-places have become its prisons.

It is, perhaps, not possible to determine how matters stand in this respect with regard to religion, because the decisive factors are not visible phenomena but the inner life of the soul. As regards Christianity specifically, what has been stated in these pages as a fundamental intellectual result of the war holds good: that it has given both inner and outer reality to those rifts which, though structurally inherent in our society, were not actualized in peacetime. We all know the great polarization that has split the religious life of our times, affecting everyone except Christians of convenience and people with absolutely no religious sense at all: the split between Christianity and a religion which repudiates any historical content, whether it be undogmatic monotheism, or pantheism, or a purely inward spiritual condition not entailing any specific beliefs. The age, with its universal religious tolerance, exerted no pressures on men to choose. If I am not mistaken, it frequently allowed a situation to arise where, on the more conscious level of the mind, a man could believe he had adopted one of these positions, while deeper down the other belief (whether old or new) was, in fact, more powerful and influential. The spiritual forces of religion have been unmistakably vitalized and enhanced by the war to a degree which demands from each and every man a decision as to where he ultimately stands. The peaceful age of gradual transitions, of hybrid forms, of that pleasant twilit zone where one can indulge alternately even in mutually exclusive attitudes—this age, we may safely assume, is past and gone. It is to be hoped that the resoluteness with which, in these years, the German people is travelling along its appointed road will also penetrate to this inmost area of decision. But nowhere will it encounter such a hollow truce as in the religious sphere, where real Christians, in obedience to some intellectual quirk, adopt an undogmatic pantheistic stance, while decided unbelievers talk themselves into a kind of Christianity by 'symbolically' adapting basic Christian teachings. Any person of some maturity will presumably have long since made his decision—except that because of the peculiar cultural broadmindedness which our situation seemed to permit, or even demand, that decision was often intermingled with, or concealed by, its opposite. This is, however, no longer possible in a period of radical eruption of man's religious depths. No matter how far either attitude is visible to the outside world: within men's souls, what is ripe for supremacy will come into its own.

In our present context the essential fact is the existence of large social groups who, in pursuit of their religious needs, are turning away from Christianity. The fact that they are turning to all sorts of exotic, far-fetched and bizarre new doctrines appears to be of no importance whatsoever. Nowhere among them, except in isolated individual cases, can I discern any genuinely viable belief providing an adequate and precise expression of the religious life. On the other hand, the widespread rejection of any fixed form of religious life is in keeping with our general cultural situation. Thus supra-denominational mysticism has by far the strongest appeal to these groups. For the religious soul hopes to find here direct spontaneous fulfilment, whether in standing naked and alone, as it were, before its God, without the mediation of dogma in any shape or form, or in rejecting the very idea of God as a petrefaction and an obstacle, and in feeling that the true religion of the soul can only be its own inmost metaphysical life not moulded by any forms of faith whatever. Like the manifestations of futurism touched on above, this wholly formless mysticism marks the historical moment when inner life can no longer be accommodated in the forms it has occupied hitherto, and because it is unable to create other, adequate forms, concludes that it must exist without any form at all.

Within the development of philosophy, this crisis seems to me to be more far-reaching than is generally admitted. The basic concepts and methodology which have been elaborated since classical antiquity and applied to the raw material of life in order to shape it into philosophical images of the world, have, I believe, achieved this to the highest degree of which they are capable. The philosophical instinct of which they were the expression has, with their help, evolved into ways of thinking, impulses and needs to which they are no longer appropriate. If the signs do not deceive us, our entire system of philosophy is beginning to become an empty shell.

It seems to me that there is one category of phenomena where one can see this particularly clearly. All the great concepts in the history of philosophy have served the task of bringing absolute unity into the fragmented, chaotic plenitude of life. But, alongside each such concept, there also exists, or arises, another concept incompatible with the first. Thus these basic concepts appear as pairs of opposites, between which one is expected to make a choice. Any phenomenon which is incompatible with one concept must of necessity be compatible with the other: one must say Yea or Nay, there is no third way. To this category belong the antinomies of the finiteness and infinity of the universe; the mechanism and teleology of organisms; free will and determinism; phenomenon and noumenon; absolute and relative; truth and error; unity and multiplicity; progress and immutability of values in human evolution. It seems to me that a great number of these pairs of opposites no longer permit a clear decision to allocate any dubious case definitely to the one concept or the other. This whole conceptual logic is felt to be so undesirably constricting, and at the same time its solutions are so rarely derived from any previously discovered third factor, but rather remain a challenge and a gap in our understanding, that this must surely indicate a profound philosophical crisis, one which brings all the specialized problems together in a general trend, albeit one which for the moment can only be negatively defined. The failure of the conceptual alternatives hitherto accepted as logically valid, and the demand for an as yet indefinable third possibility, make it more unmistakably clear than does anything else that our resources for mastering reality by giving it intellectual expression are no longer adequate to their task. They no longer accommodate what we wish to express, it transcends them, and seeks new forms, which as yet announce their arcane presence only as intuition or perplexity, desire or clumsy groping.

Perhaps the war, for all its destruction, confusion and danger, would not have had such a shattering effect had it not encountered cultural forms that were already so eroded and lacking in self-assurance. Here, also, what it has done is to make external reality give more scope and clarity to inner necessity. It has forced the individual to face the drastic decision as to whether he wishes to keep intellectual life on the old beaten track at any price, or whether he has the courage to seek new paths through the new terrain of life, whatever the risk, or whether perhaps he shall attempt what is even more perilous: to salvage the values of the former life from the collapse of their forms and carry them over into the new life. And here, at least, we can perhaps already discern the quest for a universal interpretation of life, even if as yet feeble and blurred: an illuminating basic concept, which I shall attempt to indicate in due course, which might make possible a continuity between the values of yesterday and those of tomorrow.

With more tangible significance, contemporary experience appears to play a part in the other cultural development, the elevation of means to ends in themselves. This modification of the teleological sequence has occurred, above all, in a sphere which provides the most far-reaching example in world history of the superimposition of means upon ends: the economic sphere. This example, it need scarcely be said, is *money*: a medium of exchange and balancing of values which, apart from this mediating function, is totally devoid of value and meaning, an absolute nullity. And it is precisely money which, for the majority of men in our culture, has become the supreme end. It is the possession of money which tends to be the ultimate goal, however rationally unfounded, of all the purposive activity of this majority. True, the expansion of the economy makes this dislocation of values understandable. For since it has ensured that any commodity can be obtained at any place and any time, the satisfaction of most human desires depends solely on possessing the required amount of money. In the mind of modern man, to be in need means not to be in need of material goods, but only of the money to buy them. The exclusion of Germany from the world market, which used to supply it with whatever quantities of goods were desired (making consumption purely a question of money) has brought about a most revolutionary change. Food, which used to be freely accessible provided one had money, has become scarce and its provision unreliable, and this has re-established its status as an absolute value. Money, on the other hand, which has at least forfeited its previous *unlimited* efficacy, can be seen to be in itself utterly powerless.

Even if this development is by no means complete, the bread ration-card at least symbolizes the uselessness of even the greatest wealth. In former times, the concepts of thrift and wastefulness, even when applied to particular material objects, only ever really referred to their monetary value. But now monetary value has become quite irrelevant. At last people are again being asked to economize with meat and butter, bread and wool, for the sake of these commodities themselves. This change may sound simple, but it totally reverses a sense of economic value which has been nurtured for centuries in the civilized world. A single gap has appeared in the most far-reaching example in the history of civilization of the concealment of what is really of value behind the means of obtaining it. There is, of course, no doubt that the gap will be closed again. The efficiency and omnipresence of the world economy will, in due course, make us forget that it is not money that is valuable, but things. Nobody will imagine that the grave consequences of this misconception will not reappear: the idea that everything has its price, the evaluation of things purely in terms of their monetary value, scepticism regarding any values that cannot be expressed in terms of money. The creeping crisis of culture arising from these attitudes will undoubtedly continue. But it is equally beyond doubt that the discovery that money is not what matters— is, indeed, of no use at all at the present time—will in a peculiar way jolt many people into reconsidering their attitudes. Such psychological moods and changes of mood cannot, of course, be documented. But however uncertain the consequences, and however superficial the occasion, for once a blow has been dealt to the absolute status of money value. For once it has been seen that money is no substitute for the value of economic commodities, and this mere fact in itself seems to me to be a profound psychological gain. A more sensitive, less blasé—I would even go so far as to say a more reverent—relationship to the commodities which we consume daily cannot but be felt by people who have been compelled for once to see their direct importance and the unimportance to which money is reduced the moment it ceases to function as a medium.

There is one further sense, and this time an absolute sense, in which the war reverses the relationship of ends and means. Self-preservation is customarily man's central concern. Work and love, thinking and volition, religious practices and our attempts to influence the course of our destiny: all these are aimed, by and large, at preserving the existence and development of the self, which are constantly threatened—by external danger and inner weakness, by our problematic relationships with the outside world, and by the insecurity of our material circumstances. Apart from those very rare people who really do devote their lives solely to an objective goal, the preservation of the self—which may include the selves of one's nearest and dearest—is *the* end, and all life the direct or indirect means to it. But, above this end, the war has, for millions of people, set the end of victory and the preservation of the nation, an end to which the individual life has all at once become a mere means, in respect of both its preservation and its sacrifice. The former appears even more important than the latter. The idea that a soldier goes into battle in order to sacrifice himself is emotionalism, and highly misleading. The fatherland is served not by dead soldiers, but by living ones. Where this service demands the sacrifice of life, this is, so to speak, an extreme case, which merely shows with maximum clarity that the self has lost its status as an ultimate end and, whether preserved or sacrificed, has declared itself a means to a higher end.

Of course, self-preservation will regain its old position at the head of the teleological series. But even so, one thing seems to me undeniable. The malaise of our culture, the elevation of everything that is relative and provisional into ultimate values, will not come about quite so easily in a generation which has seen for itself that it was possible even for self-preservation, usually the most autonomous of ultimate ends, to become a mere means to an end. From the very beginning of the war, there has been a prevalent feeling that, in an indefinite number of ways, it will bequeath to us a new scale of values; and in this one respect, at least, this will prove to be true. To attach ultimate significance to relatively secondary aspects of life is one of the psychological dangers of long periods of comfortable and undisturbed peace. They provide unrestricted scope for the greatest variety of activities; no violent upheavals compel men to make their choice between what is of primary and what is of secondary importance. But anyone who has once seen what is usually the most important thing in life—the self and its preservation—become a means to something higher, ought to be immune for a while to that squandering of end-status on what is relatively insignificant and peripheral.

These dangers which I have indicated converge, as if in a common symptom, in the fact that all the spheres of culture to which I have alluded have developed independently of and alien to one another—that is, until recent years, when, it is true, more unified overall tendencies have again become discernible. This is the reason for the much-discussed *lack of style* of our era. For style is always a general form which gives a common quality to a variety of individual artefacts of differing content. The more the spirit of the people (to use this problematic phrase for the sake of brevity) colours everything that is created during a particular period by virtue of its unity of character, the more style that period appears to us to have. That is why earlier centuries, which were not burdened with such an abundance of heterogenous and infinitely seductive traditions and resources, had so much more style than the present, where in innumerable cases one individual activity is completely isolated from all others. True, in recent years, perhaps since Nietzsche, a certain change has begun here. The concept of *life* now seems to permeate a multitude of spheres and to have begun to give, as it were, a more unified rhythm to their heartbeat. I believe that the war will be very conducive to this process. For, apart from the common ultimate goal which contemporary cultural movements of all kinds have embraced, they are all suffused with a passionate vitality bursting forth as if from one common source of energy.

Countless forms which had begun to harden and become immune to creative dynamism have been drawn back into the stream of life. We suspected recently that all the diverse phenomena of culture were emanations or media, heartbeats or products of the process of life itself. Now all the aspects of our consciousness seem even more palpably to have been melted down and re-fused in the increased momentum of the stream of life. It seems certain that the soldier, at least when engaged in vigorous action, feels this action to be an enormous increase in the quantity of life, so to speak, and to be in more direct proximity to its surging dynamism than he is able to feel in his usual working activities. The supreme concentration of energy pervading the life of an entire nation does not allow that independent consolidation of its diverse elements which, in peacetime, sets up these elements of culture as separate, mutually alien entities, each obeying only its particular individual laws. There is a mysterious congruence in the fact that the immense events of our day came, in a way, at the right time to vindicate this incipient spiritual tendency to seek the unity of divergent phenomena in the depths of the life process itself. Of course, the experience of these events has no direct visible effect on the rifts and internal disparities in the moral, intellectual, religious and artistic spheres of our culture. And it is equally certain that, even if such an effect occurs, it will gradually fade away again in that tragic development which appears inevitable in highly developed objective cultures. But there is to my mind no doubt that, within these limits, the war does have this positive significance, on the *form* of our culture, notwithstanding its destruction of the substance of that culture. Not only have the common goal and the common danger given our people, as the sum total of its individuals, an unsuspected unity—regardless of how far it is permanent, how far only temporary. The unprecedented enhancement and excitement in the lives of each and every one of us has also promoted this fusion, this coming together in one single stream. And, likewise, it will for a while give a new dynamic impetus to the objective elements of culture, and thus new scope and encouragement to become reintegrated, to break out of that rigidity and insularity which had turned our culture into a chaos of disjointed individual elements devoid of any common style. As I have said, we shall not, in the long run, escape this tragedy and chronic crisis of all culture. But, for a certain period, its progress will be slowed down, its intensity tempered.

Faced with the ultimate paradoxes of cultural life, we cannot, however, hope for more than this. They are, indeed, developing as if towards a crisis, and thus towards strife and gloom to which we can see no end. That mere means are regarded as ultimate ends, completely distorting the rational order of both inner and practical life; that objective culture is developing to an extent and at a pace that leave subjective culture, which alone gives significance to the perfection of objects, further and further behind; that the separate branches of culture are evolving in different directions towards mutual estrangement, that culture as a whole has already, in fact, suffered the fate of the Tower of Babel and its most profound value, which lies precisely in the integration of its parts, appears threatened with annihilation: all these things are paradoxes which are probably inseparable from the evolution of culture as such. Their ultimate logical consequence would be the continuation of this development to the point of destruction, if they were not repeatedly opposed by the positive and meaningful forces of culture, and if upheavals did not come from totally unsuspected quarters, which—often at a high price—temporarily bring cultural life, that is approaching total disintegration, to its senses.

The devastation of the war belongs, as far as we can see, to this category. It will, perhaps, once and for all remove some individual elements of contemporary culture, and create some new ones. But, as regards its effect on the fundamental inner form of all cultures, which at the summit of their development take the form of a permanent imminent crisis, it can inaugurate only a single scene or act of this endless drama. We can thus understand how this war, which seems to us to be the most momentous event since the French Revolution, with the most decisive implications for the future, can, in our prognosis, create these disparate consequences for our culture. On the one hand, it will remove certain things for ever and create certain entirely new things; but on the other hand, it will retard or reverse certain developments, which none the less seem inevitably certain to revert to their former course. The former relates to individual elements of culture, the latter to the innermost fate of its forms. Thus the merely relative and temporary quality of the latter effect does not in any way diminish the significance of the war for our culture. For this very quality integrates it into the fundamental rhythm—a tragic one, it is true—of culture, its constantly jeopardized balance, which can only be preserved by constant defensive action. Here, where it is a matter of the life of an entire form of culture, to expect any absolute, definitive solution (even within the limits of what is possible in a historical perspective) would do not more but less justice to that very life itself.

As I have said, the most basic comprehensive definition of the destiny of a highly developed culture is that it is a constant delayed crisis. I mean by this that its tendency is to cause life, in which it originates and which it is intended to serve, to disintegrate into futility and paradox. Again and again the fundamental dynamic unity of life defends itself against this tendency. Drawing on the very source of life itself, it reimposes unity on that objectivity which is alien to life and which estranges life from itself. And that is why we, in this era, stand at a high-water mark of history, because the disintegration and perversion of cultural life has reached an extreme, and life has risen in revolt against it in the shape of this war, with its unifying, simplifying and concentrated force. Even if this be only one wave in the infinite ocean of the life of mankind, no other wave has been raised to such a height and breadth by the friction of its forces. We stand deeply moved before the magnitude of this crisis, which it is utterly impossible for the individual to take the measure of. But, at the same time, the crisis is deeply familiar and intelligible to us. For in each of us it is, consciously or not, the crisis of our own soul.

[New translation. From Georg Simmel, *Der Krieg und die geistigen Entscheidungen*, Duncker & Humblot, Leipzig, 1917]

# The Idea of Europe

Is this war a paroxysm, one of those fevers by which whole peoples are seized at times as if by an epidemic, such as medieval flagellantism, and from which they awake one day shattered and unable to comprehend how such insanity was ever possible—or is it an immense breaking and ploughing of the European soil to make it yield values and developments whose nature we today cannot even guess? This was the case with the migrations of races, which to the civilized peoples of antiquity must have seemed mere senseless destruction and incomprehensible despoilation, yet which nevertheless created the conditions for a vitality and productivity of infinite value which could not have been conceived of beforehand. The fact that nobody can give a theoretical answer to this question does not lessen the urgency with which it pursues us day and night, but it does permit the practical summons to devote all our powers to ensuring that what becomes reality shall not be the senseless alternative but the meaningful one. Of course, as far as the urgency is concerned, this also represents not a diminution but only a shift of perspective—because now every moment of our lives is laden with an immense responsibility such as has never been known in peace-time. For, in peace-time, our goals and tasks are set clear and close before us, and therefore most of us consider ourselves responsible only for them, letting the impenetrable future take care of itself in a similar fashion. But now we can see no firm outline which we should be preparing ourselves to give body to, but rather the tasks facing us extend into regions that are impenetrable and thus, for us, without contour. Certainly, it is as true now as ever, and more than ever, that ripeness is all. But the world for which we need to be ripe will be a new world, perhaps one that nobody as yet has any idea of, a world of which we know only that we are responsible for it, and for making it meaningful, in everything that we do or think. Of course, losses and gains confront each other in an equation, or non-equation, that cannot yet be solved. Despite all the profundity of those philosophers of history who speculatively establish the 'necessity' of this war, I remain convinced that it would not have been sparked off had it not been for the blindness and criminal frivolity of a handful of Europeans. But now that it has happened, we have witnessed in it a blossoming of powers and an ardent capacity for self-sacrifice of unprecedented magnitude. And yet, on the other hand, in Germany itself these values are countered by those repellent manifestations of greedy selfishness that everybody is familiar with. Today, when we are paying for all present and future gains with the loss of our nearest and dearest and with the suicidal destruction of existing European values, who dares decide whether our great-grandchildren will bless or curse this disaster?—However uncertain as yet the final balance sheet of this war is for us, the living, however much it remains no more than a task to be undertaken, we have suffered *one* loss about which there is no doubt, one which is sheer loss and nothing else: the spiritual unity that we used to call 'Europe' is shattered, and no prospect of its restoration is in sight. And nobody can seriously believe that it might continue to exist without including Germany and Austria. This, I say, is an unmitigated loss; for it is certainly not the price for which increased German power and purity will be achieved. True, this is bound to be the result of the war, but what is being sacrificed to that end is merely internationalism—in its grotesquely heightened form it is mere globetrotting—which is a hotchpotch, a characterless, indiscriminate mêlée of interests and ideas, at most something abstracted from many nations by disregarding their particular individual values. The internationalist character and way of thinking, which has, alas, proved fatal to many Germans as well as others, is an altogether secondary phenomenon, arising from a simple process of either addition or subtraction, and it is the enemy of any national entity with its own roots. Europeanism, on the other hand, is an *idea*, an altogether primary phenomenon not attainable by abstraction or accumulation—however late its appearance as a historical force. It does not exist in between individual nations, it exists beyond them, and is thus perfectly compatible with any individual national life. This ideal 'Europe' is the locus of spiritual values which the contemporary cultured man reveres and which can be his if his nationality is an inalienable possession without being a blinkering limitation. It is an undeniable fact that the 'Europeans' of the last few decades have been to an extreme degree men of national character: Bismarck and Darwin, Wagner and Tolstoy, Nietzsche and Bergson. None of them is internationalist or cosmopolitan (only in Nietzsche are there the theoretical beginnings and aspirations in this direction, but in his case there is no contradiction between these and his very German nature)—but they *are* all thoroughgoing Europeans. Every one of them in fact became one of the creators of 'Europe' by developing specifically national qualities to their extreme limits! The idea of Europe, which subsumes the subtlest essence of what is intellectually mature without cutting it off from its national roots, as internationalism does, cannot be pinned down by logic or in terms of specific content. Like other 'ideas', it is not capable of tangible proof, but is accessible only to intuition, albeit intuition which can only be the reward of lengthy pursuit of the cultural values of the past and the present. The experience of the war has inescapably convinced us what sort of reality this Europe possessed: it existed in the imagination of many, in the desire of a very much smaller number, and in the possession of only a tiny handful of men, and even they did not possess the thing itself, but only its symbolic representation, because they created it for themselves.

However, the lofty supra-historical sphere in which metaphysical, artistic, religious and scientific ideas have their inviolable existence, sets no limit on the idea of Europe. It is what one might call a *historical idea*, a product of the spirit which, it is true, stands above the life from which it has arisen, but remains none the less bound to that life, from which it draws its power and significance. Certainly, the idea of Europe, this unique complexion of a nexus of spiritual achievements, distinct in character from that of the Graeco-Roman spirit of classical antiquity or the universal philosophy of medieval Catholicism—certainly this idea is immortal; but it is also vulnerable. Certainly, it can never disappear altogether—but it can become invisible, like the comet of last summer, which has not disappeared from the world either, but which perhaps may not reappear until we are all long dead. The idea of truth loses nothing of its reality and luminosity even if we all lapse into error, the idea of God is not affected if the world does not recognize Him or turns away from Him. But the idea of Europe *is* bound to those European minds which converge in it, bound in a wondrous fashion as the ship is bound to the water that sustains it: it would still be the same ship if the water were to dry up, but it would have lost its purpose as a vessel and repository for goods and values.

It is not enough that the idea of Europe cannot die: we also want it to live. And it is more manly to confess that it will not do so in the foreseeable future. This realization will, in particular, obviate the painful disillusionment in store for certain vague hopes already to be seen here and there in contemporary literature. Men's minds have been too radically sundered by hatred among the people of Europe, even the sympathies of the neutral countries have been too decisively polarized for them to provide asylum for the idea of Europe. This war will leave our adversaries also—as we are all, I imagine, convinced—too sceptical and disillusioned with one another: their common hatred of us, which at present welds them together in an unnatural makeshift alliance, will, once this conflict is resolved, flood back over them and drive them apart. No, the body whose soul was the idea of Europe has had its limbs so torn asunder that it will be impossible for Heaven knows how long for it to provide any further home for the idea. Europe has forfeited the concept of the 'good European' in which we of the older generation believed we had some share, contributing to it and benefiting from it in the confidence that we would not in so doing become in any way internationalist or cosmopolitan—or whatever other fine-sounding names are given to rootlessness in order to make men deaf to its reality—but sure, precisely through this participation, of being profoundly German. For as it is the essence of life to reach beyond life, as the spirit is most fully itself when it touches that which is more than spirit, so it seems to me—I have elaborated this idea elsewhere in these pages—that it is of the very essence of the German mind to reach out beyond what is German. Certainly, this has entailed countless dangers, distractions and losses for us: many a German tree has withered after being uprooted from its native soil for fear lest its branches might fail to reach into 'Europe'. But we must not allow these misconceptions of what we are to hide from us the fact that the yearning towards Europe does, for all that, genuinely spring from the deep of the German soul.

And it is precisely this that brings us consolation, even if the idea of Europe is on our casualty list and there remains of it only what remains of all the beloved names on that list: an admonitory reminder. The idea of Germany shall be the universal heir to those forces which reached out to that other idea, as to so many others which made our former life stray from its course in too much constriction or too much expansiveness, and which are now being brought back to their source, to spring from it anew. But it is precisely because we know that this Europeanism was no mere external pendant to the German character, that this desire to reach out beyond itself was part of its innermost vital essence—it is because we know this that we know also that Germany, grown strong within its own limits and ever more authentic within itself, will, on some distant day, breathe new life into the idea of Europe, more powerfully and expansively perhaps than was ever so in the past, and will recall it to an awareness of its immortality. It is as if a family were to close its doors to one of its sons, perhaps in estrangement and bitterness: that part of his being which came from, and related to his family is now separated from that which is truly his alone, and his future lies with the energy and growth of that part of him. But one day the moment comes when the doors open again in reconciliation, and he returns bringing riches which he could not have acquired had he not been thrown back on his own resources. And the reawakened power of the blood tells him, and them, that those things which he achieved in isolation and for himself alone were in their profoundest essence destined to flow back into the former community, now restored to life.

[New translation. From Georg Simmel, *Der Krieg und die geistigen Entscheidungen*, Duncker & Humblot, Leipzig, 1917]

# Index